DREAM AND LEGACY

DREAM AND LEGACY

Dr. Martin Luther King in the Post-Civil Rights Era

Edited by Michael L. Clemons,
Donathan L. Brown, and
William H. L. Dorsey

UNIVERSITY PRESS OF MISSISSIPPI / JACKSON

www.upress.state.ms.us

The University Press of Mississippi is a member of the
Association of American University Presses.

First printing 2017

∞

Library of Congress Cataloging-in-Publication Data

Names: Clemons, Michael L., editor. | Brown, Donathan L., editor. | Dorsey,
    William H. L., editor.
Title: Dream and legacy : Dr. Martin Luther King in the post-civil rights era
    / edited by Michael L. Clemons, Donathan L. Brown, William H. L. Dorsey.
Description: Jackson : University Press of Mississippi, 2017. | Includes
    bibliographical references and index. |
Identifiers: LCCN 2016054032 (print) | LCCN 2017020121 (ebook) | ISBN
    9781496811851 (epub single) | ISBN 9781496811868 (epub institutional) |
    ISBN 9781496811875 (pdf single) | ISBN 9781496811882 (pdf institutional)
    | ISBN 9781496811844 (hardback)
Subjects: LCSH: King, Martin Luther, Jr., 1929–1968—Influence. | King,
    Martin Luther, Jr., 1929–1968—Philosophy. | United States—Social policy.
    | United States—Foreign relations. | United States—Race relations. |
    BISAC: SOCIAL SCIENCE / Ethnic Studies / African American Studies. |
    SOCIAL SCIENCE / Discrimination & Race Relations. | POLITICAL SCIENCE /
    Public Policy / Social Policy. | POLITICAL SCIENCE / Political Freedom &
    Security / Civil Rights.
Classification: LCC E185.97.K5 (ebook) | LCC E185.97.K5 D73 2017 (print) |
    DDC 323.092—dc23
LC record available at https://lccn.loc.gov/2016054032

British Library Cataloging-in-Publication Data available

CONTENTS

ACKNOWLEDGMENTS

We wish to express our sincere thanks to all of the authors who contributed to this volume. Appreciation is extended also to Craig W. Gill, director, Katie E. Keene, associate editor, and all of the other good people at the University Press of Mississippi who worked with us to produce this volume. We sincerely appreciate their support and guidance. Much gratitude is extended to the anonymous reviewers, whose comments and suggestions were instrumental in enhancing the overall content and quality of the book.

Finally, we would be remiss not to recognize former Virginia senator Henry Marsh, the first African American mayor of the city of Richmond, who long encouraged the contemporary relevance and practicality of the work of Dr. Martin Luther King Jr.

We dedicate this book to our families, our descendants, and our ancestors. We hope that future generations in America and worldwide will hold fast to the priority of achieving the ideals of freedom, justice, equality, and tranquility for all people.

DREAM AND LEGACY

INTRODUCTION

Michael L. Clemons, Donathan L. Brown, and William H. L. Dorsey

This volume coheres around the presumption that if Dr. Martin Luther King Jr. were alive today he would have much to say about the progress and setbacks of America and the rest of the world in regards to civil and human rights, freedom and equality, and social justice. However, the question, What would Dr. Martin Luther King Jr. say? is not necessarily original. Even a cursory Google search of the internet reveals that the question has been raised previously by scholars and laypersons in a variety of contexts, at least a dozen times, although not necessarily systematically or with any marked investigatory rigor. The significance of this hypothetical query is that it leads to reflective analysis and application of a framework for analysis and problem solving codified by Dr. King during the civil rights movement in the United States. The significance of this work rests also with the fact that Dr. King's life and his work in the black struggle for freedom, perhaps unpredictably, have had a profound impact on the momentum and course of social and political history in the United States since the civil rights era. Arguably, the trajectory of society and race relations in many respects has advanced in a manner consonant with the path laid by Dr. King; this evolution has continued since the eruption of the civil rights movement in the late 1940s. Thus, Dr. King evolved a comprehensive philosophy and vision for the United States that is characterized by its universal applicability to the plight of the poor, oppressed, and downtrodden—a framework that eventually was adapted by many freedom struggles around the world. Indeed, King is a global icon of freedom, justice, and equality. He is recognized as a beacon in the struggles of peoples worldwide seeking to eradicate conditions of oppression, including entrenched poverty and social deprivation, frequently reinforced by political and economic disfranchisement.

The tentacles of Dr. King's work reach into the realm of public policy, including American foreign policy. Many of the policy issues and social developments of King's day, some of which were in their infancy during the

1960s, have blossomed in the twenty-first century and have become, in some instances, forces to undermine the political and social progress of African Americans, and, consequently, they pose potential threats to the nation's social stability. To overcome such threats, Dr. King stressed the fundamental importance of cultivating a society that would benefit from its diversity through the extension of social justice and inclusion. In keeping with this broad theme, this book describes and analyzes, through the prism of Dr. King's ideals and philosophy, some of the major contemporary policy issues and social developments emergent in the twenty-first century facing not only African Americans, but also Americans in general. We address the central question of whether change in a given area of social policy, or some social development, issue, or trend that is emergent or well underway, comports with Dr. King's vision for the black community and the nation at large. As revealed in various writings and speeches, Dr. King was lucid on the point that the lives and futures of all Americans are intertwined, regardless of cultural differences or station in life. Hence, an important contribution of this work is that it presents researched and well-reasoned speculation as to what Dr. King's reaction, response, and prescriptions might be in regards to important and problematic contemporary policy and social issues that have come to the fore in the post–civil rights era.

In his famous "I Have a Dream" speech, delivered at the August 28, 1963, March on Washington, Dr. King set forth a metric for judging the nation's social progress in race relations. He emphatically stated:

> [W]e must make the pledge that we shall march ahead. We cannot turn back. There are those who are asking the devotees of civil rights, "When will you be satisfied?" We can never be satisfied as long as the Negro is the victim of the unspeakable horrors of police brutality. We can never be satisfied as long as our bodies, heavy with the fatigue of travel, cannot gain lodging in the motels of the highways and the hotels of the cities. We cannot be satisfied as long as the Negro's basic mobility is from a smaller ghetto to a larger one. We can never be satisfied as long as a Negro in Mississippi cannot vote and a Negro in New York believes he has nothing for which to vote. No, no, we are not satisfied, and we will not be satisfied until justice rolls down like waters and righteousness like a mighty stream. (King, 1963)

This passage reveals King's preoccupation with critical policy issues and social developments facing African Americans. In some form or fashion, the problems outlined in the passage by King persist in the contemporary period. It follows, therefore, that King's vision remains relevant and can serve as a key measure for judging the progress of the nation and shaping analyses of extant social, economic, and political conditions. Not only does his vision resonate in the twenty-first century, but also more importantly, it has begun to seep into the nation's consciousness and culture. We see this evidenced and punctuated by the overt association and alignment of President Barack Obama with Dr. King's analyses and prescriptions for America during his second inauguration in January 2013. King's views and prescriptions for the ills of racial injustice in the United States have reached well beyond the civil rights community, and they have permeated the broader political culture within which the policy-making process in the United States is situated. The elevation of Dr. King to "hero status" in American history and the growing acceptance of him by the American public arguably began with the national movement to institute his birthday as a national holiday following his assassination in Memphis, Tennessee, in April 1968, while leading a strike of public-sector sanitation workers for improved wages, benefits, and working conditions. The establishment of Martin Luther King Day by the signature of Republican president Ronald Reagan in 1983 and the eventual unanimity of the states (including Arizona) on bestowing this honor ensconced King as a proponent and champion of freedom and justice for not only the nation's, but also the world's downtrodden.

However, while King's ideas have gained broad traction, there is evidence that suggests that some societal elements seek to misappropriate the symbolism of King and do not express a true recognition of and deference to his legacy. An example of such misappropriation is seen at the website of the Heritage Foundation, which promotes Webmemo #961, "Martin Luther King's Conservative Legacy," a January 2006 article by Carolyn Garris. While on its face the article appears indicative of the broad acceptance and reverential treatment that Dr. King has increasingly been accorded, it also demonstrates the misappropriation of the symbolism associated with his life. That is, while society's acceptance of King has been based on his stance on social justice and racial equality, the article reveals a clear attempt to misappropriate associated symbolism and the King legacy beyond their meaning to the black community and progressive citizens. Indeed, it is likely that such social debate and framing will continue well into the future, especially given the public's growing admiration for Dr. King and attempts by partisans to counter by absconding with his image and wielding it to their own political advantage.

In short, this anthology brings together a diverse and unique collection of multidisciplinary works by scholars from around the country that focus on contemporary social policy and issue areas in American society. This book is unique in that its chapters work to explore and amplify wide-ranging social policies and issues through the reconstructed ideation of Dr. King's perspective, analysis, and prescriptions concerning public policy and contemporary social developments. The book's multidisciplinary and interdisciplinary treatment of social policies and developments in light of King's ideals and philosophy and its attempt to glean approaches and solutions that comport with Dr. King's vision render it of essential relevance to those interested in assessing the nation's progress following the–civil rights era.

Organized sequentially into three sections, this book presents chapters focusing on selected contemporary domestic politics and policy, foreign policy and foreign affairs, and social developments that impinge upon the lives of Americans, particularly African Americans. We do not intend to leave the impression that these broad categories are exhaustive or that each is fully inclusive of the range of possible policies and social developments suitable for coverage in this book. Rather, the divisions constructed here are a matter of convenience and intended to call our attention to the pervasiveness of Dr. King's ideals and vision in both the formal or institutional realms of governance and policy making, and in the informal arena where social change is frequently pursued through mechanisms outside of formal institutional structures. The policy areas and social developments covered in this book, for the most part, are reflected in the prevailing social discourse among social analysts, government officials, and bureaucrats who are responsible for program implementation debate. We have grouped the chapters in this volume in such a way as to reflect some of the major developments that have taken place in politics and public policy, foreign policy and foreign affairs, and social issues. The sections are "I. Politics and Public Policy," "II. Foreign Affairs and Africa," and "III. Social Developments." In these contexts, we consider the contributions to racial progress and social justice that have been made to improve the quality of life for African Americans and the quality of American society in general. We sincerely hope you will find our work timely and practical and that Dr. King's legacy will be recognized and preserved for all times.

POLITICS AND PUBLIC POLICY

Part I

THROUGH THE EYES OF KING

Assessing Contemporary Challenges to Voting Rights

Donathan L. Brown

Ratified on February 3, 1870, as the third and final of the Reconstruction amendments, the Fifteenth Amendment of the US Constitution prohibits the federal and state governments from denying a citizen the right to vote based on that citizen's "race, color, or previous condition of servitude." Despite this supposed safeguard, many Southern whites orchestrated discursive maneuvers to continue African American disenfranchisement for many years to come. Even with the passage of five anti–poll tax bills in the House of Representatives from 1942 through 1949, by means of either senatorial filibusters or simply denying this legislation a floor vote, all such measures failed (Santoro, 2008). The passage of the Civil Rights Act of 1957 did little to enfranchise African Americans or increase voter turnout, as the law allowed a jury trial for those accused of denying suffrage. Because the typical all-white jury selected for these and other related trials rarely, if ever, upheld these charges, this provision was nothing more than a mirage.

Growing very impatient with Congress and fatigued by the growing resistance against African American enfranchisement, individual civil rights leaders understood that change was necessary. It became quite clear that white lawmakers and the white public in general did not view civil rights as a cornerstone issue as did African Americans. In reference to public opinion surveys that canvassed the perceived political tensions of the time, "less than 5 percent of the public listed civil rights issues as the nation's most important problem during the 40's and most of the 50's" (Santoro, 2008, p. 1396). Moreover, there were very few, if any, legal protections for African Americans following the tragic slaying of fourteen-year-old Emmett Till in Money, Mississippi, for reportedly flirting with a white woman (Crowe, 2003). As times continued to produce lackluster political outcomes, efforts by civil rights leaders began to gain more attention and momentum.

9

Hoping to force the federal government to fulfill the promises of the three-year-old *Brown v. Board of Education* decision, civil rights leaders in conjunction with the Prayer Pilgrimage for Freedom (a nonviolent demonstration for African American equality), called for a rally on the steps of the Lincoln Memorial in Washington DC. Amidst the presence of civil rights activists such as Ella Baker, A. Philip Randolph, Roy Wilkins, Adam Clayton Powell Jr., Fred Shuttlesworth, Mahalia Jackson, and Harry Belafonte, Dr. Martin Luther King Jr. was slated to speak last. Delivered on May 17, 1957, Dr. King gave one of his most memorable speeches, "Give Us the Ballot." In his address, King argued that voting rights for African Americans would result not only in a positive change for the disenfranchised, but also in the betterment of the nation. Calling for federal leadership from white moderates and liberals to jumpstart a change in political direction, King took to the bully pulpit to stake his claim by means of characterizing the problem, in hopes of eliciting a long overdue solution. As seen through King's eyes:

> All types of conniving methods are still being used to prevent Negroes from becoming registered voters. The denial of this sacred right is a tragic betrayal of the highest mandates of our democratic tradition. And so our most urgent request to the president of the United States and every member of Congress is to give us the right to vote. Give us the ballot, and we will no longer have to worry the federal government about our basic rights. Give us the ballot, and we will no longer plead to the federal government for passage of an anti-lynching law; we will by the power of our vote write the law on the statute books of the South and bring an end to the dastardly acts of the hooded perpetrators of violence. Give us the ballot, and we will transform the salient misdeeds of bloodthirsty mobs into the calculated good deeds of orderly citizens. Give us the ballot, and we will fill our legislative halls with men of goodwill and send to the sacred halls of Congress men who will not sign a "Southern Manifesto" because of their devotion to the manifesto of justice. Give us the ballot and we will place judges on the benches of the South who will do justly and love mercy and we will place at the head of the southern states governors who will, who have felt not only the tang of the human, but the glow of the Divine. Give us the ballot and we will quietly and nonviolently, without rancor or bitterness, implement the Supreme Court's decision of May seventeenth, 1954. (King, 1957)

As seen here, the political state of affairs that King describes not only belies voting rights for African Americans; it enters a grander conversation of law and order. King's brilliant message of social transformation sought to articulate the discursive dimensions of everyday life that enfranchisement can empower people with. For instance, with the right to vote, African Americans can deny the "hooded perpetrators of violence" further political influence by means of electing other officials to office. With the right to vote, African Americans can assist their own mission to end Jim Crow and no longer wait on Congress and the president to intervene.

Unfortunately, the Prayer Pilgrimage did not produce any sudden changes in political outcome. As Gilbert Jonas recounts, "the growing violence by itself should have given Congress and the Whitehouse sufficient incentive in 1957 to enact a halfway respectable civil right law. Instead, the lawmakers and executive branch interpreted that massive white resistance, including violence toward African Americans, as the will of the majority white Americans generally" (2005, p. 164). While no strong relief came from either the Eisenhower administration or Southern white segregationists, "Give Us the Ballot" not only served as King's first address given on the steps of the Lincoln Memorial, but it continues to serve as one of King's earliest exemplars of his outlook on equal access to the polls.

King often questioned the sincerity and thoroughness of some of his "supporters." The long journey toward political equality for African Americans often baffled him. Why, asked King, "is equality so assiduously avoided?" (King, 2010, p. 4). King's dismay with the wavering degrees of concern and participation by some of his "supporters" only caused him to become more involved in his quest for voter equality. He was relentless in expressing his advocacy for voting rights, even knowing the various threats waged against his life and the lives of others. While greatly monumental, the historic 1965 march from Selma to Montgomery, Alabama, which would later be referred to as "Bloody Sunday" (Lee, 2002), serves as one example where King and his supporters knew the threats against their well-being but believed the fight for equality was more important. Born out of continual frustration with white resistance, the Dallas County Voters League (DCVL) and organizers from the Student Nonviolent Coordinating Committee (SNCC) requested the assistance of King and the Southern Christian Leadership Conference (SCLC) to bring prominent civil rights and civic leaders to Selma to assist in their efforts. Civil rights leaders and their supporters knew of the challenges imposed by Alabama's segregationist governor, George Wallace (who prohibited the fifty-four-mile march from Brown Chapel in Selma, Alabama, to the state capitol in Montgomery) and a denied request for protection by federal marshals and troops.

King, who was in Atlanta, in coordination with his advisors, initially decided to postpone the demonstration; however, supporters, members of the media, and antagonists alike still convened in Selma to march. Led by John Lewis of the SNCC and the Reverend Hosea Williams of the SCLC, the estimated five hundred to six hundred supporters began their march. Earlier that morning, Dallas County sheriff Jim Clark had issued an order for all white males in the county over the age of twenty-one to report to the courthouse to be deputized prior to the march (Thornton, 2002). Law enforcement advanced on the marchers with a combination of tear gas and nightsticks. The footage of police brutality against nonviolent civil rights marchers was televised and later published in newspapers and magazines, this unfortunate episode illustrating the state of white resistance against the forces of sociopolitical equality that King's speeches and actions sought to capture.

King's effort toward the establishment of permanent black inclusion into American democracy intensified following Bloody Sunday, forcing President Lyndon Johnson's hand. With major demonstrations in Chicago, Boston, New York City, Oakland, and across the street from the White House, Johnson became wounded by widespread criticism. With the momentum generated by King and his followers, President Johnson addressed Congress on the state of the nation's democratic process, namely, voting rights for African Americans. This "destiny for democracy" and the many obstacles therein, must be quickly remedied by meaningful efforts and actions, according to Johnson. In his words,

> [S]hould we defeat every enemy, and should we double our wealth and conquer the stars, and still be unequal to this issue, then we will have failed as a people and as a nation . . . There is no Negro problem. There is no Southern problem. There is no Northern problem. There is only an American problem. And we are met here tonight as Americans, not as Democrats or Republicans, we are met here as Americans to solve that problem. (Johnson, 1965)

Taking obvious rhetorical cues from Dr. King's experienced dilemmas associated with equal access to the polls, Johnson finally sought to seize the moment in order to rescue his flagging favorability among both Democrats and Republicans.

To otherwise save a sinking presidency, congressional approval, and an awaiting world, Johnson made a calculated decision to unveil what would become one of the most important civil rights advancements since Reconstruction. In President Johnson's words,

> Wednesday I will send to Congress a law designed to eliminate illegal barriers to the right to vote . . . [T]his bill will strike down restrictions to voting in all elections: Federal, State, and local; which have been used to deny Negroes the right to vote. This bill will establish a simple, uniform standard which cannot be used, however ingenuous the effort, to flout our Constitution. It will provide for citizens to be registered by officials of the United States Government, if the State officials refuse to register them. It will eliminate tedious, unnecessary lawsuits which delay the right to vote. Finally this legislation will ensure that properly registered individuals are not prohibited from voting. (Johnson, 1965)

Again drawing upon King's rhetorical leadership, Johnson argued, "The real hero of this struggle is the American Negro. His actions and protests, his courage to risk safety and even to risk his life, have awakened the conscience of this nation. His demonstrations have been designed to call attention to injustice, designed to provoke change, designed to stir reform" (Johnson, 1965). Nick Kotz (2005) notes that "never before had the civil rights movement received the breadth of support and the strength of federal endorsement that it had during the eight days beginning with Bloody Sunday and culminating in Johnson's speech," as the efforts of King were heard loud and clear through Johnson's voice (p. 314).

Enacted by the eighty-ninth Congress and signed into law by President Lyndon Johnson, the Voting Rights Act of 1965 (VRA) was designed to eliminate rampant and widespread discriminatory voting practices largely targeted at African Americans. Specifically, the VRA prohibits states from imposing any "voting qualification or prerequisite to voting, or standard, practice, or procedure . . . to deny or abridge the right of any citizen of the United States to vote on account of race or color." Section 2 of the act contains a general prohibition on voting discrimination, enforced through federal district court litigation. Congress amended this section in 1982, prohibiting any voting practice or procedure that has a discriminatory result. Section 5 of the VRA prevents any changes in voting procedure for the nine states, and parts of seven others housed under "preclearance" (Griffith, 2008). Those states and jurisdictions in this category, chiefly because of their political history pertaining to voter disenfranchisement, must receive clearance from the Department of Justice (DOJ) in order to enforce changes in voting laws or redistricting until it is proven that the proposed changes do not deny or abridge the right to vote on account of race, color, or membership in a language minority group. Dr. King was heavily involved in early movements aimed at equal access to the polls, especially in the South; however, the political landscape continues to shift, transforming old antagonistic tactics into new policy.

KING'S DREAM DEFERRED: VOTER IDENTIFICATION LAWS

Like much of what Dr. King experienced and articulated, a large-scale shift in our nation's racial landscape, whether it be a population on the verge of receiving the overdue right to vote or a growing racial demographic (like Latinos in the United States), is often accompanied by massive waves of resistance from those who fear a possible change in the nation's balance of power. While rarely do we see protests and other forms of civil rights demonstrations that are tantamount to Bloody Sunday, nowadays, voter identification laws continue to gain retrogressive momentum, disenfranchising certain communities from political participation.

To better understand this peculiar movement, its distinct synchronicity, it is best to understand the role that shifting racial and ethnic demographics play within it. For instance, 2003 to some was no different than the years preceding it, yet to others, it marked the beginning of the end. As reported by the US Census Bureau, 2003 was the first year in American history that Latinos overtook African Americans along with all other "minority groups" to become the largest and fastest-growing group/constituency in the nation. At that time nearly one-third of the US population was nonwhite, and some projections suggested that within the next forty to fifty years whites would become a minority; this caused great concern for some. With individuals like Samuel Huntington (1981, 1996, 1997, 2004a, 2004b), Pat Buchanan (2002, 2007, 2011), and Tom Tancredo (2006) sounding the alarm, political attention at the state and local levels began to shift toward such policies as those regulating immigration (Fraga and Segura, 2006), official language legislation (Brown, 2012; Brown, 2013; Schmidt, 2000), housing ordinances (Pham, 2007), and voting rights (Hayduk, 2006). As the nation began to experience population growth across the country, questions began to quickly arise regarding how and in what ways shifting demographics could possibly correlate with a change in political direction. While Latinos are not monolithically liberal, with Cuban Americans more likely to support the Republican Party, David Leal (2007) reminds us that "Latinos are much stronger supporters of the Democratic Party than Anglos in terms of both partisan identification and voting in presidential and congressional elections," whereas "the Republican Party is worried about a future in which an expanding Latino population augments Democratic political power" (pp. 31–32). The increasingly larger Latino population, especially in the Southern states, and a growing Latino constituency that possesses the ability to shift the balance of power in many Republican stronghold districts and states are the ingredients for a perfect storm.

A cursory glance across the United States reveals disturbing trends in voter identification laws that continue to bespeak equal access to the polls. While Dr. King argued that "the basic elements so vital to Negro advancement can only be achieved by seeking redress from government at local, state and Federal levels. To do this the vote is essential," quite the retrogression has been underway for the last decade (Schlueter, 2002, p. 71). In 2003, new voter identification laws passed in Alabama, Colorado, Montana, North Dakota, and South Dakota. In 2005, Indiana, New Mexico, and Washington joined the ranks, while Georgia tightened an existing identification law. In 2006, a voter identification law passed in Ohio, while Missouri tightened an existing law, and in 2009 and 2010, Utah, Idaho, and Oklahoma passed such laws. New voter identification laws were passed in 2011 in Kansas, Mississippi, Rhode Island, and Wisconsin, while Alabama, South Carolina, Tennessee, and Texas tightened existing laws (new laws in Texas, Mississippi, and South Carolina were rejected due to DOJ preclearance) (Streb, 2013). In 2012, Minnesota, New Hampshire, Pennsylvania, and Virginia all passed new voter identification laws; however, voters ultimately rejected that of Minnesota. At the time of publication, thirty-two states have some form of voter identification laws. The range covered by these new laws includes not only photo identification requirements, but also reductions in early voting and voter registration restrictions.

In a recent study released by the nonpartisan Brennan Center for Justice at the New York University School of Law, about 11 percent of eligible voters lack government-issued photo identification needed to comply with these new laws. More disturbing, nearly 500,000 eligible voters do not have access to a vehicle and live more than ten miles from the nearest state identification-issuing office open more than two days a week. Moreover, many of these eligible voters live in rural areas with little or no public transportation (Gaskins and Iyers, 2012, p. 1). More than 10 million eligible voters live more than ten miles from their nearest state identification-issuing office open more than two days a week, with 1.2 million eligible African American and 500,000 eligible Latino voters living more than ten miles from their nearest identification-issuing office open more than two days a week (p. 1). With some projections showing that 25 percent of African-Americans, 16 percent of Latinos, and 18 percent of Americans over age sixty-five do not have the needed forms of identification to comply with these new laws (p. 1), the impact of voter identification laws becomes tantamount to a "test" or "device," restricting the opportunity to register and vote. Data sets supplied to the DOJ by Texas and South Carolina also illustrate that lower income communities and communities of color are substantially less likely to possess the kind of photo identification the proposed laws would require. While some states offered to waive the costs associated with voters seeking to obtain photo identification, this does not necessarily solve the problem. Again, while this clause to some may appear to alleviate tensions, there still is the cost of obtaining supporting documentation, like birth certificates, which critics argue that while the photo identification is "free," there still exists a cost to obtain the necessary documents. Unfortunately, these widespread findings of voter suppression continue, presenting a tremendous countervailing political force against Dr. King's staunch advocacy for barrier-free access to the polls. Neatly summarized by King's famous words, "a right delayed is a right denied," every day, month, or year that voter identification laws are upheld and allowed to fester equals another day, month, or year that voting rights are denied.

As the legal battle continues to unfold across the nation, the political stakes remain high, as the 2014 congressional and 2016 presidential elections have illustrated. Beginning in 2011, the Texas state legislature passed Senate Bill 14, a measure requiring the presentation of certain, though not all, forms of photo identification to vote. While initially introduced as an attempt to discourage "illegal immigrants" from voting, though the state failed to provide any evidence of voter fraud, the 2011–2012 actions pertaining to the Texas Voter identification law continue to garner much attention and concern. From the outset, Texas sought administrative preclearance shortly following the passage of SB 14 (SB 14), knowing that if preclearance was denied, federal law would prohibit the state from enacting the measure. Upon initial investigation and analysis of the law against the grander legal backdrop of the Voting Rights Act, the DOJ denied preclearance. Not pleased with the

DOJ's decision, the state of Texas then sought judicial preclearance, which a three-judge district court denied in August 2012. Here, the court argued that SB 14 would disproportionately burden "indigent voters," who, in turn, are disproportionately racial minorities. In what Texas officials argued was simply an attempt to require voters to produce valid photo identification at the polls, citing similar laws in states such as Georgia and Indiana, the Texas State Conference of the NAACP, the Mexican American Legislative Caucus of the Texas House of Representatives, and the DOJ saw things differently (Hasen, 2012).

Through the eyes of the law's dissenters, the details within the law itself, especially pertaining to what types of photo identifications are considered "valid" and "invalid," remained high on the list of concerns. For instance, SB 14 requires the presentation of a driver's license or personal identification card issued by the Department of Public Safety that has not expired or has expired no earlier than sixty days before the date of presentation; a US military identification card' a US citizenship certificate that contains the individual's photograph; a US passport; a license to carry a concealed handgun; or an identification card that contains the individual's photograph and has been issued or approved by the state of Texas (Texas Senate Bill 14, 2011). These restrictions to voting, claims dissenters, amount to nothing short of a thinly veiled attempt at invoking discriminatory actions against both "minority" voters and those from lower socioeconomic standings. Without federal intervention, the Texas Voter identification law, claimed the DOJ, could disenfranchise more than 1 million otherwise eligible voters (Martin, 2012). While proponents argued that SB 14 was only intended to preserve the "integrity" of voting, civil rights groups and other dissenters sided with DOJ claims that SB 14 targets racial minorities. Attorney General Eric Holder, in his address to the NAACP, "alluded to recent studies that found 8 percent of White voting-age U.S. citizens lack a government-issued photo ID, compared to 25% of black citizens," seeking to establish the existence of discrimination in the proposed law (Holley, 2012, p. 1).

In 2012, Texas state officials and the DOJ met again in court, resulting in the Supreme Court case *State of Texas* v. *Holder*. Here, the state of Texas requested that the Court strike down Congress's 2006 reauthorization of Section 5 or, at a minimum, either "discard" Section 5's prohibition on voting changes that will have a retrogressive effect on the position of racial minorities with respect to their effective exercise of the electoral franchise or bar its application to voting qualifications (*Texas* v. *Holder*, No. 12-cv-128, 2012 WL 3743676, D.D.C. Aug. 30, 2012). Critics against the proposed law refute claims over the ease of obtaining certain photo identification. Citing the seventy counties in Texas that do not have Department of Public Safety offices (the office charged with distributing drivers licenses), state proponents nonetheless sought the law's passage. Oddly enough, the passage of this 2011 law came after three previously failed attempts in 2005, 2007, and 2009. Moreover, the bill's passage came amidst Governor Rick Perry's GOP presidential bid, whereby he famously told one Tea Party crowd that the state could secede from the union should "federal mandates" keep interfering with state business.

On trial in *Texas* v. *Holder* was effect/impact and not necessarily intent. Here, the DOJ took aim at dismantling the argument that Section 5 was both outmoded and no longer needed. For instance, the state of Texas maintained that Section 5 is no longer necessary because "[segregationist] judges have retired or died, [and] federal judges throughout the South can be trusted to faithfully enforce the Fifteenth Amendment and federal voting-rights laws," further contending that Section 5 was a response to a racist federal judiciary, as opposed to it actually being enacted on account of pervasive state-sponsored racial discrimination in the covered jurisdictions that persisted in the face of increasing federal voting-rights protections and ongoing court-ordered relief (*Texas* v. *Holder*, No. 12-cv-128, 2012 WL 3743676, D.D.C. Aug. 30, 2012). During trial, the state of Texas presented extensive evidence showing that SB 14 would not have the effect of denying or abridging any citizen's right to vote on account of race or color, citing social-scientific studies as evidence. This claim was later complemented by the argument from the state of Texas citing the results of "expert-administered surveys" that those surveyed showed no disparity in photo identification possession among black, Latino, and "non-Hispanic" white voters.

With all its cards on the table, Texas was confident that SB 14, as written, would survive federal preclearance as it was confident no disparate impact existed pertaining to voter registration or turnout among communities of color. Not convinced that Texas satisfied its burden of proof, the court issued its multitiered decision. First, the Court rejected Texas's claim that SB 14 would not have a retrogressive effect on voter turnout or participation, noting that despite the evidence presented by the state of Texas, "the effect of voter ID laws on turnout remains a matter of dispute among social scientists," with no conclusive evidence in either direction (*Texas* v. *Holder*, No. 12-cv-128, 2012 WL 3743676, D.D.C. Aug. 30, 2012). Next, the Court rejected the argument that SB 14 was no different from the two current laws in Indiana and Georgia, both of which Texas lawmakers drew upon when crafting SB 14. To that effect, the Court maintained that "the circumstances in Georgia and Indiana are significantly different from those in Texas," specifically noting that SB 14 is "far stricter" than the laws in Indiana and Georgia, because a Texas birth certificate costs twenty-two dollars (compared to a birth certificate in Indiana, which costs from three to twelve dollars) and because roughly one-third of Texas's 254 counties do not have a Department of Public Safety office.

In the Court's final denial, Section 5 became the topic of conversation, as the Court explained why Senate Bill 14 would not be excluded from federal preclearance. Along with stating that "record evidence suggests that SB 14, if implemented, would in fact have a retrogressive effect on Hispanic and African American voters," the Court also explained,

> (1) a substantial subgroup of Texas voters, many of whom are African American or Hispanic, lack photo ID; (2) the burdens associated with obtaining ID will weigh most heavily on the poor; and (3) racial minorities in Texas are disproportionately likely to live in poverty. (*Texas* v. *Holder*, No. 12-cv-128, 2012 WL 3743676, D.D.C. Aug. 30, 2012)

Accordingly, SB 14 would also likely "lead to a retrogression in the position of racial minorities with respect to their effective exercise of the electoral franchise," so argued the Court, insisting that "simply put, many Hispanics and African Americans who voted in the last election will, because of the burdens imposed by SB 14, likely be unable to vote in the next election. This is retrogression" (*Texas* v. *Holder*, No. 12-cv-128, 2012 WL 3743676, D.D.C. Aug. 30, 2012). This attempt by Texas lawmakers to implement SB 14 is by no means an isolated incident. What remains most interesting throughout the pattern and frequency of these proposed laws are the statistical shifts in each state's Latino population. While Texas has long been predicted to become a Democratic-leaning state, there is already movement in some Texas counties that indicates that Texas may soon become a minority-majority state (Collins, 2012). With the momentum still present to curb the impact of certain communities of color from further impacting the political balance of power throughout the country. While these efforts did not prove successful for Texas lawmakers, officials in Arizona saw potential and orchestrated its own campaign.

As no stranger to political controversy pertaining to race, whether it be in reference to Senate Bill 1070 (Brown, 2012a), the ban on teaching ethnic studies in public schools (Biggers, 2012), the 2012 court case *Escamilla* v.

Cuello (Brown, 2013), or otherwise, the state of Arizona continues to find itself engulfed in much debate over its comingling between race and politics. With the November 2004 passage of Arizona Proposition 200, state law required prospective voters in Arizona to present proof of citizenship when registering to vote and when casting a ballot in the state. Specifically, Proposition 200 amended Arizona's voter registration procedure by (1) requiring the county recorder to reject any voter application that does not include valid proof of US citizenship and (2) requiring certain forms of identification to prove identity when a voter attempts to cast a ballot. As a result of these changes in state law, multiple parties sued the state of Arizona on the grounds that Congress had preempted the states in this area of election law with the National Voter Registration Act (NVRA). While the NVRA does not require documentary evidence of citizenship and instead requires applicants to aver, under penalty of perjury, that they are citizens, Arizona law allows officials to "reject" any application for registration that is not accompanied by concrete evidence of citizenship. Again, many previously qualified voters are now disenfranchised under the Arizona law, and only the Supreme Court can decide whether Arizona's citizenship "test" is pre-empted by the NVRA.

As many voters continue to face various political obstacles, the Supreme Court held in its hand the fate of many eager democratic participants, culminating in the 2013 Supreme Court case *Arizona* v. *Inter Tribal Council of Arizona, Inc.* For the case at hand, much tension rests within the context of interpretation, that is, how Arizona interpreted its right to evoke and enforce voter qualifications. Standing in the state's way is the NVRA, which, signed into law by President William Clinton, requires state governments to allow qualifying voters to register when they apply for or renew their driver's licenses or apply for social services. Implemented with the intention of providing greater access to voter registration, the NVRA grants greater accessibility to the polls by means of allowing voter registration by mail. Additionally, the NVRA permits prospective voters to register in elections for federal office by one of three methods: simultaneously with a driver's license application, in person, or by mail. It is confusing that Proposition 200 requires proof of citizenship upon registering to vote and the presentation of identification when voting. While the NVRA makes no mention of such requirements, Arizona law requires proof of citizenship by means of the following: (1) a photocopy of the applicant's passport or birth certificate; (2) a driver's license number, if the license states that the issuing authority verified the holder's US citizenship; (3) evidence of naturalization; (4) tribal identification; or (5) "[o]ther documents or methods of proof . . . established pursuant to the Immigration Reform and Control Act of 1986" (Ariz. Rev. Stat. Ann. §16–166(F) West Supp. 2012).

Mincing no words, the Court, in a 7 to 2 decision found that Arizona erred in its interpretation and execution of federal law and authority, positing, "Arizona's reading is also difficult to reconcile with neighboring provisions of the NVRA" (*Arizona v. Inter Tribal Council of Arizona, Inc, 2013*). Writing on behalf of the Court, Justice Antonin Scalia argued:

> Arizona's appeal to the presumption against pre-emption invoked in this Court's Supremacy Clause cases is inapposite. The power the Elections Clause confers is none other than the power to pre-empt. Because Congress, when it acts under this Clause, is always on notice that its legislation will displace some element of a pre-existing legal regime erected by the States, the reasonable assumption is that the text of Elections Clause legislation accurately communicates the scope of Congress's pre-emptive intent. (*Arizona v. Inter Tribal Council of Arizona, Inc, 2013*)

As states such as Arizona continue to experience a shifting racial and political landscape, we continue to encounter more policy efforts insistent upon requiring proof of citizenship. Attempts at altering state laws along the lines of voting continue to become more commonplace, as the issue of voter identification amidst a growing Latino population weighs heavily on the mind of many Republican lawmakers who believe their party is on the verge of extinction (Skocpol and Jacobs, 2011).

Voter identification laws, akin to what essentially amounts to a "test" or "device," have reignited debate throughout the nation. Whether it is simply retaining the right to vote or initially registering to vote, many otherwise qualified voters remain in jeopardy at the hands of sweeping voter identification laws. While it often becomes unnecessary to argue intent, a June 2012 example involving Pennsylvania Republican House majority speaker Mike Turzai does not help voter identification supporters. Referring to Pennsylvania's effort to secure its photo identification provision, Turzai remarked that securing this change will "allow Governor Romney to win the state." As debates continue to circulate over intent, with some citing a partisan voting war waged by Republicans against lower income communities and communities of color, many of whom overwhelmingly vote Democratic, intent does not trump effect, as the later can and has been proven along these lines in reference to photo identification laws.

CONCLUSION

Recent shifts in voter identification laws continue to negatively impair the state of voter participation and turnout at the polls, especially pertaining to people of color and those at the lower end of the socioeconomic ladder. With data obtained from states such as Texas and South Carolina, along with nonpartisan reports, the outcome continues to suggest that photo identification laws possess the high probability of excluding many Americans from exercising their civil duty. Amidst times like this, Dr. King's words on coalition building remind us that we are not far removed from the injustices of the past. In King's words, "in this juncture of our nation's history, there is an urgent need for dedicated and courageous leadership. If we are to solve the problems ahead and make racial justice a reality this leadership must be fourfold," naming the federal government, white Northern liberals, white Southern moderates, and African Americans as the spokes on the leadership wheel (King, 1957, p. 1). The parallels between Dr. King's efforts to receive the ballot compared to contemporary struggles to retain the ballot are by no means isolated incidences. Despite the time lapse between both episodes, many of Dr. King's words aptly describe the current state of voting wars: "We must realize that we are grappling with the most weighty social problem of this nation, and in grappling with such a complex problem there is no place for misguided emotionalism. We must work passionately and unrelentingly for the goal of freedom, but we must be sure that our hands are clean in the struggle. We must never struggle with falsehood, hate, or malice" (King, 1957, p. 1). As the debate over the intent of voter identification laws continues, this issue remains one of the most challenging social problems facing our fragile democracy in ways that threaten to silence the voices of many.

In many ways, there is very little distinction between new waves of voter identification laws and the past attempts by individuals such as George Wallace, Ross Barnett, and Orval Faubus, as each represents a formable constraint. Even when Dr. King spoke at Pennsylvania State University in 1965 about voter registration efforts, his description of the situation eerily resembled the basis that led up to the aforementioned Supreme Court case, *Arizona* v. *Inter Tribal Council of Arizona, Inc.* As Dr. King recounted to an estimated campus crowd of 8,000 people, "for almost 16,000 Negroes, . . .

only about 250 are registered to vote, not because they don't want to register, but because the registrars absolutely refuse to register Negroes as voters. On Last Monday, we led more than 800 people down to the courthouse. Not a single one was registered" (King, 1965, p. 1). Remembering the incident in Arizona whereby state law sought to supersede federal law (the NVRA) by means of denying individuals voter registration without photo identification, we cannot help but to see peculiar parallels.

Dr. King's dream of voter equality continues to escape reality, as more individuals who lack "proper" identification no longer possess that legal safeguard in some states. While we do not know what tomorrow will hold, from what today tells us, Dr. King's dream remains nothing short of deferred.

REFERENCES

Ariz. Rev. Stat. Ann. §16–166(F) (West Supp. 2012).

Arizona v. Inter Tribal Council of Arizona, Inc, 2013.

Biggers, J. 2012. *State Out of the Union: Arizona and the Final Showdown over the American Dream*. New York: Nation Books.

Brown, D. L. 2012a. "An Invitation to Profile: *Arizona v. United States*." *International Journal of Discrimination and the Law* 12, (2): 117–27.

———. 2012b. "The Strange Life of Assimilation in the National Language Debate." *Journal of Race and Policy* 8(1): 6–17.

———. 2013. "When English Is Not Enough: *Cabrera v. Cuello*." *Harvard Journal of Hispanic Policy* 25 (1): 49–68.

Brundage, W., and P. Wallenstein, eds., 2012. *The Folly of Jim Crow: Rethinking the Segregated South*. Arlington: University of Texas Press.

Buchannan, P. 2002. *The Death of the West: How Dying Populations and Immigrant Invasions Imperil Our Country and Civilization*. New York: St. Martin's Griffin.

———. 2007. *State of Emergency: The Third World Invasion and Conquest of America*. New York: St. Martin's Griffin.

———. 2011. *Suicide of a Superpower: Will America Survive to 2025?* New York: Thomas Dunne Books.

Collins, G. 2012. *As Texas Goes . . .: How the Lone Star State Hijacked the American Agenda*. New York: W. W. Norton.

Crowe, C. 2003. *Getting Away with Murder: The True Story of the Emmett Till Case*. New York: Penguin Books.

Feagin, J. 2006. *Systemic Racism: A Theory of Oppression*. New York: Routledge.

Fraga. L., and G. Segura. 2006. "Culture Clash? Contesting Notions of American Identity and the Effects of Latin American Immigration." *Perspectives on Politics* 4(2): 279–87.

Frederickson, K. 2011. *The Dixiecrat Revolt and the End of the Solid South, 1932–1968*. Chapel Hill: University of North Carolina Press.

Gaskins, K., and S. Iyer. 2012. "The Challenge of Obtaining Voter Identification." New York: Brenan Center for Justice. http://www.brennancenter.org/sites/default/files/legacy/Democracy/VRE/Challenge_of_Obtaining_Voter_ID.pdf.

Grantham, D. 1992. *The Life and Death of the Solid South: A Political History.* Lexington: University of Kentucky Press.

Griffith, B., ed. 2008. *America Votes!: A Guide to Modern Election Law and Voting Rights.* Chicago: American Bar Association Publishing.

Hasen, R. 2012. *The Fraudulent Fraud Squad: Understanding the Battle over Voter ID: A Sneak Preview from the Voting Wars, from Florida 2000 to the Next Election Meltdown.* New Haven: Yale University Press.

Hayduk, R. 2006. *Democracy for All: Restoring Immigrant Voting Rights in the United States.* New York: Taylor and Francis.

Holley, J. 2012. "NAACP Convention; Holder Likens Voter ID Law to Poll Tax." *Houston Chronicle,* July 11, p. 1.

Huntington, S. 1981. *American Politics: The Politics of Disharmony.* Cambridge: Belknap Press of Harvard University Press.

———. 1996. *The Clash of Civilizations and the Remaking of World Order.* New York: Simon and Schuster.

———. 1997. "The Erosion of American National Interests." *Foreign Affairs* 76(1): 28–49.

———. 2004a. "The Hispanic Challenge." *Foreign Policy* (March/April): 2.

———. 2004b. *Who Are We? The Challenges to America's National Identity.* New York: Simon and Schuster.

Jonas, G. 2005. *Freedom's Sword: The NAACP and the Struggle against Racism in America, 1909–1969.* New York: Routledge.

Johnson, L. B. 1965. *We Shall Overcome.* Speech delivered at United States Capitol, Washington, DC.

King, M. L., Jr. 1957. *Give Us the Ballot: We Will Transform the South.* Speech delivered at the Abraham Lincoln Monument, Washington, DC.

———. 1965. *Remarks at Penn State.* Speech delivered at Pennsylvania State University, State College, PA.

———. 2010. *Where Do We Go from Here?: Chaos or Community?* Boston: Beacon.

King, K. 2010. *African American Politics.* Cambridge: Polity.

Kotz, N. 2005. *Judgment Days: Lyndon Baines Johnson, Martin Luther King Jr., and the Laws That Changed America.* Boston: Houghton Mifflin.

Leal, D. 2007. "Latino Public Opinion: Does It Exist?" In R. Espino, D. Leal, and K. Meier. *Latino Politics: Identity, Mobilization and Representation.* Charlottesville: University of Virginia Press, 27–43.

Lee, T. 2002. *Mobilizing Public Opinion: Black Insurgency and Racial Attitudes in the Civil Rights Era.* Chicago: University of Chicago Press.

Martin, G. 2012. "Voter ID Law: Foes Say Bill Was Rushed by GOP." *San Antonio Express News.* July 11, p. 1A.

Pham, H. 2008. "The Private Enforcement of Immigration Laws." *Georgetown Law Review* 96(3): 77–82.

Santoro, W. 2008. "The Civil Rights Movement and the Right to Vote: Black Protest, Segregationist Violence and the Audience." *Social Forces* 86(4): 1391–1414.

Schmidt, R. 2000. *Language Policy and Identity Politics in the United States*. Philadelphia: Temple University Press.

Schlueter, N. 2002. *One Dream or Two?: Justice in America and in the Thought of Martin Luther*. Lanham: Lexington Books.

Schultz, M. 2005. *The Rural Face of White Supremacy: Beyond Jim Crow*. Urbana: University of Illinois Press.

Skocpol, T., and L. Jacobs, eds. 2011. *Reaching for a New Deal: Ambitious Governance, Economic Meltdown, and Polarized Politics in Obama's First Two Years*. New York: Russell Sage.

Smith v. Allwright, 321 U.S. 649 (1944).

Streb, M., ed., 2013. *Law and Election Politics: The Rules of the Game*. New York: Routledge.

Tancredo, T. 2006. *In Mortal Danger: The Battle for America's Border and Security*. Nashville, TN: WND Books.

Texas Senate Bill 14, 2011.

Texas v. Holder, No. 12-cv-128, 2012 WL 3743676, (D.D.C. Aug. 30, 2012).

Thornton, J. 2002. *Dividing Lines: Municipal Politics and the Struggle for Civil Rights in Montgomery, Birmingham and Selma*. Tuscaloosa: University of Alabama Press.

Tolbert, C., and J. Grummel, 2003. "Revisiting the Racial Threat Hypothesis: White Voter Support for California's Proposition 209." *State Politics and Policy Quarterly* 3(2): 183–202.

THE IDEALS AND VISION OF THE LATE DR. MARTIN LUTHER KING JR.

Crime and Social Justice

Jason M. Williams and Helen Taylor Greene

I think with all these challenges being met and with all of the work, and determination going on, we will be able to go this additional distance and achieve the ideal, the goal of the new age, the age of social justice.
—MLK, JR. DECEMBER 18, 1963, WESTERN MICHIGAN UNIVERSITY (WALLIS, 2010)

In 1998, Reginald Wilkinson, president of the American Correctional Association (ACA), paid tribute to Dr. Martin Luther King Jr. at the opening session of its Winter Conference noting that King had great concern for justice, equality, peace, harmony, and the realization of the American dream for all. Pollard described King's vision of justice as one that includes a fair criminal justice system, economic and environmental justice, gender equity, unity between diverse communities, full participation for all, and peace.

Although known for his nonviolent philosophy, King often was on the wrong side of both the law and justice, repeatedly jailed for violating "unjust laws" prevalent throughout his involvement with the American civil rights movement. In his "Letter from a Birmingham Jail," King addressed issues of justice and injustice, as well as just and unjust laws. Eight months later, in a speech given at Western Michigan University that is quoted above, he identified the coming age of social justice. The University of California, Berkeley, School of Welfare Social Justice Symposium defines social justice as a process, not an outcome, which (1) seeks fair (re)distribution of resources, opportunities, and responsibilities; (2) challenges the roots of oppression and injustice; (3) empowers all people to exercise self-determination and realize their full potential; and (4) builds social solidarity and community capacity for collaborative action.

Since King's death, academicians, practitioners, and nongovernmental organizations have been involved in the social justice movement both in the United States and abroad. Yet the age of social justice is still in its nascent stage of development. In fact, until very recently social justice was marginalized in many disciplines due at least in part to (1) the status of conflict, critical and "radical" scholars in their respective disciplines, and (2) the apolitical posture of professional organizations. In the study of criminology, criminal justice, and the administration of justice, social justice remains a lofty goal. It is just in the past twenty years that social policy has become an important focus in professional organizations, including the American Society of Criminology and the Academy of Criminal Justice Sciences. Through research, numerous crime and justice scholars have impacted social justice.

The purpose of this chapter is to (1) examine what has transpired during the past fifty years for African Americans and the administration of justice, (2) reflect on what Dr. King might think about crime and social justice today, and (3) identify policy solutions to the justice dilemma. It begins with a brief historical overview of African Americans and the administration of justice, before, during, and after the 1960s (herein referred to as the era of Dr. Martin Luther King Jr.). It documents key developments in the administration of justice in the context of Dr. King's philosophy of social justice from his untimely death in 1968 until the present. In this chapter, "administration of justice" refers to the processes that govern justice and the implicit sociopolitical influences that are attached to them. Three important policy issues during the past fifty years are analyzed: the drug war, black-on-black crime and victimization, and mass incarceration. The chapter concludes with an overview of peacemaking criminology, restorative justice, and several policy-oriented recommendations. A brief historical overview of African Americans and the administration of justice is presented next.

A BRIEF HISTORICAL OVERVIEW OF AFRICAN AMERICANS AND THE ADMINISTRATION OF JUSTICE

The administration of justice in the United States has been a "peculiar institution" since colonial times that has undergone numerous changes, some in hopes of bettering justice, but often making matters of justice much worse. Oshinsky (1996) suggests that with regard to African Americans, the administration of justice always has been a questionable system impacted by the need to maintain control over enslaved populations. African Americans were almost always the targets of such rules and regulations, although white indentured servants and Native Americans could be disciplined as well. Feagin (2010) states that this control was necessary and supported by the law to keep the system of slavery and white supremacy intact. Laws during this period were primarily set forth by plantation masters, a process of justice known as "plantation justice." Over time, slavery became viewed as inhumane, especially by abolitionists in the North. Many slaves escaped from some plantations believing the North was a place of freedom and detachment from life in the South. Some were captured by slave patrols, one of the uniquely American contributions to policing.

Oshinsky (1996) posits that while Northerners frowned upon the institution of slavery even though some had slaves, they believed that enslaved and free African Americans should be encouraged to stay in the South. This attitude would later be vividly acknowledged in the passing of the Fugitive Slave Act of 1850, a federal law commanding that runaway slaves be branded as fugitives and returned to their masters if captured. Some, including President Abraham Lincoln, believed newly emancipated slaves and free "Negroes" should be colonized to either Liberia or Central America.

During the Civil War and after, the administration of justice was unsystematic, especially in the South. After plantation justice dissolved, there was no distinct system in place for administering justice. White Southerners understood that the law could be used as a mechanism of control to preserve their way of life. After the Civil War, the absence of a viable system of justice and the need for economic recovery in the South contributed to the convict leasing system, a punitive system of vicious racist social control. The Black Codes and Pig's Law are examples of unjust draconian laws targeting African Americans in an aggressive attempt to keep them "in their place." Unjust laws, the convict leasing system, lynching, and pervasive denial of legal rights defined the administration of justice for African Americans in the North and South well into the future. Muhammad notes that beliefs about the inferiority and criminality of African Americans exacerbated the justice dilemma. It is within this historical context that Dr. King began his nonviolent crusade against racial injustice.

THE ADMINISTRATION OF JUSTICE DURING THE ERA OF DR. MARTIN LUTHER KING JR.

The model of administering justice that began during slavery and continued throughout the twentieth century can be characterized as state-sponsored racial violence. In the South, protestors against Jim Crow were brutalized by police. During the 1960s social unrest was deeply attached to social, economic, and political exclusion of African Americans and other groups. Dr. King's "Letter from a Birmingham Jail," written in 1963, is useful for understanding his social philosophy in a criminological context. Within it, King connects racial injustice to the need for a progressive social justice movement. For example, early within his letter he stated quite clearly, "I am in Birmingham because injustice is here" (University of Pennsylvania). The injustice he is explaining refers to the racial subjugation African Americans faced daily and violence inflicted on those who dared to protest with him. He further alluded to the greater consciousness of his recipients by stating, "I cannot sit idly by in Atlanta and not be concerned about what happens in Birmingham. Injustice anywhere is a threat to justice everywhere" (ibid.), thus noting that there is a geographical connectedness concerning injustice and that this connectedness requires the attention of all. Moreover, Dr. King felt that the failure to recognize the connectedness results in the acceptance of the status quo, to the detriment of analyzing what King calls the "underlying causes" (ibid.).

While paying close attention to the administration of justice, King noted, "Negroes have experienced grossly unjust treatment in the courts" (ibid.). He also took issue with the suggestion of African Americans waiting for change, when he noted that "this wait" has almost always meant "never" (ibid.). King's thoughts on African Americans not needing to wait any longer clearly are representative of his continued work in spite of going to jail and the other negative consequences of his actions. Regarding the breaking of laws, King noted that "there are only two types of laws: just and unjust" (ibid.). He supported this assertion by suggesting that "one has not only a legal but a moral responsibility to obey just laws. Conversely, one has a moral responsibility to disobey unjust laws" (ibid.), suggesting that the movement that began in Birmingham was one of moral good.

King also took aim at segregation and the voting system in the letter. He stated, "segregation is not only politically, economically and sociologically unsound, it is morally wrong and sinful" (ibid.). He identified and attacked devious methods used to prevent Negroes from becoming registered voters, especially in counties where "Negroes constitute a majority of the population" (ibid.). Toward the end of the letter King spoke profoundly on the refusal of many to see the acts of the Birmingham police force for what they were. While speaking to his fellow clergymen who sought to thank the police force for its careful watch of the protest King noted,

You warmly commended the Birmingham police force for keeping "order" and "preventing violence." I doubt that you would have so warmly commended the police force if you had seen its dogs sinking their teeth into unarmed, nonviolent Negroes. I doubt that you would so quickly commend the policemen if you were to observe their ugly and inhumane treatment of Negroes here in the city jail; if you were to watch them push and curse old Negro women and young Negro girls; if you were to see them slap and kick old Negro men and young boys; if you were to observe them, as they did on two occasions, refuse to give us food because we wanted to sing our grace together. I cannot join you in your praise of the Birmingham police department. (ibid.)

What is strikingly profound about King's letter is that his words were in defense of African Americans who were brutalized physically, psychologically, politically, economically, and socially, each of which to some degree was legal and justified by the governing social norms of his time. The last sentence of his letter is the essential logic on which King's push for social justice is based. The need to institute a more egalitarian system of social participation for all and on all levels is what fueled King and his followers in the freedom movement.

CRIME AND SOCIAL JUSTICE AFTER THE ERA OF DR. MARTIN LUTHER KING JR.

After Dr. King's death in 1968, racial injustice in the criminal justice system aptly described by Tonry as "punishing race" continued and arguably worsened. During the 1970s punitive policies became more severe, reversing the pro-human rights record the United States had as a result of its Supreme Court rulings during the 1960s. The Omnibus Crime Control and Safe Streets Act passed in 1968 and designed to improve and ameliorate deficiencies in the administration of justice was not as effective as intended. Race baiting, a tactic that dates back to Barry Goldwater, who utilized the Southern Strategy to capture the Southern white vote away from the more liberal and socially conscious Democrats during the 1964 presidential election led to politicians playing to the white angry base in local, state, and national elections. By the 1980s, the moral panic against drugs and drug control laws obliterated reforms achieved in the two previous decades. Crime control legislation enacted in 1984 specifically targeted violent crime, controlled substances and sentencing that impacted the "War on Drugs," and mass incarceration in the following decades.

AFRICAN AMERICANS AND THE WAR ON DRUGS

Tonry, Alexander, and Butler argue that statistics on African American arrests for drug offenses suffice as proof of discrimination and substantiate that they are a targeted group. For example, between 1980 and 2009 drug possession/use arrests statistics show that while in 1980 the black arrest rate was twice that of whites, later in the decade the disparity increased to about four black arrests to one white (see figure 2.1). Between 1980 and 1989, the white arrest rate increased by 56 percent while for blacks the rate was four times higher (219 percent). Overall, from 1980 through 2009 the white rate doubled, while the black rate tripled. The statistics corroborate what some scholars view as the racialization of drug enforcement.

The statistics on drug sales and manufacturing are no better than those recorded for possession and use. According to the same source, when controlling for drug sale/manufacturing arrest rates in 1980, blacks were arrested at a rate about four times higher than whites (see figure 2.2). Within that ten-year period, the white rate increased by 127 percent, while for blacks it increased by 363 percent. In 1989 blacks made up an astonishing 52 percent of all drug sales and manufacturing arrests. Ironically, between 1989 and 2009, the decline rate was greater for blacks (59 percent) than for whites (27 percent). However, in 2009 the rate for blacks was about four times that of whites, making it comparable to disparity rates in 1980.

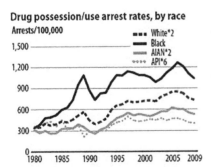

Figure 2.1 Source: H. Snyder, *Arrest in the United States, 1980–2009 (9/2011)* at www.bjs.gov. Bureau of Justice Statistics, Washington, DC. Note: AIAN=American Indian/Alaskan Native; API=Asian/Pacific Islander.

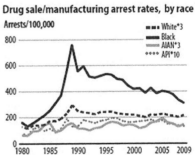

Figure 2.2 Source: H. Snyder, *Arrest in the United States, 1980–2009 (9/2011)* at www.bjs.gov. Bureau of Justice Statistics, Washington, DC. Note: AIAN=American Indian/Alaskan Native; API=Asian/Pacific Islander.

BLACK-ON-BLACK CRIME AND VICTIMIZATION

Dr. King did not specifically address the problem of crime and victimization in black communities. Rather, in the context of social justice, he opted for a more comprehensive approach to ameliorating factors that contributed to crime and other social problems. Understanding the involvement of some African Americans in drug behavior and the War on Drugs is important to understanding black-on-black crime (and victimization) before, during, and after the era of Dr. King. Although not new, the disproportionate representation of African Americans in crime and victimization statistics continues to be disconcerting. Gabbidon and and Greene (2005) state that in 1960, there were an estimated 1,064,814 Negroes arrested (of approximately 3.5 million arrests), and by 1994 there were 3,705,713 blacks arrested (of approximately 11.8 million arrests). Since then, all arrests continue to fluctuate (see table 2.1). In light of this fluctuation and the limitations of the Federal Bureau of Investigation's arrest data, it is impossible to say definitely that black-on-black crime is "better" now than in 2000, although it does appear to have improved since the 1990s.

Table 2.2 provides some evidence that limited progress has been made, at least in the arrests for violent crimes (murder and nonnegligent manslaughter,

Table 2.1 Black Arrests 1960, 1970, 1980, 1990, 2000, 2010

	1960	1970	1980	1990	2000	2010
Total	3,498,926	6,257,104	9,683,672	11,151,368	9,068,977	10,177,907
Black Arrests	1,064,814	1,688,389	2,375,204	3,224,060	2,528,368	2,846,862

Source: Gabbidon and Greene. 2009. Appendix A.1, pp. 300-03, and Gabbidon and Greene. 2013. Appendix A.1, p. 319.

Table 2.2 Trend of Black Arrests, 1995–2010

	1995		2000		2005		2010	
	Arrests	% Black	Arrests	% Black	Arrests	% Black	Arrests	% Black
Total	11,386,627	30.9	9,068,977	27.9	10,189,691	27.8	10,177,907	28.8
Homicides	16,691	54.4	8,683	48.8	10,093	48.6	8,641	48.7
Aggravated Assault	437,686	38.4	315,729	34	329,247	34.3	317,435	33.5
Rape	26,519	42.4	17,859	34.1	18,405	32.7	15,503	31.8
Robbery	137,761	59.5	72,149	53.9	84,785	56.3	87,587	55
Drug Abuse Violations	1,143,148	36.9	1,039,086	34.5	1,330,802	33.9	1,082,301	11.5

Source: Compiled from US Department of Justice, Federal Bureau of Investigation, *Crime in the United States, 1995, 2000, 2005, 2010.* Retrieved from www.fbi.gov on July 11, 2013.

aggravated assault, robbery, and rape), as well as drug abuse violations. The percentage of blacks arrested for these offenses has decreased since 1995.

Even though African Americans are less likely to be arrested for homicide, intraracial—"black-on-black"—homicide rates are important. Research has noted that the high levels of murder rates within the African American community are partly due to their spatial confinement to the ghetto. Scholars such as Curtis (1967) and Wolfgang and Ferracuti (1969) note that violent crime is specific to a type of culture that makes such acts acceptable. Braithwaite (1975), Hawkins (1985), and Staples (1986) point to structural attributes such as poverty, breakdown of the family, and poor schools, that often elude the mainstream discourse on African American violence. Although numerous explanations are available on the issue of African American violence, not enough has been done to reduce and prevent intraracial homicide.

African American homicide victimization trends have fluctuated over the years and are much lower today than when King was alive. For instance, according to Cooper and Smith (2011), in 2008, the murder rate for blacks (19.6 homicides per 100,000) was at least six times higher than the rate for whites (3.3 homicides per 100,000). Also the victimization rate for blacks peaked in the early 1990s, reaching a high of 39.4 homicides per 100,000 in 1991 (see figure 2.3). After 1991, the victimization rate for blacks went down until 1999, when it stabilized at about 20 homicides per 100,000. In addition, in 2008, the homicide offending rate for blacks (24.7 offenders per 100,000) was seven times higher than the rate for whites (3.4 offenders per 100,000) (see figure 2.4). The offender rate for blacks showed a similar pattern to the victimization rate, peaking in the early 1990s at a high of 51.1 offenders per 100,000 in 1991. Moreover, after 1991, the offender rate for blacks declined

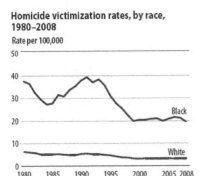

Figure 2.3 Source: A. Cooper and E. L. Smith, Homicide Trends in the United States, 1980–2008 (11/2011) at www.bjs.gov. Bureau of Justice Statistics, Washington, DC.

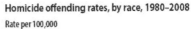
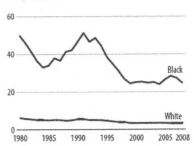

Figure 2.4 Source: A. Cooper and E. L. Smith, Homicide Trends in the United States, 1980–2008 (11/2011) at www.bjs.gov. Bureau of Justice Statistics, Washington, DC.

until it reached 24 per 100,000 in 2004. The rate has fluctuated, increasing to 28.4 offenders per 100,000 in 2006 before falling again to 24.7 offenders per 100,000 in 2008.

AFRICAN AMERICANS AND MASS INCARCERATION

Several scholars refer to the twenty-first century as the "age of mass incarceration," examining incarceration and race (see, e.g., Tonry, 2011; Alexander, 2010; Perkinson, 2010; Barker, 2009; Pratt, 2009; Clear, 2007; Harris and Miller, 2003; Mauer, 1999; Wacquant, 2009). For example, according to Carson and Sabol (2012), in 2011 blacks and Hispanics were imprisoned at higher rates than whites in all age groups for both sexes. Furthermore, regarding males eighteen and nineteen years old, black males were imprisoned at more than nine times the rate of white males. Hispanic and black male prisoners age sixty-five or older were imprisoned at rates between three and five times those of white males. Between the ages of twenty and twenty-four, black males were imprisoned at about seven times that of white males. Moreover, black females were imprisoned at between two and three times the rate of white females, while Hispanic females were imprisoned at between one and three times the rate of white females.

The collateral consequences of mass incarceration are well known. For these individuals, their families, and communities, imprisonment is costly. Ex-offenders experience great difficulty when they leave prison. In spite of their reentry efforts, legal barriers to successful reentry remain. Dr. King probably would be concerned about mass incarceration, reentry, and felon disfranchisement. He would view denial of rights for ex-offenders in a manner similar to his perspective on the denial of voting rights to African Americans during the 1960s.

When drugs, homicide, and mass incarceration are taken into consideration, it becomes clear that Dr. King's vision for the age of social justice has not occurred. There have been several attempts within criminological inquiry to restore order and peace to selected communities and populations that have been historically mistreated and negatively affected by the criminal justice system. Such perspectives are neither popular nor acceptable to most mainstream criminologists, policy makers, and justice practitioners. The next section will review peacemaking criminology and restorative justice and their implicit connection to King's ideas and vision for social justice.

PEACEMAKING CRIMINOLOGY AND RESTORATIVE JUSTICE AS SOCIAL JUSTICE REMEDIES

Peacemaking criminology was an idea invented during the late 1980s in a variety of writings by Pepinsky and Quinney (1991) that became more relevant by challenging dominant mainstream perspectives in the early 1990s. At the time, crime control and prevention models dominated criminological inquiry. Proponents believed that critical criminology did not go far enough in acknowledging underlying causes of crime and that a comprehensive critique of societal and governmental responses to crime was nonexistent. According to Quinney (1991), peacemaking criminology is "a criminology that seeks to alleviate suffering and thereby to eliminate crime" (qtd. in Wozniak, 2000, p. 284). According to Wozniak (2000) peacemaking criminology requires one to "extend beyond mere ideas to include the personal and moral dimensions of a scholar" (p. 270). The criminologist operates as a social justice advocate and thus emerges as a conscious technocrat on crime with an implicit connection to social issues. Peacemaking criminology examines in real-time the impact of social institutions and their broader connection to criminality and human suffering. Wozniak (2000) noted "peacemaking criminologists offer a conception of justice defined in terms of equal well-being for all, where the needs of all are met equally but differentially, that is, according to the unique needs of each" (p. 271)(see table 2.3).

Table 2.3 Descriptions of Peacemaking Criminology
It offers a global critique of the entire criminal justice system and its warlike history.
It shows how everything is connected.
It turns the premises of traditional criminology upside down.
It seeks to preserve the dignity of individuals.
It focuses on what actually works to create a safe community of goodwill and respect for all human beings.
It concentrates on building rather than serving social ties.
It is criminology of compassion for and of empathy with all who suffer.
It defines the role of police as peace officer rather than as crime fighter.
It is interested in avoiding structural conditions that exclude people from having their needs met and defines such unresponsiveness as a form of structural violence.
It attempt to negate power relations in all its forms and seeks ways to structurally and interpersonally minimize violence, harm, and the negation of democracy.
Source: J. F. Wozniak. 2000. "The Voices of Peacemaking Criminology: Insights into a Perspective with an Eye toward Teaching." *Contemporary Justice Review*, pp. 267-89.

Theoretically speaking, the inquiry of peacemaking criminologists is the opposite of that of mainstream criminologists. As Wozniak explains:

> Mainstream criminologists accept existing legal categories and then seek to use the scientific method to define, oversee, study, and control the "criminals" specified by law and to explore the cause of crime within that framework. Peacemaking criminology is less interested in such a narrow view of etiology of "crime." Such inquiry, inevitably value-laden, must start by asking not what is "crime" but what is social harm and what are the political, economic, and social arrangements that bring about such harm. (p. 271) (see table 2.4)

Table 2.4 Contrasting Peacemaking and Mainstream Criminologies
Peacemaking challenges the status quo
Peacemaking challenges inequality and society and illuminates structurally-based injustices. It questions the acceptability of existing social arrangements.
Peacemaking questions state definitions of "who is the criminal," especially as these definitions ignore the harms and violations of human rights perpetrated by the powerful. Mainstream criminology accepts existing legal categories as real and focus more on the "causes" of "criminal" behavior.
Peacemaking examines the world in a power-reflexive modality, taking into account how power shapes and penetrates virtually all aspects of social life, including work of criminologists. Mainstream scholars assume that criminology can escape the influence of power and ideology, and that knowledge is best understood through a "value-free" scientific method.
Peacemaking conceptualizes social change through liberation and change in the oppressive criminal justice system. Mainstream criminology emphasizes social control and mechanisms instrumental in sustaining ongoing criminal justice processes.
Peacemaking focuses on change from the inside out; from the one to many rather than grand design, from the top down. The focus is on individual and community empowerment.
Peacemaking emphasizes social justice rather than criminal justice. There is a desire for a better society—one that is socialist, not capitalist.
Peacemaking includes a spiritual perspective. It is more about connections than dissection. It concentrates on building rather than severing social ties, on what to do rather than whom to blame, on positive empowerment rather than negative disaffection. It is concerned with the resolution of conflict, not the identification and processing of "criminals." It emphasizes healing.
Peacemaking emphasizes nonviolence and peace instead of violence, law, and order. It is critical of the entire criminal justice system, especially its warlike history and profit structure.
Peacemaking has a great sympathy for the needs of all involved in a harm situation.
Source: J. F. Wozniak. 2000. "The Voices of Peacemaking Criminology: Insights into a Perspective with an Eye toward Teaching." *Contemporary Justice Review* pp. 267–89.

Another school of thought within criminological inquiry that relates to King's message on social justice is restorative justice. Like peacemaking criminology, restorative justice aims at correcting harms done to victims, it "seeks to bring together the victim, the offender, and the community in a process whereby a harm done can be addressed and the victim/or the community made whole again" (Hanser, 2009, p. 191). Restorative justice and peacemaking criminology are theoretically in harmony, though implemented differently. For instance, restorative justice responds to crime in pursuit of righting wrongs and making the community whole, while peacemaking criminology according to Quinney (1991, p. 11) suggests that "crime is suffering . . . the ending of crime is only possible with the ending of suffering" (qtd. in Hanser, 2009, p. 192). Therefore, they differ in the sense that peacemaking criminology sees crime as a symptom of social decay at the hands of social institutions that must be fixed to alleviate social harm, while restorative justice is more reactive as opposed to preventative.

Restorative justice puts the community and its role in administering justice back into the justice discourse. Under this paradigm social justice governs because communities affected by social harms are best able to address such issues unique to their living space. Although both schools of thought are vast, it is difficult to fit them into the confines of this chapter. Many scholars have written on restorative justice and its different dimensions (see, e.g., Wheeldon, 2009; Palvich, 2005; Harris, 2004; Takagi and Shank, 2004; Braithwaite, 2002; McCold and Wachtel, 2002; Van Ness and Strong, 1997; Van Ness, 1993), as well as peacemaking criminology (see, e.g., Klenowski, 2009; Braswell, Fuller and Lozoff, 2001; Pepinsky, 1999; Fuller, 1998; Sullivan and Tifft, 1998; Quinney, 1995; Friedrichs, 1994; Braswell, 1990) and their connection to peace, justice, and the revitalization of society.

Both share a kinship to King's message on social justice in the sense that they advocate for an understanding of the root causes of crime that goes beyond the definitions ascribed by the state. Peacemaking criminology associates crime and harm with social institutions, much like King when he acknowledged the role of white supremacy in state responses to African American concerns. More importantly, both schools of thought advocate nonviolent responses to oppression and social harm as did Dr. King.

Restorative justice demands reconciliation between the perpetrator and the affected and pursuit of less and/or nonpunitive approaches to punishment. King's philosophy on social justice, in combination with peacemaking criminology and restorative justice, allows for society to recognize human suffering and crime in their fullest context. Each fosters a dialogue about holistic approaches to rectify root causes instead of continuing ineffective piecemeal responses. Many of the root causes are the result of racial and class divisions inadequately addressed in our society and others.

DISCUSSION AND FUTURE POLICY RECOMMENDATIONS

As we reflect upon what Dr. King would think about crime and social justice if he were alive today, we believe he would agree that there is much more to be done. Yes, there has been progress but not enough. Ross (2008) states that social justice fosters fairness and collectivity and includes the prevention of conditions that contribute to criminal behavior. When a black male teenager can be shot and killed while walking home in Sanford, Florida, because he was mistaken for a burglar; when a black female teenager can be gunned down by a stray bullet in her Chicago, Illinois, neighborhood; or when police violence and racial profiling continue to occur, are we really in a social justice era? Within the context of King's philosophy, social justice requires the analysis (and elimination) of the root causes of oppression and the complete resuscitation of oppressed people(s). For African Americans this means the revitalization of schools and communities, economic stability, racial equality under the law, and the dismantling of the police as a tool of racialized social control.

In spite of the Kerner Commission, the Civil Rights Acts of 1964, the 1967 President's Commission on Law Enforcement and the Administration of Justice, the 1968 Omnibus Crime Control and Safe Streets Act, the 1994 Violent Crime Control and Law Enforcement Act as well as more recent crime and justice legislation, social justice and distributive justice in the United States continue to be elusive goals. It is in this context that we recommend policy solutions for issues presented earlier in this chapter.

One policy recommendation is advocating for the adoption of Racial Impact Statements (RIS) that are designed to inform policy makers about the potential "harm" of legislation before it is enacted. For example, Connecticut, Iowa, Minnesota, and Wisconsin use RIS to reduce racial disparities in sentencing. Mauer and others believe that RIS provide an opportunity for alternatives to be considered that will have fewer disparate consequences for racial minorities. He suggests that legislation that prohibits the sale of drugs in school zones has a negative impact on racial minorities. While no one disagrees with the intent of the legislation, Mauer believes the focus of sentencing policy should not just be penalties. The adoption of RIS provides legislators in states with disproportionate confinement of minorities in prisons (and on probation and parole) with a proactive approach to reducing sentencing disparities.

Our second policy recommendation calls for a White House conference or other national symposium on mass incarceration to identify effective strategies for reducing the imprisonment conundrum. This symposium would address sentencing reforms, the school-to-prison pipeline, felon disenfranchisement, prisoner reentry, and disproportionate minority confinement. Those jurisdictions that have made progress in reducing their prison and jail populations will be an important part of this gathering. The Pew Center on the States found that state prison populations declined for three consecutive years (2010–2012), due, at least in part, to research and public opinion in favor of policy reforms. Gelb notes that these research-based reforms are less costly prison alternatives proven to reduce recidivism. Those states that have successfully adopted new criminal justice policies provide models for reducing prison populations and costs.

In keeping with Dr. King's philosophy of justice and social justice, peacemaking criminology and restorative justice should be an integral part of the conference/symposium. When citizens, practitioners, and researchers involved in justice come together in harmony to alleviate crime and their collateral consequences, institutions will be rebuilt in ways that potentially will bring about a truly egalitarian society. As King noted many times, institutions must be studied and if necessary rebuilt.

Our third policy recommendation calls for policies that strengthen families, communities, and schools in order to prevent and control African American crime and victimization. Tonry and others believe that drug, crime, and social welfare policies exacerbate rather than prevent crime. In the past, crime control policies devoid of prevention strategies have proven ineffective. Even though successful policies and programs that prevent delinquency and crime have been identified, they do not receive enough national attention and replication (see for example www.crimesolutions.gov). Citizens must work with elected officials to insure that research that demonstrates "what works" and "best practices" is available and replicated, especially in communities that continue to experience neighborhood effects of crime and delinquency.

In conclusion, we believe efforts to obtain Dr. King's vision of a fair criminal justice system require more involvement by citizens in the policy-making process. In the future, policies should be guided by both sound research and public opinion. The role of justice agencies, their organizational culture, and personnel in impeding social justice can no longer be ignored. It is well known that certain criminal justice policies have produced unintended consequences. Tonry has suggested that such consequences are foreseeable during the policy-making process but are ignored. In the words of Dr. King in an address to Lincoln University in 1961, "[B]lack criminality is environmental and not racial since poverty, disease, and ignorance breed crime whatever the racial group may be" (qtd. in Dyson, 2000, pp. 19–20).

REFERENCES

Alexander, M. 2010. *The New Jim Crow: Mass Incarceration in the Age of Colorblindness.* NY: New Press.

Auletta, K. 1982. *The Underclass.* NY: Random House.

Barker, V. 2009. *The Politics of Imprisonment: How the Democratic Process Shapes the Way America Punishes Offenders.* NY: Oxford University Press.

Braithwaite, J. 1979. *Inequality, Crime and Public Policy.* London: Cambridge University Press.

———. 2002. *Restorative Justice and Responsive Regulation.* NY: Oxford University Press.

Braswell, M. C. 1990. "Peacemaking: A Missing Link in Criminology." *The Criminologist* 15: 3–5.

Braswell, M., J. Fuller, and B. Lozoff. 2001. *Corrections, Peacemaking, and Restorative Justice: Transforming Individuals and Institutions.* Cincinnati: Anderson.

Bruce, M. A., V. J. Roscigno, and P. L. McCall. 1998. "Structure, Context, and Agency in the Reproduction of Black-on-Black Violence." *Theoretical Criminology* 2(1): 29–55.

Burke, R. H. 2012. *Criminal Justice Theory: An Introduction.* NY: Routledge, 2012.

Bursik, R. J. 1984. "Urban Dynamics and Ecological Studies of Delinquency." *Social Forces* 63: 393–413.

Butler, P. 2009. *Let's Get Free: A Hip-Hop Theory of Justice.* NY: New Press.

Carson, E. A., and J. Sabol. 2012. *Prisoners in 2011.* Washington, DC: Bureau of Justice Statistics.

Clear, T. R. 2017. *Imprisoning Communities: How Mass Incarceration Makes Disadvantaged Neighborhoods Worse.* NY: Oxford University Press.

Cooper, A., and E. L. Smith. 2011. *Homicide Trends in the United States, 1980–2008.* Washington, DC: Bureau of Justice Statistics.

Curtin, M. E. 2000. *Black Prisoners and Their World, Alabama, 1865–1900.* Charlottesville: University Press of Virginia.

Curtis, Lynn A. 1975. *Violence, Race, and Culture.* Lexington: Lexington Books.

Dyson, M. E. 2000. *I May Not Get There with You: The True Martin Luther King, Jr.* New York: Free Press.

Duffee, D., and E. R. Maguire. 2007. *Criminal Justice Theory: Explaining the Nature and Behavior of Criminal Justice.* NY: Routledge.

Feagin, J. R. 2010. *The White Racial Frame: Centuries of Racial Framing and Counter-Framing.* NY: Routledge.

Friedrichs, D. O. 1994. "Crime Wars and Peacemaking Criminology." *Peace Review* 6: 159–64.

Fuller, J. R. 1998. *Criminal Justice: A Peacemaking Perspective.* Boston: Allyn and Bacon.

Gabbidon, S. L., and H. T. Greene. 2005. *Race and Crime*. Thousand Oaks, CA: Sage.

Garland, D. 2001. *The Culture of Control: Crime and Social Order in Contemporary Society*. Chicago: University of Chicago Press.

Gelb, Adam. 2013. *U.S. Prison Population Drops for Third Year as States Adopt New Policy Strategies*. Washington, DC: Pew Center.

Hanser, Robert D. 2009. "Peacemaking Criminology: A Special Issue Part I Conflicts and Geographical Flashpoints around the World: The Effective Application of Restorative Justice and Peacemaking Criminological Perspectives." *Contemporary Justice Review* 12(2): 191–205.

Harris, M. Kay. 2004. "An Expansive, Transformative View of Restorative Justice." *Contemporary Justice Review* 7(1): 117–41.

Harris, O., and R. R. Miller. 2003. *Impacts of Incarceration on the African American Family*. New Brunswick: Transaction.

Hawkins, D. F. 1985. "Black Homicide: The Adequacy of Existing Research for Devising Prevention Strategies." *Crime and Delinquency* 31: 83–103.

Hudson, B. 1993. "Racism and Criminology: Concepts and Controversies." In *Racism and Criminology*, ed. D. Cook and B. Hudson. London: Sage. 1–27.

Jeffrey, C. R. 1971. *Crime Prevention through Environmnetal Design*. Beverly Hills: Sage.

Klenowski, P. M. 2009. "Peacemaking Criminology: Etiology of Crime or Philsophy of Life?" *Contemporary Justice Review* 12(2): 207–22.

Mauer, Marc. 1999. *Race to Incarcerate*. NY: New Press.

———. Winter 2009. "Racial Impact Statements Changing Policies to Address Disparities." *Sentencing Project*. July 2013. <www.sentencingproject.org/doc/rd_abaarticle.pdf>.

McCold, P., and T. Wachtel. 2002. "Restorative Justice Theory Validation." In *Restorative Justice: Theoretical Foundations*, ed. E. Weitekamp and H. J. Kerner. Cullompton: Willan, 2002. 110–142.

Miller, Walter B. 1958. "Lower Class Culture as a Generating Milieu of Gang Delinquency." *Journal of Social Issues* 14(3): 5–19.

Moses, E. R. 1936. "Community Factors in Negro Delinquency." *Journal of Negro Education* 5: 220–27.

Moynihan, D. P. 1965. *The Negro Family*. Washington, DC: United States Department of Labor.

Muhammad, K. G. 2010. *The Condemnation of Blackness: Race, Crime, and the Making of Modern Urban America*. Cambridge: Harvard University Press, 2010.

Oshinsky, D. M. 1996. *Worse Than Slavery: Parchman Farm and the Ordeal of Jim Crow Justice*. NY: Free Press, 1996.

Packer, H. L. 1968. *The Limits of the Criminal Sanction*. Stanford: Standford University Press.

Pavlich, G. 2005. *Governing Paradoxes of Restorative Justice*. London: Glass House.

Pennsylvania, University of. 2012. "Letter from a Birmingham Jail [King, Jr.]." n.d. *African Studies Center*.19 12. http://www.africa.upenn.edu/Articles_Gen/Letter_Birmingham .html.

Pepinksy, H. E., and R. Quinney. 1991. *Criminology as Peacemaking*. Bloomington: Indiana University Press.

Perkinson, R. 2010. *Texas Tough: The Rise of America's Prison Empire*. NY: Metropolitan Books.

Pollard, III, A. B. *Martin Luther King in Sociological Context*. August 15, 2003. A paper presented at the annual meeting of the Association for the Sociology of Religion, Atlanta, Georgia.

Pratt, Travis C. 2009. *Addicted to Incarceration: Corrections Policy and the Politics of Misinformation in the United States*. Los Angeles: Sage.

Quinney, R. 1988. "Crime, Suffering, Service: Toward a Criminology of Peacemaking." *The Quest*: 66–75.

———. 1991. "The Way of Peace: On Crime, Suffering, and Service." In *Criminology as Peacemaking*, ed. H. E. Pepinsky and R. Quinney. Bloomington: Indiana University Press. 3–13.

———. 1995. "Socialist Humanism and the Problem of Crime: Thinking about Erich Fromm in the Development of Critical/Peacemaking Criminology." *Crime, Law and Social Change* 23(2): 147–56.

Ross, J. I. 2009. "Social Justice." In *The Encyclopedia of Race and Crime*, ed. Helen T. Greene and Shaun L. Gabbidon. Thousand Oaks: Sage. 765–66.

Sellin, T. 1938. *Culture Conflict and Crime*. NY: Bulletin No. 41 Social Science Research Council.

Shaw, C. R., and H. D. McKay. 1942. *Juvenile Delinquency in Urban Areas*. Chicago: University of Chicago Press.

Snyder, H. 2011. *Arrest in the United States, 1980-2009*. Washington, DC: Bureau of Justice Statistics.

Staples, R. 1986. "The Masculine Way of Violence." In *Homicide among Black Americans*, ed. Darnell Hawkins. NY: University Press of America. 137–53.

Stark, R. 1987. "Deviant Places: A Theory of the Ecology of Crime." *Criminology* 25: 893–909.

Sullivan, D., and L. Tifft. 1998. "Criminology as Peacemaking: A Peace-Oriented Perspecitve on Crime, Punishment, and Justice That Takes into Account the Needs of All." *The Justice Professional* 11(1–2): 5–34.

Takagi, P., and G. Shank. 2004. "Critique of Restorative Justice." *Social Justice* 31(3): 147–63.

Tonry, M. H. 1995. *Malign Neglect: Race Crime and Punishment in America*. New York: Oxford University Press.

———. 2009. "Explanations of American Punishment Policies." *Punishment and Society*: 377–94.

———. 2011. *Punishing Race: A Continuing American Dilemma*. New York: Oxford University Press.

Unnever, J. D., and S. L. Gabbidon. 2011. *A Theory of African American Offending: Race, Racism, and Crime*. New York, NY: Routledge.

Van-Ness, D., and K. H. Strong. 1993. "New Wine in Old Wineskins: Four Challenges of Restorative Justice." *Criminal Law Forum* 4(2): 251–76.

———. 1997. *Restoring Justice*. Cincinnati: Anderson.

Wacquant, L. 2009. *Punishing the Poor: The Neoliberal Government of Social Insecurity*. Duke: Duke University Press.

Wheeldon, J. 2009. "Finding Common Ground: Restorative Justice and Its Theoretical Construction(s)." *Contemporary Justice Reivew* 12(1): 91–100.

Wolfgang, M. E., and F. Ferracuti. 1969. *The Subculture of Violence: Towards an Integrated Theory in Criminology.* London: Tavistock.

Wozniak, John F. 2000. "The Voices of Peacemaking Criminology: Insights into a Perspective with an Eye toward Teaching." *Contemporary Justice Review* 3(3): 267–89.

A VISION FOR RACIAL CONGRUENCE

Reflecting on the Underrepresentation of Faculty of Color in the Academy

Alonzo M. Flowers III and Rosa M. Banda

All progress is precarious, and the solution of one problem brings us face to face with another problem.
—DR. MARTIN LUTHER KING JR.

During the 1960s, an era of great social change, Dr. Martin Luther King Jr. spoke candidly about the direction of race relations in the United States. King's foresight about the precarious nature of progress and the inherent problem-solution-problem cycle remains pertinent at institutions of higher education. While there are a myriad of issues that are reflective of this problem-solution-problem cycle in postsecondary education, this chapter focuses on faculty diversity or the lack thereof. As a national leader in the movement for social equality, Dr. King played a critical role in providing a voice for the *voiceless*. Today, Dr. King's vision for racial congruence—"going beyond purely civil rights questions to questions of human rights"—still remains true, particularly in academe, even though the conversations about race and equality have become more antiquated and increasingly covert (Harvey, 2003; Bensinon, 2004; Gillborn, 2008). One of the conundrums of the discussion of affirmative action in higher education is that it is often conceptualized as strictly a policy-centered argument that does not take into account the true need for a diversified academy, in particular the recruitment and retention of faculty of color. R. Downing and colleagues (2002) explain,

In the past decade affirmative action in education has provoked more strong sentiment in the nation than has affirmative action in employment. Even though the number of Americans who are directly touched by affirmative action programs in education is only about one quarter the number of those directly touched by affirmative action in employment, issues of equity and merit in higher education can ignite intense feelings. (p. 256)

As noted by Moody (2010), minority students account for approximately 28 percent of the overall student body, while college faculty of color make up *only* 12 percent. Over the past several decades, there has been an unprecedented increase in the enrollment of a diverse student (gender, racial, and ethnic) population in higher education, while faculty diversity continues to remain stagnant (Moses and Chang, 2006; Berry and Bonilla-Silva, 2008).

Many researchers have explained why faculty of color remain underrepresented in the academy. One of the most pervasive arguments, by Trower and Chait (2002), notes the marginal numbers of students of color earning doctorates. Trower and Chait also assert that individuals of color often find both their academic and professional experiences to be "uninviting, unaccommodating, and unappealing" (p. 34). This is further corroborated by the admission of faculty members of color who continue to encounter racist ideologies and racially discriminatory behaviors. Stanley (2006) summarized these challenges to include (a) low numbers of minorities in the professoriate and on campus, (b) barriers to tenure and promotion, (c) feelings of "otherness," and (d) experiences of racial and ethnic bias. Conversely, Jackson (1991) asserted,

> Racist perceptions, both in an individual and institutional sense, are still rather dominant, and subsequently have a tendency to not only restrict access for those who possess the requisite credentials but also stifle the professional growth of those already in academia such that they become less visible signs of success. (p. 145)

As such, antidiscrimination policies such as affirmative action were created as a protection against the racialized social structure; more specifically to help ensure that qualified diverse groups would be given an equitable opportunity to perform their job function (Turner, 2003; Quezada, 2004).

While affirmative action policies have provided students of color increased opportunities (e.g., admissions) in higher education, it is vital to make the connection to Dr. King's words that "all progress is precarious and the solution of one problem brings us face to face with another problem," as seen in the lack of representation of faculty of color at institutions of higher education. Nevertheless, efforts to diversify both student and faculty populations have remained controversial (Turner and Myers, 2000; Slaughter, Ehrenberg, and Hanushek, 2004) specifically to the enactment of affirmative action policies. Consequently, six states have forbidden the use of affirmative action in public university admissions, hiring and government contracts either through ballot referenda or legislation (Hajdin, 2002).

Despite the design and purpose of affirmative action, its policies have had an adverse effect on the recruitment and retention of faculty of color for multiple reasons. Turner (2002) notes that faculty of color have more stringent performance expectations than white faculty; are held to a higher standard with regard to their academic credentials; are viewed as tokens; "lack support or validation" for their research; and are "expected to handle minority affairs" (p. 24). Often, academic departments and education leaders are reluctant to address faculty diversity questions on campus due to issues regarding the "legality of affirmative action as promoting preferential treatment based upon race and ethnicity" (Wood, 2008, p. 2). One of the most pragmatic issues with affirmative action policies is that they undermine the basic principles of meritocracy upon which the United States was founded (Holzer and Neumark, 2006). For instance, studies conducted by both Fine and colleagues (1997) and Pierce (2003) found that their white male participants indicated that affirmative action policies allowed people of color the opportunity to take their jobs. Such sentiment shared by participants in the aforementioned studies illustrates how white males fail to acknowledge their inherent privilege in society's social structure (Pelham and Hetts, 2002).

With this in mind, the purpose of this chapter is to utilize Dr. King's prolific words to frame a discussion about affirmative action policies and how the recruitment, tenure, and promotion of faculty of color remain complex issues within institutions of higher education. Specifically, we focus on problems that faculty of color continue to encounter in the academy, namely, the search-and-hire process, search committee members, scholarship, tenure, and promotion. After a discussion of affirmative action polices and court rulings, we establish diversity in the faculty ranks as a compelling interest for institutions of higher education. Last, we delineate some of the problems that faculty of color encounter in the academy (e.g., search-and-hire process, search committee members, scholarship, tenure and promotion) and how these problems are poorly conceived and misguided based on narrow applications of affirmative action policies (Stanley, 2006; Umbach, 2006; Wood, 2008).

AFFIRMATIVE ACTION

Although Dr. King never discussed "affirmative action," he was in support of social programs that sought to achieve parity between races. In a 1967 speech titled "Where Do We Go from Here?" Dr. King offered this poignant thought: "A society that has done something special *against* the Negro for hundreds of years, must now do something special *for* him, in order to equip him to compete on a just and equal basis" (King, 1967)." As noted in the aforementioned quote, Dr. King explicitly discussed the duty of society to create programs that supported and actively promoted equality in a time of inequality. Dr. King's vision and keen awareness of the need for social programs to achieve equitable opportunities in times of racial discrimination are inextricably linked to affirmative action in the realm of public policy in the early 1960s.

"Affirmative action" refers to a set of policies and institutional actions that provide underrepresented groups (women and minorities) with increased access to employment, education, and business opportunities which were previously inhibited by discriminatory practices. In this chapter, we utilize the federal definition of affirmative action as issued from Executive Order 10925:

> A set of procedures designed to eliminate unlawful discrimination between applicants, remedy the results of such prior discrimination, and prevent such discrimination in the future. Applicants may be seeking admission to an education program or looking for professional employment.

Supporters of affirmative action acknowledge the impact of the policy but contend that there remains a preference for white male hegemonic ideology within the academy specifically the ideas held by senior colleagues (Reyna, et al., 2005).

In 1961, President Kennedy issued Executive Order 10925, which introduced the phrase "affirmative action" into public policy; this order encouraged employers to take action to ensure nondiscriminatory hiring practices (Bergmann, 1999). It is vital to note that the affirmative action debate in the context of higher education is fundamentally different when compared to the context of employment. For instance, institutions of higher education are expected to consider the "moral argument" for affirmative action, while private employers are not expected to consider such a position. The moral argument is connected to Flores and Rodriguez's (2006) assertion that, "affirmative action policies aim to identify individuals from a group that has experienced past discrimination in an attempt to balance access and opportunities for all, although the particular target groups, mechanism, and practice of various programs vary" (p. 303). Unfortunately, the misconceptions that exist on the topic of affirmative action often overshadow the purpose of the mandate, thus misleading and dividing the American public.

Despite the divisive nature of affirmative action programs, the federal mandate serves as a tool that institutions of higher education can choose to utilize when attempting to diversify the demographic landscape of their respective institution (Glazer, 2000). As a means to increase enrollment of underrepresented groups, for instance, institutions of higher education have routinely utilized affirmative action in the admissions process (Moody, 2010). One of the goals for affirmative action in higher education was to remedy past discriminatory practices that occurred by giving underrepresented groups (minorities and women) preference in employment and college admissions over white males when candidates are similarly qualified (Slaughter, Ehrenberg, and Hanushek, 2004). As a result, affirmative action triggered a series of legal challenges in higher education that weakened the diversity argument. Major judiciary rulings followed. Notably, in *Regents of the University of California v. Bakke* (1978) the Supreme Court ruled that institutional policies that set aside a specific number of places for minority students violated the Fourteenth Amendment of the US Constitution. The California ruling bars states from using quotas as a method of decision making, but the construct of race as an influential factor in the college admission process remained intact.

While the Supreme Court decision in *Regents of the University of California v. Bakke* (1978) ruled against the use of a quota system but left race as an influential factor in the college admissions process, a subsequent ruling by the Supreme Court further strengthened the need for diversity. In *Grutter v. Bollinger* (2003) the Supreme Court ruled that diversity was of "compelling interest." The educational benefits, for instance, that flow from a racially and ethnically diverse student body in higher education is a "compelling interest" that can constitutionally support race-sensitive actions. *Grutter v. Bollinger* (2003) continued to offer judiciary rulings on affirmative action policies principally in regard to the use of race and ethnicity as a factor to consider in the student admission and recruitment processes. The divisive and heated debate on affirmative action not only triggered federal court cases but also flooded many states with ballot initiatives.

Many institutions and states continue to operate under the auspice of affirmative action, but a growing number of policies were prevented by ballot initiatives or popular referenda (e.g., California's Proposition 209, Michigan's 2 Proposal) from using race-based strategies to increase their minority representation in higher education. In 2006, Michigan voters decided to adopt a constitutional amendment through a ballot proposal that prohibited all public institutions from using affirmative action programs that granted preferential treatment on the basis of race or sex in employment, education, or contracting. Public institutions that were affected by Michigan's 2 Proposal included state government, local governments, public colleges and universities, community colleges and school districts.

As in Michigan, institutions of higher education remained at the center of affirmative action debates as seen in *Fisher v. University of Texas* (2013). In *Fisher v. University of Texas* (2013), the US Supreme Court deliberated the constitutionality of a race-conscious university admissions policy under the Equal Protection Clause of the Fourteenth Amendment. In the ruling of the case the Court left intact the two central components of the *Grutter* case: (1) that obtaining the educational benefits of student body diversity is a compelling state interest that can justify the use of race in university admissions and (2) that a university may consider the race of its applicants only in a manner narrowly tailored to achieve that compelling interest (Moses and Chang, 2006). A brief excerpt of the majority opinion, delivered by Justice Kennedy, reads,

> In determining whether summary judgment in the University's favor was appropriate, the Fifth Court Circuit must assess whether the University has offered sufficient evidence to provide that its admissions programs is narrowly tailored to obtain the educational benefits of diversity. (pp. 8–13)

In addition, the Court placed a conspicuous emphasis on the second holding where the Court asserted that the burden of proof falls on the university. As such, a Supreme Court ruling was vacated and remanded to the Fifth Circuit Court so that the University of Texas can provide sufficient evidence of the benefits of diversity within this case. According to Horn, Flores, and Orfield (2006), when institutions say that they have ended affirmative action, they are almost always talking about one part of an interrelated process, while continuing affirmative policies on other fronts, either through direct action or by adopting "race-attentive" recruitment policies focused on largely minority communities and schools (p. 9). Assuredly, merit has become one of the pervasive arguments in the affirmative action debate. Berry and Bonilla-Silva (2008) assert that "malleable notions of qualification [and] merit" are simply means of "perpetuating racial inequality" (p. 237).

A "COMPELLING INTEREST" FOR FACULTY DIVERSITY

The aforementioned landmark court cases have offered controversial and broad judiciary rulings on affirmative action, namely, in regards to how race and ethnicity factor in the admission process of college students. However, the court set the precedent in *Grutter v. Bollinger* (2003) where diversity was established as a "compelling interest" for institutions of higher education. While this decision was in reference to students, Springer (2002) argues that the "many elements of the decisions lend support to the faculty diversity legal debate" (p. 5). Few would argue that faculty diversity is not a "compelling interest" for institutions of higher education.

The compelling interest for a diverse faculty is beneficial for students and postsecondary institutions alike. There is a plethora of research that notes the importance of faculty of color in academe, particularly if institutions of higher education wish to adequately prepare students for a diverse society and increasing global society (Antonio, 2002; Stanley, 2006; Turner, González, and Wood, 2008; Umbach, 2006). Namely, students benefit from taking courses from diverse faculty because of the varied teaching approaches that faculty of color employ (Antonio, 2000; Garcia, 2000; Turner, 2000; Umbach, 2006; Vargas, 2002). In addition to instructional approaches, faculty of color are more likely to infuse diversity in the curriculum (Hurtado, Ponjuan, and Smith, 2003) by being inclusive of texts and research written by minorities and women (Milem, 2003). A diverse faculty, research has shown, also influences minority students' persistence in college (Castellanos and Jones, 2003; Hernandez, 2000; Osegura, Locks, and Vega, 2009) primarily because faculty of color are often mentors and role models for their students (Stanley, 2006).

A diverse faculty is also beneficial to institutions. In most cases, faculty of color are used to entice students of color to attend their respective institutions. This suggests that faculty of color not only aid in the recruitment of students of color but can also influence the retention issues with which institutions of higher education continue to struggle. In addition to recruitment and retention efforts, faculty of color also bring innovative scholarship to academe (Turner, 2000; Urrieta and Mendez Benavidez, 2007). Moreno and colleagues (2006) posit that postsecondary institutions "must tap the kind of intellectual power and innovation that comes from a professoriate that is racially and ethnically diverse" (p. 2). This latter benefit to institutions of higher education via the scholarship that faculty of color typically engage in is not always valued by majority faculty, which can be problematic, a discussion that will be further developed in a subsequent section.

The burden of proof to reaffirm the compelling interest of diversity for universities is no small task. While progress has been made in regards to infusing diversity within the higher education realm, it has been precarious in nature as low numbers of faculty of color exist in the academy. This reality remains reflective of King's foresight that cautioned against the precarious nature of progress. The inherent problem-solution-problem cycle, particularly in regards to achieving parity between races, extends further than establishing a compelling interest used to diversify the student enrollment at postsecondary institutions. Equally important and relevant to King's foresight are the on-going challenges that minority faculty encounter in their journey through the faculty pipeline. What follows is an explication of the challenges that diverse faculty encounter in academe, despite the verified compelling interest they bring to students and institutions alike.

DIVERSE FACULTY

Dr. King's quote about the precarious nature of progress and the inherent nature of problem-solution-problem remains a relevant and powerful reflection of reality, particularly in regards to the diversity of faculty, or lack thereof, found at institutions of higher education. The National Center for Education Statistics (2008) reports that faculty of color, specifically black/African Americans, Latina/os (used interchangeably with Hispanic), Asian Americans, and American Indians comprise *only* 6 percent, 4 percent, 6 percent, and .5 percent, respectively, of the 16 percent of full-time faculty. Further disaggregation of data reveals that only 5.3 percent of the full professors in the United States are African American, Hispanic, or Native American (Ryu, 2008). Even though faculty of color are more prevalent on college campuses today when compared to the 1960s, national and state data suggest that there has been insignificant change in the percent of minority faculty (Moreno, et al., 2006). As a result, faculties of color continue to be underrepresented in the academy (Harvey, 2001; Trower and Chait, 2002; Turner, 2003; Turner and Meyers, 2000; Quezada, 2004).

Even though progress has been made in the number of minorities who have attained terminal degrees, for those who seek faculty positions, problems prior to and upon their arrival on college campuses have made the promise of social equality stagnant in nature. As previously noted, affirmative action policies were enacted to increase parity in regards to diversity in society—a sentiment that profoundly undergirded Dr. King's struggle in the civil rights movement. To the dismay of social justice advocates, the minimal increase of faculty of color at postsecondary institutions and subsequent accolades earned (e.g., scholarship, tenure, and promotion) brings about deep-rooted prejudices that continue to slow the true progress of social equality. The precarious nature of progress noted in Dr. King's words depicts the challenges that faculty of color encounter throughout their time in the academy via the faculty pipeline. What follows is a brief explication of those, albeit limited, challenges faculty of color encounter which include faculty search process, search committee members, scholarship, and tenure and promotion.

Faculty Search Process

Make no mistake that a viable pool of scholars of color exists; however, their entrance into the academy is often hindered by the faculty search process. Smith (2000) asserts that the traditional hiring practices most universities employ often impede the recruitment and hiring of faculty of color. Such an impediment is residual of the arbitrary nature of the selection process of potential candidates. The traditional search-and-hire process, both complex and subjective (Smith, 2000), is not based on "true meritocracy" (Simplicio, 2007). The traditional search-and-hire process presents faculty of color with a new problem as, despite their terminal degree attainment, they continue to be overlooked for tenure-track faculty positions. To mediate this issue, departments must proactively recruit a pool of candidates that purposively includes faculty of color as a means to counter the traditional search-and-hire process that is overwhelmingly found at institutions of higher education. Bilimoria and Buch (2010) posit that "[h]iring outcomes may be diversified by increasing the range of candidates in the early stages in the faculty search process" (p. 28). Still, the reality of true progress of diversifying faculty only materializes if institutions and departments are genuinely committed to *true* diversity.

Search Committee Members

Faculty who possess expert subject knowledge are often charged with finding viable candidates for faculty appointments within their respective departments. As search committee members, faculty not only bring forth expert subject knowledge but also consciously embrace a "color-blind" perspective when assessing candidates' qualifications (Kayes, 2006). A color-blind perspective, though conscious in nature, often promotes biased-prone conceptualizations about candidates (Bilimoria and Buch, 2010; Moody, 2004) without search committees' knowledge. Crosby, Iyer, and Sincharoen (2006) assert that the unconscious nature of search committees' bias is difficult to correct if unexamined. Such unconscious biases, as a result, continue to promote, replicate, and preserve the culture found in the department. Kayes (2006) posits that the unconscious (and, at times, conscious) bias that search committee members possess often undermines the goal of diversifying faculty. Smith (2000) similarly notes, "Faculty search committees that hold unverified assumptions cause campuses to engage in self-fulfilling prophecies regarding the recruitment of minority faculty" (p. 51). Unsurprisingly, tension and conflict often arise when discussing the qualifications of candidates if search committee members lack an understanding of the importance of diversifying faculty (Bilimoria and Buch, 2010).

Scholarship

While the prior two subsections discuss problems faculty of color encounter prior to their arrival on college campuses, the next two subsections explicate the problems that they encounter upon their arrival and matriculation in the faculty pipeline. The inherent privilege in a faculty appointment is that scholars can remain autonomous in the type of research they pursue. Still, the "autonomous" nature of scholarship remains limited in that "mainstream" forms of scholarship are often privileged over scholarship that is not viewed as "traditional." Faculty of color, more often than not, engage in scholarship that examines and produces "new knowledge about sociocultural differences" (Robinson-Armstrong, 2010, p. 37). Stanley (2006) similarly asserts that faculty of color focus on research that benefits communities of minorities which is not considered to be "mainstream" and is less apt to be published in "top tier" journals. Such scholarship, Turner (2003) posits, is often not respected or valued by majority faculty. The latter part of this statement is problematic on multiple levels and is of increasing concern to how it possibly can influence tenure and promotion decisions.

Tenure and Promotion

Despite the "autonomy" of research agendas, the "nontraditional" scholarship that faculty of color conduct often counters traditional paradigms of thought found within university departments and can jeopardize tenure and promotion (Stanley, 2006). For faculty of color, in other words, having values, knowledge, and interests divergent from those of the majority of the faculty can be detrimental to professional advancement (Diggs, et al., 2009). Faculty of color, for example, are often expected to advise and mentor students of color as well as take part in committee work that addresses issues of diversity. While such expectations are valuable in nature, this work is often not rewarded when placed on tenure dossiers. Designed to serve as a mechanism to safeguard academic freedom in times of political unrest, the awarding of tenure has been morphed into what some believe to be a process that is not solely based on merit. A recent study conducted by Trower (2009) found that African American and Hispanic faculty did *not* believe that tenure and promotion decisions were *only* based on performance. She observed,

> [S]ome minorities are skeptical about the claim that tenure decisions are entirely merit-based. They may have experienced chilliness, hostility, or outright racism, or they may have minority colleagues or friends who have. They may also be all-too-familiar with unconscious or implicit bias. (p. 44)

Whether unconscious or implicit, faculty of color remain cognizant of the bias that infiltrates the institutional departments and universities in which they belong. To be certain, there are several reasons why faculty are not awarded tenure but minority faculty and especially, female minority faculty encounter much more "psychological minefields" while in the academy (Ruffins, 2007) and on their trajectory to tenure and promotion. Being worthy of tenure by faculty members who have divergent values and interests, more often than not, undermines the work that faculty of color typically engage in—leaving the decision to award and promote via tenure a heavily arbitrary process.

CONCLUSION

There is no doubt that if Dr. Martin Luther King Jr. were alive today he would be pleased with the progress this country has made in regards to diversity. Yet, he would be quick to reiterate his belief about the precarious nature of progress. While strides have been made in regards to faculty diversity, more problems have surfaced as a result despite an established argument that situates diverse faculty as a "compelling" interest for both students and institutions. First, gaining entrance in the elite academy of institutions of higher education continues to be challenging for faculty of color. Second, faculty of color who enter the academy continue to encounter embedded racist (and gendered) ideals that make their interests and values (via scholarship and committee work) a risk to their promotion and tenure. Solutions—or at least improvements—to the aforementioned problems are feasible, but once solved other obstacles are certain to surface. Achieving diversity—as seen through the vision of Dr. King—remains elusive to an extent. Tatum offered this poignant perspective: "Twenty years ago, a lack of diversity within a university was a consequence of unequal opportunity in American society. Today, a lack of diversity within a university faculty suggests unequal opportunity in that university" (p. 2). To put it simply, institutions must be willing to change more than the mere complexion of their faculty. While progress is always good, Dr. King's foresight of its precarious nature remains truer than ever today.

REFERENCES

Antonio, A. L. 2000. "Faculty of Color and Scholarship Transformed: New Arguments for Diversifying Faculty." *Diverse Digest* 3(2): 6–7.

Bensimon, E. M. 2004. "The Diversity Scorecard: A Learning Approach to Institutional Change." *Change* 36(1): 45–52.

Bergmann, B. R. 1999. "The Continuing Need for Affirmative Action." *Quarterly Review of Economics and Finance* 39: 757–68.

Berry, B., and E. Bonilla-Silva. 2008. "They Should Hire the One with the Best Score: White Sensitivity to Qualification Differences in Affirmative Action Hiring Decisions." *Ethnic and Racial Studies* 31(2): 215–42.

Bilimoria, D., and K. K. Buch. 2010. "The Search Is On: Engendering Faculty Diversity through More Effective Search and Recruitment." *Change* 42(4): 27–32.

Castellanos, J., and L. Jones, eds. 2003. *The Majority in the Minority: Expanding the Representation of Latina/o Faculty, Administrators and Students in Higher Education.* Sterling, VA: Stylus.

Cook, B. J., and D. I. Córdova. 2006. *Minorities in Higher Education: Twenty-Second Annual Status Report*. Washington, DC: American Council on Education.

Crosby, F. J., A. Iyer, and S. Sincharoen. 2006. "Understanding Affirmative Action." *Annual Review Psychology* 57: 585–611.

Diggs, G. A., D. F. Garrison-Wade, D. Estrada, and R. Galindo. 2009. "Smiling Faces and Colored Spaces: The Experiences of Faculty of Color Pursuing Tenure in the Academy." *Urban Review* 41: 312–33.

Downing, R., M. Lubensky, S. Sincharoen, P. Gurin, F. Crosby, S. Queirolo, and J. Franco.2002. "Affirmative Action in Higher Education." *The Diversity Factor* 10(2): 13–18.

Executive Order. No. 10925, 13 C.F.R.1960 1961.

Fine, M., L. Weis, L. Powel, and M. Wong, eds. 1997. *Off White: Readings on Race, Power, and Society*. New York: Rouledge.

Flores, A., and C. M. Rodriguez. 2006. "University Faculty Attitudes on Affirmative Action Principles toward Faculty and Students." *Equity and Excellence in Education* 39(4): 303–12.

Garcia, M., ed. 2000. *Succeeding in an Academic Career: A Guide for Faculty of Color*. Westport, CT: Greenwood.

Glazer, N. 2000. "Society Needs Affirmative Action in Higher Education." In *Affirmative Action*, ed. B. J. Grapes, pp. 14–22. San Diego: Greenhaven.

Gillborn, D. 2008. Racism and Education: Coincidence or Conspiracy? Abingdon: Routledge.

Hajdin, M. 2002. "Affirmative Action, Old and New." *Journal of Social Philosophy* 33(1): 83–96.

Harvey, W. B. 2001. *Minorities in Higher Education: Eighteenth Annual Report*. Washington, DC: American Council on Education.

———. 2003. *Minorities in Higher Education 2002–2003: 20th Annual Status Report*. Washington, DC: American Council on Education.

Hernandez, J. C. 2000. "Understanding the Retention of Latino College Students." *Journal of College Student Development* 41(6): 575–88.

Holzer, H. J. and D. Neumark. 2006. "Affirmative Action: What Do We Know?" *Journal of Policy Analysis and Management* 25(2): 463–90.

Horn, C. L., S. M. Flores, and G. Orfield, eds. 2006. *Latino Educational Opportunity*. San Francisco: Jossey-Bass

Hurtado, S., L. Ponjuan, and G. Smith. 2003. *Women and Faculty of Color on Campus: Campus Diversity and Civic Engagement Activities*. University of Michigan Diverse Demographic Project. Retrieved from http://www.umich.edu/~divdemo/.

Jackson, K. W. 1991. "Black Faculty in Academia." In *The Racial Crisis in American Higher Education*, ed. P. G. Altbach and K. Lomotey, pp. 3–17. Albany, NY: State University of New York Press.

Kayes, P. E. 2006. "New Paradigms for Diversifying Faculty and Staff in Higher Education: Uncovering Cultural Bias in the Search and Hiring Process." *Multicultural Education* 14(2): 65–69.

King, M. L., Jr. 1967. "Where Do We Go from Here?" Annual Report delivered at the 11th Convention of the Southern Christian Leadership Conference, August 16, Atlanta, GA.

Lee, W. Y. 2002. "Culture and Institutional Climate: Influences on Diversity in Higher Education." *The Review of Higher Education* 25(3): 359–68.

Milem, J. F. 2003. "The Educational Benefits of Diversity: Evidence from Multiple Sectors." In *Examining the Evidence on Racial Dynamics in Higher Education*, ed. M. Chang, D. Witt, J. Jones, and K. Hakuta. Palo Alto, CA: Stanford University Press.

Moody, J. 2010. "Rising above Cognitive Errors: Guidelines to Improve Faculty Searches, Evaluations, and Decision-Making." In *Diversity on Campus*. San Diego, CA.

Moody, J. A. 2004. *Faculty Diversity: Problems and Solutions*. New York: Routledge.

Moreno, J. F., D. G. Smith, A. R. Clayton-Pedersen, S. Parker, and D. H. Teraguchi. 2006. "The Revolving Door for Underrepresented Minority Faculty in Higher Education: An Analysis from the Campus Diversity Initiative." In *Association of American Colleges and Universities*. Claremont Graduate University, 1–18.

Moses, M. S., and M. J. Chang. 2006. Toward a Deeper Understanding of the Diversity Rationale." *Educational Researcher* 35 (1): 6–11.

National Science Foundation, Division of Science Resources Statistics. 2008. *Bachelor's Degrees, by Race/Ethnicity, Citizenship, Sex, and Field: 2008*. Washington, DC: National Science Foundation.

Oseguera, L., A. M. Locks, and I. I. Vega. 2009. "Increasing Latina/o Students' Baccalaureate Attainment: A Focus on Retention." *Journal of Hispanic Higher Education* 8(23): 23–53.

Pelham, B. W., and J. J. Hetts 2002. "Underworked and Overpaid: Elevated Entitlement in Men's Self-Pay." *Journal of Experimental Social Psychology* 37: 93–103.

Pierce, Jennifer L. 2003. "Racing for Innocence: Whiteness, Corporate Culture, and the Backlash against Affirmative Action." *Qualitative Sociology* 26: 53–70.

Quezada, R. L. 2004. "The Absence of Diversity in the Academy: Faculty of Color in Educational Administration Programs." *Education* 125(2): 213–21.

Robinson-Armstrong, A. 2010. "Benefits of a Diverse Faculty: A Review of the Literature." *A Collection of Papers on Self-Study and Institutional Improvements in Higher Education*. The Higher Learning Commission.

Reyna, C., A. Tucker, W. Korfmacher, and P. Henry 2005. "Searching for Common Ground between Supporters and Opponents of Affirmative Action." *Political Psychology* 26(5): 667–82.

Ryu, M. 2008. *Minorities in Higher Education 2008: 23rd Status Report*. Washington, DC: American Council on Education.

Ruffins, P. 2007. "The Shelter of Tenure Is Eroding and for Faculty of Color Gaining Membership May Be Tougher than Ever." Retrieved Oct. 18 from http://diverseeducation.com/article/8333/.

Simplicio, J. S. C. 2007. "A Closer Look at the Truth behind the Hiring Practice: How Colleges Really Hire." *Education* 128(2): 256–61.

Slaughter, J. B., R. G. Ehrenberg, and E. Hanushek. 2004. "The Underrepresentation of Minority Faculty in Higher Education: Panel Discussion [Electronic version]." *American Economic Review* 94(2): 302–06.

Smith, D. G. 2000. "How to Diversify the Faculty." *Academe* 86(5): 48–52.

Springer, A. 2002. *How to Diversify Faculty: The Current Legal Landscape*. Washington, DC: American Association of University Professors.

Stanley, C. A. 2006. "Coloring the Academic Landscape: Faculty of Color Breaking the Silence in Predominantly White Colleges and Universities." *American Educational Research Journal* 43: 701–36.

Tatum, C. 2003. "The Recruitment and Retention of a Diverse Faculty: A Proposal by the Dean's Diversity Subcommittee." http://w3.coh.arizona.edu/coh/diversity_initiatives/DiversityProposal.pdf.

Trower, C. A. 2009. "Toward a Greater Understanding of the Tenure Track for Minorities." *Change* 41(5): 38–45.

Trower, C. A., and R. P. Chait. 2002. "Faculty Diversity: Too Little for Too Long." *Harvard Magazine* (March-April), 33ff.

Turner, C. S. 2000. "New Faces, New Knowledge: As Women and Minorities Join the Faculty, They Bring Intellectual Diversity in Pedagogy and in Scholarship." *Academe* 86(5): 34–37.

———. 2003. "Incorporation and Marginalization in the Academy: From Border toward Center for Faculty of Color?" *Journal of Black Studies*, 34: 112–25.

Turner, C. S., J. C. González, and J. L. Wood. 2008. "Faculty of Color in Academe: What 20 Years of Literature Tells Us." *Journal of Diversity in Higher Education* 1(3): 139–68.

Turner, C. S., and S. L. Myers. 2000. *Faculty of Color in Academe: Bittersweet Success*. Des Moines, IA: Longwood Division, Allyn and Bacon.

Umbach, P. D. 2006. "The Contribution of Faculty of Color to Undergraduate Education." *Research in Higher Education*, 47: 317–45.

Urrieta, L., Jr., and L. Mendez Benavidez. 2007. "Community Commitment and Activist Scholarship: Chicana/o Professors and the Practice of Consciousness." *Journal of Hispanic Higher Education* 6: 222–36.

Vargas, L., ed. 2002. *Women of Faculty of Color in the White Classroom: Narratives on the Pedagogical Implications of Teacher Diversity*. New York: Peter Lang.

Wood, J. L. 2008. "Ethical Dilemmas in African-American Faculty Representation." *Journal of Education Policy*. https://www4.nau.edu/cee/jep/journalterms.aspx?term=1andyear=2008.

AFRICAN AMERICAN HEALTHCARE

Assessing Progress and Needs through Martin Luther King's Perspective on Social Justice and Equality

Marcus L. Martin, Audrey E. Snyder, Jamela M. Martin,
Taj'ullah Sky Lark, Hannah Firdyiwek, and Leslie Walker

INTRODUCTION AND BACKGROUND

Since Dr. Martin Luther King Jr.'s death in 1968, the US population has grown substantially, with a marked increase in the percentage of people of color. It is estimated that by 2050, more than half of the American population will be people of color (US Census Bureau, 2008). The United States has the largest per capita expenditure on health care of any nation in the world ($8,233 per capita versus $3,268 average per capita in other developed nations), yet the United States ranks below many developed countries in health care outcomes (Kane, 2012). These statistics, as dramatically shown in Figure 4.1, sparked discussion among students and faculty involved in two University of Virginia programs.

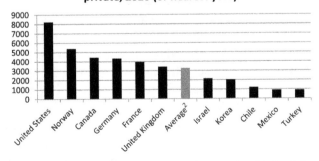

Figure 4.1 The average is based on data from the thirty-four member nations of the Organization for Economic Co-operation and Development. Sample excerpted from OECD (2012), OECD Health Data 2012: How Does the United States Compare at www.oecd.org/health/healthdata.

Students from the University of Virginia, who were either enrolled in the institution's study abroad program UVA in St. Kitts and Nevis January Term (J-Term) 2013 or who conducted research in the UVA Jefferson Public Citizens' summer 2012 research project in St. Kitts and Nevis were asked to reflect on the question, "What might Dr. King say about health care today?" Students researched Dr. King's speeches and data to develop their viewpoints and were asked to discuss their views with others in their group and with faculty and then write group reports.

The educational relationship between UVA and St. Kitts and Nevis originated with a visit from the federation's minister of health to Charlottesville during October 2007. The minister of health expressed an interest in collaborating with UVA on health care education. For the university, this partnership would become an opportunity to further diversify the cultural content of the undergraduate curriculum and to expand options for studying abroad in St. Kitts and Nevis. Of note, Marcus L. Martin and Audrey E. Snyder served as guest editors for the *Special Edition of the Journal of Race and Policy* Proceedings of the UVa in St. Kitts and Nevis Program" 7(1)(Summer 2011). During the first two weeks of J-Term, UVA offers a study abroad program on disaster preparedness in St. Kitts and Nevis. Students studying in St. Kitts and Nevis during J-Term 2013 participated in this research.

The second group of students participated in the Jefferson Public Citizens (JPC) Program at UVA, which was established to provide undergraduate students the opportunity to conduct public service projects and research. The JPC Program inspires students to act as engaged citizens through active community partnerships, research service projects, and scholarly reflections and encourages them to prepare to work with local, national, and international communities to effect positive change in the world. Authors of this chapter Marcus L. Martin, Audrey E. Snyder, and Jamela M. Martin served as mentors to the JPC students who conducted research in St. Kitts and Nevis in the summer of 2012. The JPC students' research project was titled Enhancing Primary and Preventative Care through Increased Utilization of Community Health Centers in St. Kitts and Nevis. They studied the views of patients, health care providers, and policy makers regarding the health system through surveys and interviews. These students gained an appreciation and awareness of cultural differences and health care nuances of the developing West Indies Federation compared to those of the United States of America. A manuscript reporting the results of this study was published in the 2013 edition of the Jefferson Public Citizens' journal, *Public* (www .virginia.edu/jpc).

The Federation of St. Kitts and Nevis is a developing nation. There, unlike the United States, the health care expenditure per capita is very modest and focused on primary and preventive care. Students in the study abroad program and Jefferson Public Citizens research team made comparisons between the health care system of a small federation with much lower financial resources and the health care system in the United States while reflecting on the study question.

In his talk on January 4, 2013, to students of the UVA in St. Kitts and Nevis Program, Dr. Patrick Martin of the Ministry of Health and chief medical officer of St. Kitts and Nevis noted that comparatively, the public and private health expenditures are contradistinctive between the Federation of St. Kitts and Nevis (SKN) and the United States. Total health care expenditure in SKN is $691 per capita versus $8,233 in the United States, and represents 5.6 percent of the GDP versus 17.3 percent in the United States (table 4.1).

Table 4.1		
	SKN	USA
Total Health Expenditure (% GDP)	5.6 (2010)	17.3 (2009)
Total Health Expenditure (US$)	691 (2010)	8,233 (2009)
Table 1. Total Health Care Expenditure per capita in St. Kitts and Nevis and the United States		
Source: Chief Medical Officer of St. Kitts and Nevis, Dr. Patrick Martin, of the Ministry of Health during his talk on January 4, 2013, to UVa nursing students.		

The guiding principles of health care policy in St. Kitts and Nevis are consistent with the principles espoused by the World Health Organization (WHO) as central to a primary health care-based health system. These include social justice, responsiveness to legitimate needs, quality orientation, participation, intersectionality, sustainability, and government accountability. The overall themes of service delivery incorporate prevention, health promotion, care of the family throughout the life cycle, and the health of the environment. More specifically, the core structural and functional elements of the primary health care orientation include the following: guaranteed universal coverage and access; optimal organization and management based upon sound policy and legal and institutional frameworks; high-quality programs and services that are available, accessible, affordable, acceptable, and quality-enhancing; decision making based on the well-being of families and communities; participation by families and communities in decision making; and an emphasis on health promotion, prevention, and health maintenance. The ultimate vision for population health and personal medical service delivery is comprehensive, holistic, and integrated care rendered by coordinated teams of knowledgeable and skilled providers.

Access to health care and behavioral modifications are two important determinants of health outcomes in any health system. While in recent years the uninsured and underinsured in the United States total about 20 percent of the population (approximately 61 million US citizens) the Patient Protection and Affordable Care Act (PPACA), also known as ObamaCare, has the potential of providing health insurance to 30 million more Americans (Patient Care and Affordable Care Act, 2010).

The Affordable Care Act is perhaps the single most important governmental legislation of the past fifty years to have an impact on the health of those living in the United States. Compared to fifty years ago, the United States today has made great strides with health care access, quality of clinical care, research, and diversity within our health professions' training programs and workforce. Although the United States has made much progress, there is still much work to do, particularly with access to health care, health care insurance coverage, and representation of minorities in the health professions.

METHODS

We postulated that if Dr. King were alive his focus on health care would center on issues of access. Considering this hypothesis, we asked students and faculty engaged in study abroad in the St. Kitts and Nevis J-Term and JPC summer research programs to participate in this project on what might Dr. King say about health care today. Several steps were utilized in compiling data and opinions on this topic. Thirty-four undergraduate students with various academic majors at UVA, enrolled in the 2013 J-Term course, conducted literature reviews and participated in focus groups to condense the pertinent literature into six papers. These students also held discussions with six UVA faculty members teaching in the St. Kitts and Nevis J-Term. Five additional students, who participated in the JPC summer research, comprised a peer review group to edit and further condense the six papers into one manuscript. Finally, three of the six faculty mentors further edited the manuscript for accuracy and completion.

Students in the UVA in St. Kitts and Nevis study abroad program learned how a developing nation focuses resources on primary and preventative care in comparison with health care in the United States. UVA faculty and the St. Kitts and Nevis minister of health gave pertinent lectures to the students on various health-related topics including the following: an overview of health care and culture in St. Kitts and Nevis; global health and global research methodologies; infant mortality as an indicator of population health; emergency and disaster management; current health disparities; and what might Dr. King think about health care today. Students were immersed in local health care culture through field experiences at St. Kitts and Nevis hospitals and community health clinics. A total of thirty-nine students and six faculty members participated in the project.

Students in the UVA in St. Kitts and Nevis J-Term course were divided into six teams of five or six students each. They conducted literature searches on Dr. King's speeches and reviewed current literature relevant to health care access. Student teams met daily over the course of the two-week January term to debate pertinent findings related to Dr. King's speeches. Daily team focus groups fostered communication, teamwork, and consensus.

The JPC group of five students interacted frequently from November 2011 during planning and implementation of summer research, through their May 2013 final presentation on access to community health centers in St. Kitts and Nevis. This group of students served as peer reviewers, critiquing the summarized opinions expressed in the six papers written by the January Term students.

RESULTS OF STUDENT LITERATURE SEARCHES

Equality and justice for all are common themes resonating from Dr. King's speeches. Although the focus of each speech was specific to a particular issue at hand, the themes are overarching in relevance to the human condition and inalienable rights. Quotations from Dr. King's speeches are applicable to the disparities and underpinnings of the state of health of minorities in both the United States and the Federation of St. Kitts and Nevis, and possible remedies thereof. Dr. King was able to see the interdependency of our human existence and how the denial of human and civil rights threatens the overall health of all mankind.

> Let us march on poverty until no American parent has to skip a meal so that their children may eat. March on poverty until no starved man walks the streets of our cities and towns in search of jobs that do not exist.
>
> "Address at the Conclusion of the Selma to Montgomery March on Alabama State Capital," Montgomery, AL, March 25, 1965

Because the goal of America is freedom, abused and scorned tho' we may be, our destiny is tied up with America's destiny.
"Letter from a Birmingham Jail," Birmingham, AL, April 16, 1963

We've come a long, long way, but we have a long, long way to go in economic equality.
"A Realistic Look at the Question of Progress in the Area of Race Relations," St. Louis, MO, April 10, 1957

Of all forms of inequity, injustice in health care is the most shocking and inhuman.
"Speech to the Medical Committee for Human Rights," Chicago, IL, March 25, 1966

All I'm saying is simply this, that all life is interrelated, that somehow we're caught in an inescapable network of mutuality tied in a single garment of destiny. Whatever affects one directly affects all indirectly. For some reason, I can never be what I ought to be until you are what you ought to be. You can never be what you ought to be until I am what I ought to be. This is the interrelated structure of reality.
"Eulogy for the Martyred Children," Birmingham, AL, September 18, 1963

How long? Not long, because the arc of the moral universe is long, but it bends toward justice.
"How Long, Not Long," also known as "Our God Is Marching On," Montgomery, AL, March 25, 1965

The good neighbor looks beyond the external accidents and discerns those inner qualities that make all men human and, therefore, brothers.
Strength to Love, 1963

Injustice anywhere is a threat to justice everywhere.
"Letter from a Birmingham Jail," Birmingham, AL, April 16, 1963

Now, I say to you today my friends, even though we face the difficulties of today and tomorrow, I still have a dream. It is a dream deeply rooted in the American dream. I have a dream that one day this nation will rise up and live out the true meaning of its creed: "We hold these truths to be self-evident, that all men are created equal."
"I Have a Dream," Washington, DC, August 28, 1963

If any of you are around when I have to meet my day, I don't want a long funeral. And if you get somebody to deliver the eulogy, tell them not to talk too long. Every now and then I wonder what I want them to say ... I'd like somebody to mention that day, that Martin Luther King, Jr., tried to give his life serving others. I'd like for somebody to say that day, that Martin Luther King, Jr., tried to love somebody. I want you to be able to say that day that I did try to feed the hungry. I want you to say that I tried to love and serve humanity.

"The Drum Major Instinct," Atlanta, GA, February 4, 1968

In a sense we've come to our nation's capital to cash a check. When the architects of our republic wrote the magnificent words of the Constitution and the Declaration of Independence, they were signing a promissory note to which every American was to fall heir. This note was a promise that all men—yes, black men as well as white men—would be guaranteed the unalienable rights of life, liberty and the pursuit of happiness.

"I Have a Dream," Washington, DC, August 28, 1963

These quotations (Washington, 1986; King, 1965, 1957; PNHP, 2014) as examples of Dr. King's sentiment about human rights and social justice, coupled with current literature regarding health disparities and access issues, served as the basis for six brief papers written by the student teams. This chapter on what might Dr. King say about health care today was written excerpting from the following student papers:

TEAM 1: "Infant Mortality Rates in African American Women: What Would Dr. King Say?"

TEAM 2: "That Our Destinies Are One: Exploring African American Mistrust of Health Care and a Response from a Civil Rights Perspective"

TEAM 3: "Access: A Crucial Multidimensional Component of Healthcare"

TEAM 4: "Dreaming of Equality: Those Excluded by the Affordable Care Act"

TEAM 5: "The Affordable Care Act—What Would Dr. King Say?"

TEAM 6: "United States Healthcare: Accessibility and Affordability"

DISCUSSION

Health Disparities

A health disparity is an inequality in health outcomes or mortality. Disparities can also be viewed as a lack of equal opportunity or treatment within a
health care system. Generally, health disparities are a measure of inequity and
are typically deemed unfair, unjust, unnecessary, and often avoidable. Close
to 20 percent of the US population in recent times has been either uninsured
or underinsured. There is a disproportionate share of minorities enrolled in
lower-end health care insurance plans. Minorities tend to be underinsured
with higher deductibles, higher premiums, and likely no dental coverage,
no catastrophic coverage, and no prescription plan. The most important
predictor of quality of care is access to care.

While some health disparities are associated with poverty, education, and
housing, some are genetically linked, and others are directly associated with
implicit biases in health care. African Americans have the highest overall
incidence of death rates from cancer of the lung, colon, rectum, prostate, and
breast than any other ethnic/racial group. African Americans also have the
highest incidence of and death rate from HIV-AIDS. Heart disease, diabetes
and infant mortality rates are highest among African Americans. African
Americans have the highest rates of homicide deaths. Latinos have the highest rate of cervical cancer. Asian Americans have the highest rate of gastric
cancer (National Cancer Institute, 2008; Friedan, 2011).

Infant Mortality

"Infant mortality [defined as the death of a child before the age of one] is
an important indicator of the health of a nation or community because it is
associated with a variety of factors such as maternal health, quality and access to medical care, socioeconomic conditions, and public health practices"
(MacDorman, et al., 1994). In 2010, the US infant mortality rate (IMR) was
6.14 infant deaths per 1000 live births (Miniño and Murphy, 2012). The 2010
IMR in comparison to the 1990s' IMR has decreased, yet the rates are not
practical.

Between 2006 and 2008, the IMR for non-Hispanic blacks was 13.1 per
1,000 live births and 5.6 for non-Hispanic whites, with infant mortality occurring 2.3 times more in non-Hispanic blacks in the United States (MacDorman and Mathews, 2012). In 2010, the US Department of Health and Human

Services (USDHHS) launched its Healthy People 2020 targets, which aimed to improve the health of all Americans along a decade-long initiative. Its goal of fewer than six infant deaths per 1,000 live births highlights the scope and importance of critically addressing this issue for African Americans.

According to the USDHHS, among white women with live births, 79.2 percent began care in the first trimester of pregnancy, and 4.9 percent received late or no care. Conversely, far fewer black women began early care (60.6 percent), and twice as many obtained late prenatal care (11.3 percent) (Kiely and Kogan, 1994). African American women are also more likely to give birth to low-weight babies, a factor which is closely linked to infant mortality. A focus on adequate and consistent prenatal care for African American women is essential to lowering infant mortality rates in this population.

It is well established that prenatal care is connected to birth outcomes. The American Association of Pediatrics (AAP) and the American College of Obstetrics and Gynecology (ACOG) assert that women who receive early and regular prenatal care deliver healthier infants (10). It is during prenatal care that comorbidities such as maternal hypertension and diabetes, which can lead to infant death, are prevented and/or addressed (Lockwood and Lemons, 2007; Johns, et al., 2007). The Institute of Medicine estimates that for every additional $1.00 spent on prenatal care, $3.37 is saved on health care spending for neonates (Lantos and Lauderdale, 2011).

Without prenatal care and surveillance, conditions such as gestational diabetes (GDM) and preeclampsia may go unrecognized in poor, uneducated, and/or vulnerable populations. Otherwise healthy women should be at lower risk of developing comorbidities such as GDM. However, income, education level, and ethnicity are significant social determinants of the development of these conditions (Goldenberg, et al., 1996). Controlling for factors such as poverty, education, housing, employment, and medical risks such as high blood pressure and diabetes mellitus, 90 percent of the difference between black and white infant mortality rates in our country cannot be accounted for.

Studies show that education level is a significant contributor to infant mortality, and women of all races tend to have higher infant mortality rates if they have less than a high school education. Unfortunately, in African American women, even with college and/or professional degrees, the infant mortality rate is still greater than that of all other races. There is also a potential familial tie between low birth weight and premature births in African American women. Mothers who were low birth weight babies give birth to low birth weight babies. There is also an association with high blood pressure and diabetes (Jaber, Melchior, and Rutledge, 1992). According to Singh and van Dyck (2010):

> The leading causes of infant death in 2007 were congenital anomalies (birth defects), short gestation and low birth weight, Sudden Infant Death Syndrome (SIDS), maternal complications of pregnancy, unintentional injuries, chord and placental complications, and [respiratory distress syndrome]. Together these causes accounted for 62.1 percent of all infant deaths in 2007 and 57.9 percent of all infant deaths in 1970.

There can never be a quality health care system, based on equality, unless all people are given resources to maintain a healthy life. Because infant health spans the breadth of a health system's services, providers, and levels of care, the African American infant mortality rate may reflect inherent and interrelated issues within our health care system. To establish the best-quality health care system and to reach Healthy People 2020 goals, an expanded and exigent focus on infant mortality in underserved populations, including African Americans, is critical.

Age-Adjusted Mortality

Age-adjusted mortality rates per 100,000 persons by race and ethnicity for three health-focused areas in the United States would indicate that African Americans have a higher mortality rate from heart disease, cancer, and stroke. The white population has a higher heart disease and cancer mortality rate than all other race ethnicities with the exception of African Americans in the United States. African American men have DNA variants that place them at increased risk for prostate cancer when these variants occur in combination (Freedman, et al., 2006). African American men are twice as likely to develop prostate cancer as white men (Jones, 2001). The age-adjusted death rate for diabetes mellitus of African Americans is 40.4 per 100,000, for American Indian-Alaska natives 34 per 100,000, and for Hispanics 25.6 per 100,000. Age adjusted death rates related to HIV/AIDS is 20.4 per 100,000 for African Americans, which is twice that of American Indian-Alaska natives, twenty times that of Asian-Pacific Islanders, ten times that of whites, and four times that of Hispanics. Age-adjusted mortality from homicide is 20 per 100,000 for African Americans compared to 3.6 per 100,000 for whites (Kochanek, et al., 2011).

Minorities, particularly African Americans, receive fewer referrals for renal transplant evaluation and fewer transplants, less adequate pain medication for cancer, fewer admissions to cardiac care units, and fewer revascularization procedures, especially coronary artery bypass grafts. Studies also show that African Americans and Latinos are less likely to receive pain medication in the emergency department for fractures compared to white patients (Betancourt, 2007). These statistics reflect the inherent disparities in health care for minority populations.

Physician Shortage

By 2015, the Association of American Medical Colleges (AAMC) approximates that the United States will be have a deficit of 62,900 doctors. This lack of physicians is expected to multiply two-fold by 2025. Historically, there have been approximately 24 physicians per 100,000 people in communities where there are high numbers of African Americans and Hispanics versus other communities where there are 69 physicians per 100,000 with a low proportion of Hispanics and African Americans. The shortage is escalating as a result of numerous factors including time investment for someone to become a doctor, the aging baby boomers (which will substantially increase the need for care), and the extension of health care insurance to all US citizens (Lowrey and Pear, 2012). Similarly, there is also a significant shortage of minority physicians. AAMC found that in 2008 only 6.3 percent of practicing physicians were African American, 5.5 percent Hispanic or Latino, and 0.5 percent American Indian/Alaska Native (Castillo-Page, 2010). To increase the number of physicians overall, loan forgiveness and funding for scholarship programs could be strengthened.

Distrust

People of color, particularly African Americans, are less trusting than whites of hospitals; of reasons physicians use or withdraw life-sustaining therapies; of the organ donation system; and have a profound mistrust of medical research. The US Public Health Service conducted The Tuskegee Study of Untreated Syphilis between 1932 and 1972. Before this study, which aimed to determine the effects of untreated syphilis, men had little access to health care. Six hundred African American men from the rural community of Tuskegee, 399 with syphilis and 201 without, were told they were being evaluated for what was commonly termed "bad blood," a blanket diagnosis referring to syphilis, anemia, or fatigue. Patients were never told that they had syphilis, but were given free medical exams, vitamins, meals, and burial insurance. Despite the widespread introduction of penicillin as a powerful antibiotic after World War II and the subsequent 1947 discovery of its efficacy in treatment of syphilis, it was, in accordance with the purpose of the study, never used to treat the men. This unethical practice was continued for forty years, during which time the men passed syphilis on to their partners, and their children developed congenital syphilis. The study might have never come into the public light if not for the efforts of Dr. Peter Buxton, who leaked details to the press in 1972 after fruitless efforts to end the study through review by a board of physicians, all but one of whom deemed the study fit to continue (Parker, Alvarez and Thompson, 2003).

In 1974 Congress passed the National Research Act, which both created the National Commission for Protection of Human Subjects in Biomedical and Behavioral Research (NCPHSBBR) and required the establishment of institutional review boards for any institution receiving federal aid (Hoyert and Xu, 2012). Four years after its founding, the NCPHSBBR issued the Belmont Report, which focused on the distinction between research and practice and led to the establishment of three ethical principles: respect for persons, beneficence, and justice. The report also detailed guidelines for informed consent, increased assessment of risks and benefits, and appropriate subject selection in medical research (National Commission for the Protection of Human Subjects of Biomedical and Behavioral Research, 1978).

The mistrust in the medical establishment led to fewer African Americans participating in research and seeking medical care. This mistrust has had a noted impact in public opinion in light of the AIDS epidemic of the 1990s, such as the suspicion within the African American community that the government had manufactured and introduced the disease.

While correlation of reduced participation in medical studies and a negative approach to care cannot signify direct causation, one can reason that increased research participation and greater utilization of care would be useful both to improve quality of life and to identify factors that could be utilized to lessen health disparities. Studies show more blacks than whites know about the Tuskegee syphilis study. More blacks than whites are reluctant to enter into research trials. Lack of adequate minority participation in research studies hampers progress toward understanding disease processes, the effects of medications or treatment, and ultimately a better health care system and delivery.

Access to Care

"One size fits all" health care systems cannot meet the needs of the increasingly diverse US population. Access to care issues must be addressed, culturally appropriate written materials distributed, and interpreter services provided. Convenient hours of operation, accessible clinic locations, and culturally sensitive policies, practices, and settings are important for health care delivery. Currently about 70 million low-income Americans, mostly pregnant women and children, individuals with disabilities, and the elderly who need help at home and those living in nursing homes, are recipients of Medicaid. The Affordable Care Act (ACA) now requires states to cover the very low income population within their Medicaid programs, including adults without dependent children. The government provides 100 percent of this new cost coverage with federal funds for states who elect to expand their Medicaid programs. This provision will happen over approximately three years, subsequently dropping down to around 90 percent, requiring states to pick up a portion of the cost. With the passage of the ACA, up to 17 million new Americans would be expected to gain Medicaid coverage under the new health law. Medicaid expansion is one part of the laws that changed significantly with the US Supreme Court ruling in June 2012. The justices asserted that states can refuse to expand Medicaid to all low-income adults without losing all federal funding or existing Medicaid programs. Some states have opted out, leaving some of the poorest people without Medicaid coverage. The ACA creates a national Medicaid minimum eligibility level of 133 percent of the federal poverty level (approximately $31,000 for a family of four) approximately $15,000 for individuals under the age of sixty-five, including adults without dependent children (Patient Care and Affordable Care Act, 2010). This change ends the longstanding coverage gap for low-income adults.

The eligibility standards now also include people who were previously ineligible, such as low-income adults with or without dependents, and low-income children who heretofore would have lost their Medicaid benefits when they were reclassified as adults at age nineteen. The ACA includes protections which outlaw some practices that have previously left people uninsured. Insurers can no longer cancel insurance policies if a person gets sick, a practice previously known as rescission. In January 2014, annual dollar limits previously set by insurance companies on how much they would pay for an individual's medical expenses each year were eliminated. In addition, lifetime limits have been eliminated. High medical bills resulting from major or long-term illness are no longer subject to payment limits from insurers. In 2007, 62.1 percent of all bankruptcies were due to unpaid medical expenses, a number that these measures seek to decrease (Himmelstein, et al., 2009).

The new health care law promotes free preventive care and annual check-ups which hopefully will keep people healthier through preventative health screenings and early identification and treatment of health concerns. New private health plans now must cover and eliminate cost sharing such as co-payments, co-insurance, or deductibles for proven preventive measures such as immunizations and cancer screenings, which will encourage people to seek preventative care.

Older adults with Part D drug coverage will find it less expensive to pay for their medications in the future. Americans who can afford coverage will be required to have health insurance or pay a tax penalty. As of January 2014, insurers cannot deny coverage to anyone regardless of pre-existing conditions, and they cannot charge more because of gender. More primary care doctors will be promoted and supported with a higher income from the Medicaid program. Funding for scholarships and loan-forgiveness pro-grams for primary care physicians choosing to serve underserved and rural communities will encourage doctors to practice in these areas (Assistant Secretary of Public Affairs, 2015). Some people who are required to purchase insurance who have not done it before may qualify for subsistence through the government to help pay for the insurance. By raising the Medicaid eligi-bility ceiling to 133 percent of the poverty level, the ACA targets low-income families and allows nearly 17 million additional people access to health insur-ance (Patient Care and Affordable Care Act, 2010; Martin, 2013).

Kathleen Sebelius, secretary of Health and Human Services stated: "When the average African American child born today will live five fewer years than the average white child, with a greater likelihood of illness, we are still falling far short of Dr. King's vision" (Sebelius, 2011). Dr. King's dream was that all children would have the chance to reach their full potential, no matter the color of their skin or where they were born. The ACA, with its emphasis on providing attainable health care costs for typically underserved populations, comes close to fulfilling his dream of equality of care.

We are at the beginning of a new era in terms of health care in the United States. There are still those who will not benefit from the health care law, such as those who are undocumented or not considered legal in the United States. Unfortunately, an estimated 11 million undocumented immigrants in the United States remain unable to access health care under this act (Preston,

2008). These immigrants provide necessary services, often in farming and the service industry. Dr. King, who spoke out strongly for certain basic rights afforded to all people, would likely support the ACA but would object to the fact that it does not allow access for undocumented immigrants. Since Dr. King is quoted as saying that access to basic health care is a universal human right, we believe he would want the ACA to be revised to incorporate undocumented immigrants (Zuber, 2012).

One way of extending health care to undocumented immigrants would be to grant them access to Medicaid. While this action would add a significant financial burden to the US health care budget, it would ensure that undocumented immigrants could get necessary health services without fear of being deported. Considering the strained nature of our nation's health care budget, however, this option would almost invariably be unpopular with members of Congress and/or the general public. A more appealing and potentially cost-effective option would be to implement the Development Relief and Education for Alien Minors (DREAM) Act, allowing undocumented minors the ability to buy insurance.

In August 2010, Congress began to develop the DREAM Act. Under this act, children of illegal immigrants would be given access to higher education, citizenship, and all the benefits that American citizenship affords (Barron, 2011). Should this act pass, it would be a significant step toward both health care and education equality. By allowing the children of undocumented immigrants to gain citizenship through sustained education, the act would allow immigrant minors to acquire steady jobs, livable incomes, and necessary health care. Although this method may be less efficient than providing Medicaid for immigrants, it would create a sustainable system to provide undocumented immigrants both citizenship and health care.

There are several practical reasons to expand care to all people, regardless of citizenship status. Many individuals who do not have health coverage delay seeking care and resort to obtaining treatment in costlier emergency departments, which raises the overall cost of care. With a total annual cost of $113 billion to provide emergency care for undocumented immigrant treatment, a government decision to treat these individuals through primary care would lower overall costs significantly (Zuber, 2012). Furthermore, undocumented immigrants who do not have access to primary health care may develop preventable life-threatening conditions that are expensive to treat. Solving this dilemma by increasing access to primary care would increase the overall health of society in the United States. In addition, these undocumented immigrants, though not US citizens, likely work, and the taxes they would pay as citizens could apply to some level of health insurance to benefit the country's health system.

While the ACA increases the coverage of many Americans and is moving toward a concept of universal health care, there is room for improvement. Critics of the ACA believe that it will "extend a new entitlement without clear cost-control mechanisms and the result will be that spending exceeds expectations" (Trumbull, 2010). This is largely due to the fact that the act extends Medicaid to millions of families just above the poverty line and extends subsidies to help millions more comply with the mandate to buy insurance. In addition, employers have the choice to offer health insurance as a benefit or pay a penalty. Those preferring to pay the fee would force employees to purchase coverage on new insurance exchanges (Patient Care and Affordable Care Act, 2010).

An essential provision of the ACA is expanding Medicaid coverage to low-income Americans (those with incomes less than 138 percent of the federal poverty level). However, a Supreme Court decision in 2012 made Medicaid expansion optional for states, and as of February 2015, only 28 states and the District of Columbia agreed to do so. From 2014 to 2016, the federal government will cover 100 percent of expansion cost. Afterward, federal support will decline each year, reaching and remaining at 90 percent by 2020 (Barofsky, 2015). Uninsured community health center (CHC) visits have decreased, and Medicaid-covered visits have increased in states that expanded Medicaid in 2014, whereas CHCs in states opting out of the expansion have maintained a high rate of uninsured visits. This suggests that ACA-related Medicaid expansions have been successful in decreasing the number of uninsured safety net patients in the United States (Angier, et al., 2015).

Results from the Commonwealth Fund Biennial Health Insurance Survey, 2014, indicate that the ACA's subsidized insurance options and consumer protections reduced the number of uninsured working-age adults from an estimated 37 million people, or 20 percent of the population, in 2010 to 29 million, or 16 percent, by the second half of 2014. Conducted from July to December 2014, for the first time since it began in 2001, the survey found declines in the number of people who report cost-related access problems and medical-related financial difficulties. The number of adults who did not get needed health care because of cost declined from 80 million people, or 43 percent, in 2012 to 66 million, or 36 percent, in 2014. The number of adults who reported problems paying their medical bills declined from an estimated 75 million people in 2012 to 64 million people in 2014. In 2014, 6.7

million people enrolled in health plans sold through the ACA's marketplaces, with most signing up through the federal marketplace website (Collins, et al., 2014).

These new subsidized options for people who lack insurance from employers are helping to reverse national trends in health care coverage and affordability. Uninsured rates have declined to their lowest levels in more than a decade, and rates among young adults and low-income adults are at their lowest levels in fourteen years. For the first time since 2003, when the question was first introduced, there was a decline in the number of adults who reported not getting needed care because of cost. And for the first time, there was a decline in the number of people who had problems paying their medical bills or who were paying off medical debt over time (Collins, et al., 2014).

On June 25, 2015, the US Supreme Court delivered a major victory to the Obama administration and congressional Democrats, as it handed down its decision on *King v. Burwell*, the biggest legal challenge to the Affordable Care Act (ACA) since the Supreme Court upheld the constitutionality of the law in 2012. The Court ruled six to three that federal tax subsidies to help consumers purchase health insurance are permitted under the ACA regardless of whether insurance is purchased through a state-run exchange or an exchange facilitated by the federal government. After passage of the ACA, thirty-four states chose not to establish state-run exchanges and instead directed residents to so-called federally facilitated exchanges.

CONCLUSION

Dr. Martin Luther King Jr. would suggest that there be a way for all Americans, regardless of their socioeconomic status, to have equal access to health care at an affordable rate. He would be pleased with the establishment of the Affordable Care Act, which is providing coverage to millions of people who were previously uninsured. This allows for low-income families to afford health care through the expansion of Medicaid, affordable health insurance, and tax aid.

However, because health care is not simply a "citizen's" right but rather a human right, we conclude that Dr. King would be disheartened at the fact that undocumented immigrants are still denied Medicaid or subsidies (Patient Care and Affordable Care Act, 2010). He would be disheartened over the shortage of health care providers, particularly the vast underrepresentation of minority physicians and other health care providers, and the persistence of underserved communities. He would also be disheartened by the mistrust of health care systems by minorities. Dr. King would desire a reduction in health disparities inclusive of infant and age-adjusted mortality rates among all citizens. He would advocate for health care that is community-based and culturally sensitive to the minority populations in the United States that contribute to the diversity and greatness of this country. Specifically, we believe Dr. King would advocate for the following:

- Equitable health care that is affordable, free to those without income, accessible, sustainable, and portable.
- Diverse health care providers and administration reflective of the racial demographics of the communities served.
- Health prevention through comprehensive education, beginning as early as kindergarten to completion of compulsory education, and via community information sessions and workshops.
- Increasing and expanding health centers within low-income communities.
- Employment opportunities for the unemployed/underemployed and the poor with a living wage which would position individuals with the means to pay for health care.

ACKNOWLEDGMENTS

The following students participated in the work of this project: Hadeel Al-wani, Lauren Baetsen, Carlo Basilio, Lynasia Braxton-Doggett, Margaret Brown, Paige Calodney, Fiona Charles, Jeffrey Chidester, Teshara Clemons, Lauren Coleman, Jasmine Drake, Claire Finkel, Asmita Gautam, Sarah Haas, Jacqueline Hall, Amber Hamilton, Rachel Henderson, Elizabeth Herbst, Brittany Jackson, Shakye Jones, Rose Krieger, Ha Lai, Yizhen Liu, Maria Melnyk, Kasonde Mwaba, Renee Redman, Eric Richwine, Abigail Rieman, Blair Ross, Kelsey Shea, Caroline Stewart, Lindsey Tyler, Ashley Wright, Tsewang Yang-zom, Elizabeth Ball, Lehanne Giffin, Rachel Hanna, Kenny Perez Lorenzo, and Suraj Mishra.

This chapter was originally printed in the book *West Indies Health Care and Disaster Preparedness*, which was edited by Marcus L. Martin, Audrey Snyder,

Anna Walker Jones, and Leslie U. Walker, and published by CreateSpace in 2015. The authors of this chapter are very grateful for the contributions of the UVA faculty, students, and staff. We are particularly grateful for the administrative support provided by the Office for Diversity and Equity. We thank Gail Prince-Davis, Anna Jones, and Barbara Blum for their clerical assistance with the manuscript. We also thank Dr. Patrick Martin, chief medical officer, Ministry of Health of St. Kitts and Nevis, for his informative lecture to the 2013 UVA in St. Kitts and Nevis students. In addition, we thank UVA faculty: Dr. Nate Charlton, Mr. Kostas Alibertis and Ms. Elisabeth Wright for their contributions to the UVA in St. Kitts and Nevis January-term course and for their valued interaction and stimulating discussions with student groups related to this study. The University of Virginia International Studies Office and the Provost Office (sponsor of the Jefferson Public Citizen's Program) supported education and research activities in St. Kitts and Nevis. If we have overlooked someone in our acknowledgments, we apologize.

REFERENCES

Angier, H., M. Hoopes, R. Gold, S. R. Bailey, E. K. Cottrell, and J. Heintzman. 2015. An Early Look at Rates of Uninsured Safety Net Clinic Visits after the Affordable Care Act. *Annals of Family Medicine.* 13(1): 10-6.

Assistant Secretary of Publics Affairs, Digital Communications Division. 2015. *Creating Jobs by Addressing Primary Care Workforce Needs.* United States Department of Health and Human Services. http://www.hhs.gov/healthcare/facts/factsheets/2013/06/jobs06212012.html.

Barofsky, J. 2015. *What Are the Effects of Not Expanding Medicaid?.* Washington, DC: Brookings Institution. http://www.brookings.edu/blogs/health360/posts/2015/02/20-effects-not-expanding-medicaid-barofsky.

Barron, E. 2011. "The Development, Relief, and Education for Alien Minors (DREAM) ACT." *Harvard Journal on Legislation.* 48(2): 625-55. Index to Legal Periodicals and Books Full Text (H. W. Wilson), EBSCOhost.

Betancourt, Maina A., Jr. 2007. "Barriers to Eliminating Disparities in Clinical Practice." In *Eliminating Healthcare Disparities in America: Beyond the IOM report,* ed. R. A. Williams. Totowa, NJ: Humana. 83-85.

Castillo-Page, L. 2010. *Diversity in the Physician Workforce: Facts and Figures 2010.* Washington, DC: Association of American Medical Colleges; 2010. https://members.aamc.org/eweb/upload/Diversity%20in%20the%20Physician%20Workforce%20Facts%20and%20Figures%202010.pdf.

Collins, S. R., P. W. Rasmussen, M. M. Doty, and S. Beutel. 2015. *The Rise in Health Care Coverage and Affordability since Health Reform Took Effect: Findings from the Commonwealth Fund Biennial Health Insurance Survey, 2014. The Commonwealth Fund* 1800(2): 1-15.

Freedman, M. L., C. A. Haiman, N. Patterson , G. J. McDonald, A. Tandon, A. Waliszewska, et al. 2006. "Admixture Mapping Identifies 8q24 as a Prostate Cancer Risk Locus in African-American Men." *Proceedings of the National Academy of Sciences of the United States of America* 103(38): 14068-73. Epub 2006 Aug 31.

Friedan, T. R. 2011 Jan 14. CDC Health Disparities and Inequalities Report—United States." *Morbity and Mortality Weekly Report.* 60, supp. http://www.cdc.gov/mmwr/pdf/other/su6001.pdf.

Goldenberg, R. L., S. P. Cliver, F. X. Mulvihill, C. A. Hickey, H. J. Hoffman, L. V. Klerman, et al. 1996 Nov. "Medical, Psychosocial, and Behavioral Risk Factors Do Not Explain the Increased Risk for Low Birth Weight among Black Women." *American Journal of Obstetrics and Gynecology* 175(5): 1317-24.

Himmelstein, D. U., D. Thorne, E. Warren, and S. Woolhandler. 2009 Aug. *Am J Med.* 122(8):741-46. doi: 10.1016/j.amjmed.2009.04.012.

Hoyert, D. L., and J. Xu. 2012. "Deaths: Preliminary Data for 2011." *National Vital Statistics Reports* 61. http://www.cdc.gov/nchs/data/nvsr/nvsr61/nvsr61_06.pdf.

Jaber, L. A., W. R. Melchior, and D. R. Rutledge. 1992 Jul–Aug. "Possible Correlation between Glycemia and Blood Pressure in Black, Diabetic, Hypertensive Patients." *Annals of Pharmacotherapy* 26(7-8): 882-86.

Johns, B., K. Sigurbjörnsdóttir, H. Fogstad, J. Zupan, M. Mathai, and T. Tan-Torres Edejer. Apr 2007. "Estimated Global Resources Needed to Attain Universal Coverage of Maternal and Newborn Health Services." *Bulletin of the World Health Organization.* 85(4): 256–63.

Jones, J. 2001 Mar 7. "African-Americans and Prostate Cancer: Why the Discrepancies?" *Journal of the National Cancer Institute* 93(5): 342-44.

Kane, J. 2012 Oct 22. "Health Costs: How the US Compares with Other Countries." In PBS Newshour. The Rundown: A Blog of News and Insight. Washington, DC: NewsHour Productions, LLC. c2003-2014. [about 10 screens]. http://www.pbs.org/newshour/rundown/2012/10/health-costs-how-the-us-compares-with-other-countries.html.

Kiely, J. L., and M. Kogan. 1994. "Reproductive Health of Women: Prenatal Care." In From Data to Action: CDC's Public Health Surveillance for Women, Infants, and Children, ed. L. S. Wilcox and J. S. Marks. Atlanta, GA: Centers for Disease Control and Prevention; 1994. 105-18. http://stacks.cdc.gov/view/cdc/11354/.

King, M. L., Jr. 1965. "Address at the Conclusion of the Selma to Montgomery March." http://kingencyclopedia.stanford.edu/encyclopedia/documentsentry/doc_address_at_the_conclusion_of_selma_march/index.html.

———. King, M. L., Jr. 1957. "A Realistic Look at the Question of Progress in the Area of Race Relations." Address delivered at St. Louis freedom rally. http://kingencyclopedia.stanford.edu/primarydocuments/Vol4/10-Apr-1957_ARealisticLook.pdf.

Kochanek, K. D., J. Xu, S. L. Murphy, A. M. Miniño, and H-S. Kung. 2011. "Deaths: Final Data for 2009." *National Vital Statistics Report* 30(3). Hyattsville, MD: National Center for Health Statistics. http://www.cdc.gov/nchs/data/nvsr/nvsr60/nvsr60_03.pdf

Lantos, J. D., and D. S. Lauderdale. What Is Behind the Rising Rates of Preterm Birth in the United States? Rambam Maimonides Med J. Oct 2011; 2(4): e0065. doi: 10.5041/RMMJ.10065.

Lockwood, C. J., and J. A. Lemons, eds. 2007. *Guidelines for Perinatal Care*. 6th ed. Elk Grove Village, IL: American Association of Pediatrics and American College of Obstetrics and Gynecology. 83-137.

Lowrey, A., and R. Pear. 2012 Jul 28. "Doctor Shortage Likely to Worsen with Health Law." *New York Times*. http://www.nytimes.com/2012/07/29/health/policy/too-few-doctors -in-many-us-communities.html?_r=0&.

MacDorman, M. F., and T. J. Mathews. 2012. "Infant Mortality Statistics from the 2008 Period Linked Birth/Infant Death Data Set." *National Vital Statistics Reports* 60(5). Hyattsville, MD: National Center for Health Statistics. http://www.cdc.gov/nchs/data/nvsr/nvsr60/ nvsr60_05.pdf.

MacDorman, M. F., D. L. Rowley, S. Iyasu, J. L. Kiely, P. G. Gardner, and M. S. Davis. 1994. "Birth Outcomes: Infant Mortality." In *From Data to Action: CDC's Public Health Surveillance for Women, Infants, and Children*, ed. L. S. Wilcox and J. S. Marks. [Internet]. Atlanta, GA: Centers for Disease Control and Prevention. 231-49. http://stacks.cdc.gov/view/ cdc/11354/.

Martin, M. Health disparities. 2013. Lecture during January Term. St. Kitts and Nevis Jan 2-14.

Miniño, A. M., and S. L. Murphy. 2012. *Death in the United States, 2010*. NCHS data brief, no. 99. Hyattsville, MD: National Center for Health Statistics. http://www.cdc.gov/nchs/ data/databriefs/db99.htm.

National Cancer Institute at the National Institutes of Health. *Cancer Health Disparities*. Reviewed March 11, 2008. http://www.cancer.gov/cancertopics/factsheet/disparities/ cancer-health-disparities.

National Commission for the Protection of Human Subjects of Biomedical and Behavioral Research. 1978. The Belmont Report: Ethical Principles and Guidelines for the Protection of Human Subjects of Research. DHEW Publication No. (OS) 78-0012. Bethesda, MD. http://videocast.nih.gov/pdf/ohrp_belmont_report.pdf.

Parker L., S. H. K. Alvarez, and S. Thompson. 2003. "Module 2: The Legacy of the Tuskegee Syphilis Study." In *Ethics and Public Health: Model Curriculum*, ed. B. Jennings, J. Kahn, A. Mastroianni, and L. S. Parker. Rockville, MD: Health Resources and Services Administration. 37-73. http://www.aspph.org/wp-content/uploads/2014/02/ EthicsCurriculum.pdf.

Patient Care and Affordable Care Act of 2010. 2010. Pub. L. 111 Stat. 148 March 23.

Physicians for a National Health Program (PNHP). 2014. "Dr. Martin Luther King on Healthcare Injustice." http://www.pnhp.org/news/2014/october/dr-martin-luther-king -on-health-care-injustice.

Preston, J. 2008. "Decline Seen in Numbers of People Here Illegally. *The New York Times*." July 31. http://www.nytimes.com/2008/07/31/us/31immig.html?_r=0.

Sebelius, K. 2011. *A Tribute to Dr. King*. USDHHS. January 17. http://www.hhs.gov/healthcare/ facts/blog/2011/01/drking-tribute.html.

Singh, G. K. van Dyck PC. 2010. *Infant Mortality in the United States, 1935-2007: Over Seven Decades of Progress and Disparities*. Rockville, MD: Health Resources and Services Administration, Maternal and Child Health Bureau. http://www.hrsa.gov/healthit/ images/mchb_infantmortality_pub.pdf.

Trumbull, M. 2010. "New Healthcare Bill Pros and Cons: Will It Cut Costs?" *Christian Science Monitor*. March 22 [cited 2015 Jul 1]. http://www.csmonitor.com/USA/2010/0322/New-health-care-bill-pros-and-cons-Will-it-cut-costs.

United States Census Bureau. 2008. *An Older and More Diverse Nation by Midcentury.* Updated 2013 June. http://www.census.gov/newsroom/releases/archives/population/cb08-123.html.

Washington, J. M., ed. 1986. *A Testament of Hope: The Essential Writings of Martin Luther King, Jr.* San Francisco: Harper and Row.

Zuber, J. 2012. "Healthcare for the Undocumented: Solving a Public Health Crisis in the US." *Journal of Contemporary Health Law and Policy* 28(2)(Spring):350-80.

Part II

FOREIGN AFFAIRS AND AFRICA

TOWARD FOREIGN POLICY JUSTICE?

A Dream Unfulfilled

Michael L. Clemons

It is fascinating that social scientists and historians have paid such little attention to Dr. Martin Luther King Jr.'s vision for contemporary American foreign policy. In this regard, perhaps most significant are his ideas regarding "foreign policy justice," although he never employed the notion directly. The paucity of research and punditry on the subject may simply be a narrow reflection of Americans' general preoccupation with life and their lack of interest in the subject of foreign policy. However, due to their historical oppression and economic exploitation in specific national contexts, some racial and ethnic groups have been prone to developing an international or transnational perspective. Jewish Americans and African Americans perhaps represent the most concrete examples, with the former group firmly in recognition of the historical significance and practicality of the state of Israel, and the latter evolving a simultaneous universalism and sense of pan-African globalism. These key developments have contributed to their political outlook and agenda for action. Suffice it to say, African Americans have long embraced the global arena as a forum for articulating not only their views about international issues, but also their domestic interests and concerns. In many cases, international appeals were prompted by the lack of legal standing of African Americans. However, while they frequently made such appeals as deprived citizens on their own behalf as former slaves and people of African descent, they also in some instances have done so on behalf of the United States as official representatives (Clemons, 2010, pp. 33–34).

King's foreign policy views were undergoing formation before the Vietnam War. As illustrated by James H. Cone, they unfolded in two distinct phases. The first phase is marked by the December 1955 Montgomery bus boycott, and the second phase, initiated in 1963, concluded with passage of the 1965 Voting Rights Act. In the second phase, King questioned more profoundly the nexus of racism, poverty, and militarism in US domestic and foreign policies. During both phases, his ideas about domestic and foreign affairs were undergirded by his deep faith in a God that embodied justice, love, and hope. According to Cone, the principal difference between the two phases was the shifting emphases given by Dr. King to each of these theological attributes as he developed a nonviolent philosophy of social change that would eradicate racial and economic exploitation in the United States and facilitate the establishment of peace in America and throughout the world (Cone, 1987, pp. 456–60). The leadership articulated by King was ardently opposed to the Vietnam War. His public visibility on the issue reached a crescendo with "Beyond Vietnam," a major speech he delivered at New York's Riverside Church on April 4, 1967.

King's conception of global politics was consistent with the theological principles of justice, love, and hope. This conception was unifying in that it was instrumental in helping to connect the international interests of people of African descent. Ronald Walters has noted, however, that, in concert with the principles of Christianity, the "manner in which blacks came into U.S. citizenship, the dynamics of their original and evolving American identity, the continuing ties with Africa and other peoples of African descent, and the prospects of a Pan-African relationship" served also as significant unifying factors (Walters, 2012, p. 1).

PURPOSE

The so-called war on terrorism is one of the most important and difficult challenges to face contemporary US foreign policy. Inevitably, the situation lends import to questions of fairness, equity, and justice in international as well as domestic terms, and specifically raises questions about "foreign policy justice" and the utility of this ideal for the success or lack thereof of American foreign policy making. Thus, in considering developments in the war on terrorism from George H. W. Bush to Barack H. Obama, I weigh the nation's tendency to foster policies and practices that contribute to or detract from progress toward the achievement of foreign policy justice. In doing so, I draw upon the works and praxis of Dr. King and employ the notion of "foreign policy justice." The term, "foreign policy justice," first articulated by Ronald Walters Jr., is applicable in both the pre- and post–September 11 contexts, and it is broadly relevant for shedding light on the era of globalization. Given the conception of foreign policy justice, I consider the Bush administration's declaration of the war on terrorism in the aftermath of the

September 11 attack, and the process and progress of disengaging from an increasingly unpopular policy stance. Indeed, the war on terrorism ushered the United States into two costly major conflicts with Iraq and Afghanistan. Thus, at issue is whether there has been a positive change toward foreign policy justice since the election of Barack Obama. Specifically I query, does America's handling of the war on terrorism since the election of President Obama comport with the vision espoused by Dr. King and the ideal of foreign policy justice?

This chapter proceeds as follows. First, I focus on the development and evolution of King's global vision. Next, I examine the development and application of the concept of foreign policy justice. Following this, the major tenets distilled from the thought of King are employed to further develop the notion of foreign policy justice. The synthesis of Walters' and King's ideals and perspectives yield a framework that enables an appraisal of America's progress in ending the war on terrorism. In this context, we identify the predominant explanations for September 11 and demonstrate their utility for understanding the principal interests and positions of key actors and the possibilities of and obstacles to foreign policy justice. The chapter concludes with a discussion about the prospect for foreign policy justice.

KING'S GLOBAL VISION

Martin Luther King Jr. was the product of a society premised operationally on white supremacy, an ideology that presupposes the legitimacy of subjugating entire groups of people in economic, social, and political terms. His views about race, society, and the fundamental importance of social justice and human rights emerged early on with his socialization as the son of a Baptist preacher in the segregated Southern city of Atlanta, Georgia. As an undergraduate student pursuing the educational path of his father, he attended the prestigious Morehouse College in Atlanta, Georgia, a private, all-male historically black institution. The college's president, Dr. Benjamin E. Mays, encouraged the development of King's spirituality and social activism, and in his last semester at Morehouse, he was ordained. From 1948 to 1951, he attended Pennsylvania's Crozer Theological Seminary where he grappled with and eventually gravitated toward the neo-orthodoxy of Reinhold Niebuhr, which stressed the "intractability of social evil" (King Center Archives, 2014). From Crozer, King moved on to earn a doctorate degree in theology at Boston University (1951–1955), where he further developed his knowledge of such philosophers as Emmanuel Kant, St. Thomas Aquinas, Aristotle, and Karl Marx (see Clayborne Carson, 1998).

King's vocation as a Baptist minister was fundamental to shaping his ideas about America's role in the world. His acceptance of the Nobel Peace Prize only nine years following his entrée to the civil rights movement is revelatory of his extraordinary rise to international prominence. It may be that his acceptance of the prestigious award bestowed upon him an even greater sense of obligation to people at home and abroad. Thus, King's acceptance of the globally distinguished Nobel Peace Prize elevated him to the global stage and reinforced opinions as well as his own belief that he, "was called by God to speak for the voiceless, for the weak, and even for the people around the world whom the U.S. government labeled terrorists and the enemy" (Hopkins, 2008, p. 70; also see Cone, 1987). King later humbly acknowledged that he, "[could not] forget that the Nobel Prize for Peace was also a commission—a commission to work harder than I had ever worked before for 'the brotherhood of man.' This is a calling that takes me beyond national allegiances, but even if it were not present I would yet have to live with the meaning of my commitment to the ministry of Jesus Christ" (King, 1967).

In 1967, exactly one year before he was assassinated, Dr. King, in a speech at Riverside Church in Harlem, New York, stridently rejected violence as a means for resolving conflict. He observed the problem of US militarism in Vietnam, and in this watershed speech, he stated, "Perhaps the more difficult, but no less necessary, task is to speak for those who have been designated as our enemies. . . . [T]he true meaning and value of compassion and nonviolence [is] when it helps us to see the enemy's point of view, to hear his questions, to know his assessment of ourselves" (King, 1967).

Along with empathy and reciprocity of perspective, King implored the rejection of violence as a means to bring about social change. He challenged powerful states when dealing with a less powerful state to exercise compassion and to seek to understand issues from the adversarial point of view. King's vision, therefore, was that as a global superpower, the United States is obliged to assume a constructive role vis-à-vis smaller, less powerful, nation-states for purposes of advancing the ideals of global freedom and justice. He came to view as intertwined the domestic dimensions of freedom and justice and the ideal of freedom and justice abroad. Significantly, however, King's civil rights leadership and his conception of violence and war abroad were guided by the principles of Christianity.

The challenge before Dr. King rested largely with whether and how he could operationalize his Christian worldview in the contemporary context and turmoil of the civil rights movement and the Vietnam War. His religious orientation would not allow for the rationalization of the war as an effort to defend democracy. Neither would it permit one to disavow the connection between domestic and foreign affairs, particularly pertaining to the constituents of the movement, whom King represented. Increasingly, the American public perceived that the resources being expended to fight the war were draining the national economy and that the population as a whole was being negatively impacted.

The crystallization of the antiwar movement at the height of the civil rights movement facilitated the efforts of antiwar activists to demonstrate that African Americans were bearing the brunt of the burden associated with the war, which was the basis of the country's economic dislocation. Specifically, it was pointed out that among the front-line soldiers, African Americans comprised a share disproportionate to their representation in the population as a whole. Consequently, the Vietnam War, and in particular the nature of US involvement, presented King with a profound moral quandary in reference to his stance on violence. Hopkins (2008) reported, "The white power structure and most of the major civil rights organizations urged him to harangue black communities about nonviolence. Yet the same powerful institutions cautioned him to remain silent on the U.S. war initiative in Vietnam, where he called the United States the greatest purveyor of violence in the world" (p. 70). King reasoned that as the world's "greatest purveyor of violence," it would be difficult for the United States to continue to justify maintaining a huge military advantage against its adversary and the infliction of escalating violence that transpired during the latter years of the administration of President Johnson. His adherence to the ideal of compassion and the complete rejection of violence were fundamental to his opposition to the Vietnam War, as was his view of the need to respect and understand the position of the "enemy," whom he deemed brothers. The military might and the broader policing power of the United States relative to those of North Vietnam were gargantuan; thus, it was the power differential and the odds that motivated King to publicly denounce the war.

King's vocal opposition to the war and his leadership in the antiwar movement reflected a global vision of "The Beloved Community," a notion of philosopher-theologian Josiah Royce, founder of the Fellowship of Reconciliation, which became a central theme of King's activism. In 1956, King spoke before Student Nonviolent Coordinating Committee (SNCC) members and emphasized that in the aftermath of successful nonviolent direct action redemption and reconciliation would flourish, bringing forth the Beloved Community (The King Center Archives, 2014). King's deployment of the concept proliferated and stressed that all peoples of the world were entitled to share in its wealth. He expounded the meaning by saying,

> In the Beloved Community, poverty, hunger and homelessness will not be tolerated because international standards of human decency will not allow it. Racism and all forms of discrimination, bigotry and prejudice will be replaced by an all-inclusive spirit of sisterhood and brotherhood. . . . [I]nternational disputes will be resolved by peaceful conflict-resolution and reconciliation of adversaries, instead of military power. Love and trust will triumph over fear and hatred. Peace with justice will prevail over war and military conflict. (The King Center Archives, 2014)

It is interesting that for King, the Beloved Community "was not devoid of interpersonal, group or international conflict"; rather, conflict is assumed inevitable, and all conflict can be resolved through nonviolent means.

The preceding overview demonstrates the reverberation of King's ideals about domestic and global affairs and their relevance in the twenty-first century. His perspective on these matters as arguably the most prominent leader of the US civil rights movement congealed during his relatively short but impactful life forming the embryo of the notion of foreign policy justice. The major tenets of King's thought can be distilled as follows: (1) might does not necessarily make right; (2) in situations of bargaining, as well as conflict where the parties are of considerable unequal power and resources, the powerful and well-resourced must seek to balance the scales of fairness and equity to avoid taking unfair advantage; (3) given that domestic politics is inextricably intertwined with foreign affairs, care must be taken to ensure that domestic conditions for the poor are not overlooked or exacerbated as a consequence of the nation's foreign policy program; and (4) the powerful should respect and understand the needs and motivations of the weak and its perceived enemies. Taken together, these ideals form the basis of foreign policy justice.

Thus, unlike the vast majority of black and white leaders of the period, King grew increasingly aware of the entanglement of freedom and justice at the domestic and international levels. Interestingly, his tendency toward black nationalism and the goal of integration comported with his practice of Christianity and secular humanism. King recognized domestic politics and policy as integral to interstate relations, and consequently to the ideal of foreign policy justice. In the section below, I focus on Ronald Walters' conception of foreign policy justice and move toward the formulation of a more comprehensive understanding that is inclusive of Dr. King's philosophy, ideals, and values.

UNDERSTANDING FOREIGN POLICY JUSTICE

In the most encompassing sense, the notion of justice is intrinsic to American values, or at least the portrayal of these values. A review of the research literature shows that the term "foreign policy justice" is obscure, if not absent, from the work of historians, political scientists, and others who specialize in foreign affairs, international relations, and US foreign policy. The edicts laid down by King, particularly in the era of the Vietnam War, when he challenged some and isolated others by virtue of his opposition to the war, have had a penetrating effect on American society. Political scientist and activist Ronald W. Walters Jr. (2002) first advanced the notion of foreign policy justice. He used the term to amplify researchers' and analysts' lack of consideration of the "moral content or the racial interests of a policy in their determination of which party to a dispute should be advantaged." In addition to the fundamental question of the humanity of foreign policy is whether and how white supremacist ideology operates to subvert the achievement of foreign policy justice. In explaining the concept, Walters articulates the view that

> the condition of slavery placed blacks at the bottom of American society, and racism kept them there. Consequently, blacks' interests were shaped in both domestic and foreign affairs as rehabilitative projects to construct positive relations between Africans and peoples of African descent, and between the nations and continents that contain such peoples. *Thus, the counterpoise to this has caused blacks to construct the same paradigm of justice seeking in foreign affairs as in the domestic arena.*" (Emphasis mine; Walters, 2002, p. 1)

Hence, the dynamics of African American life have contributed to the evolution of a constructed view of foreign policy justice in the twenty-first century, which extends not only to the states encompassing the African Diaspora, but well beyond.

Walters' notion of foreign policy justice is rooted in the historical context of the Western world and the United States in particular. It raises the question of whether the outcomes of foreign policy reflect the expressed commitment to freedom, democracy, and justice, without conscious or institutional consequences tied to race, ethnicity, or geopolitical wealth and resources. Walters' conception of "racial foreign policy justice" evolved out of the convergence of racial repression at the domestic level and the belief in the United States as the principal purveyor of justice and democracy. Foreign policy justice is therefore a norm endemic to the particular experience of African Americans and Americans generally as a people. Inherent to freedom, democracy, and justice are the twin pillars of fairness and equity, both of which are essential ingredients for maintaining basic social stability and peace among a diverse populace.

The prevalence of foreign policy justice among diverse nation-states can be viewed as the antithesis of Samuel Huntington's postulation that the "principal conflicts of global politics will occur between nations and groups of different civilizations," and thus, "[t]he clash of civilizations will dominate global politics" (Huntington, 1993). Contrary to the Huntington thesis, foreign policy justice is realistically achievable. It assumes that humankind can manage and/or resolve conflict that sometimes further sharpens apparent group differences such as race, culture, class, and religion, which may be indicative of economic, political, and other social forms of discrimination, and in the contemporary United States even more insidious forms of institutionalized discrimination are present. Given the origin and the importance of constructed group differences, it is useful to recognize that foreign policy justice rejects both ethnocentrism and xenophobia as explanations or justifications for decisions and foreign policy making.

Moreover, the perception of the pursuit of foreign policy justice is critical as a single action indeed may help ward off group conflict in domestic society and in the global arena. Most importantly, confidence can be instilled by the perception that foreign policy justice is a goal, especially during times of social instability stemming from inequalities linked to race, ethnicity, and/or class by perception and/or empirical observation. Along these lines, it is important to consider whether the foreign policy behavior and decisions of the United States comport with the sense of values, morality, and justice that Americans have been socialized to believe comprise the basis of their country's foreign affairs. In this respect, the post–September 11 era poses a major challenge as there has been growing concern about whether the United States has moved away from or toward a posture and foreign policy that exemplifies a "might makes right" approach. This consideration highlights the contradictions inherent in policy formulations that readily expose the United States as incapable, for example, of mediating global disputes between and among adversarial groups due to confusion over its roles as ally and "honest broker" or mediator of disputes.

Thus, foreign policy justice is inherently moral, and it takes into account social differentiation based on dimensions of race, class, and gender. In theoretical terms, the directional tendency of foreign policy justice is away from realism and toward idealism. Foreign policy justice is therefore part of the global vision of idealist theory, which emphasizes morality, the altruistic nature of human beings, and community (Goldstein and Pevehouse, 2013, pp. 35–36). Consistent with Dr. King, it rejects the notion that "might makes right" and inherently seeks to achieve outcomes that are perceived as or in reality are fair and equitable, especially in situations where the parties have unequal power and consequently, without the application of justice, would suffer massive unequal loss and defeat. Foreign policy justice subscribes also to St. Thomas Aquinas' "proportionality doctrine," which stipulates that "the means used were proportional to the ends" (Roskin and Berry, 2005, p. 55). Finally, foreign policy justice rejects ethnocentrism and xenophobia. It assumes that no one culture is better than another; rather, it asserts that they are only different. The idea that all people are of the same race—the human race—takes precedence over any inclination to devalue another cultural, religious, or other type of group.

Within the context of both domestic America and the West, people of African descent experienced a form of political, social, and economic repression that inordinately influenced their global perspective and sense of foreign policy justice. The forces of history that have impinged upon their rights, freedom, and general well-being have been not only of domestic origin, but are also international in their dimensions, extending beyond the parochial boundaries of culture and geography. The experience of economic and political repression based on fallacious interpretations of cultural differences and the imposition of race as a social construction helped evolve a particularly insidious social condition within which the African American experience has unfurled. Beginning with the era of African enslavement and into the period of Jim Crow, African Americans were uniquely exposed to the underbelly of domestic society. As chattel, black people were not afforded any of the basic legal and political rights and protections typically bestowed by citizenship, and their economic opportunities were highly limited. For the most part, the legal and political disenfranchisement of African Americans was reinforced by a capitalist economic system, which was largely the exclusive domain of whites, especially those with established financial wherewithal. The resultant domestic system of white political and social domination, and black subordination, was tied to global economic structures and forces. As such, it combined with the latter as a major force to help shape African Americans' outlook, perceptions, interpretations, and probable prescriptions for relevant foreign policy developments and international decision making. It is the momentum and force of these developments that propel and continue to advance African American domestic interests and their interests abroad (Walters, 2010, p. 1).

Before turning attention to the war on terrorism and foreign policy justice, I briefly examine US foreign policy in the period prior to the devastation that occurred on September 11, 2001, and a discussion of President George W. Bush's response to the devastation follows.

PRE-SEPTEMBER 11 US FOREIGN POLICY

The end of the global stalemate between the United States and the Soviet Union left a vacuity that enabled virtually unfettered assertion of American global influence through the pursuit of an imperialist agenda. This was possible because the United States emerged from the Cold War era as the only power with the capacity to manage international justice (Johnson, 2002; Boggs, 2005; Hardt and Negri, 2001). However, to exert said capacity, the United States had to balance its global interests with acting convincingly as an objective global manager and defender of international justice. This objective, accomplished in part by the facade of American exceptionalism, allowed for both the dismissal and consequent embracement of imperialism by asserting the generally accepted view that the United States has a special leadership role to play in the world (Johnson, 2004). The belief in American exceptionalism by Westerners in general offsets and may even supplant the negativity associated with traditional forms of US global intervention. However, while exceptionalism may dictate a special role for the United States in human history (McCrisken, 2004), one of its key features in the post-Cold War era has been massive military buildup and expansion of global US capacity through involvement in international institutions. For example, the development and assertion of the concept of "global security" was to justify American imperialist interests and actions. The concept was operationalized during the first Gulf War when the United States was able to initiate and utilize its function as "international police" and wield military supremacy

(Hardt and Negri, 2001). The presidency of George W. Bush constituted an important link in the chain of the institutionalized imperialist trajectory on which the United States has been since the end of the Cold War (Farwell, 2012, p. 1).

The continuity and consistency of American foreign policy are remarkable, especially considering the ideological ebb and flow of politics, and consequently, an executive branch of government that is continuously in flux. Nonetheless, from one presidential administration to the next, there seems to be a perspective and vision advanced in global affairs fostered only by virtue of occupying the position of president of the United States. Perhaps it is the context and inherent opportunities and constraints of the office that lend themselves to the incredible consistency of the nation's foreign affairs, even in the face of anomalous tragedies such as the September 11 attacks.

For decades, an edict of American foreign policy has been that the United States' role in the Middle East largely centers on the protection and promotion of its interests in maintaining access to oil resources. While oil is indisputably a vital American interest, in some ways the preoccupation with it has diverted the attention from other prominent interests, including the problem of global terrorism. Moreover, globalist expansion, a foreign policy posture that largely has been rejected by the United States since the Vietnam War, has been allowed to fester. The pervasiveness of the Cold War's influence in global affairs, to a significant degree, held in check the imperialist aspirations of both the Soviet Union and the United States. However, unlike colonialism, which connotes the foreign physical occupation of a state, imperialism transcends the necessity of physicality since it entails "the practice, theory, and the attitudes of a dominating metropolitan centre ruling in a distant territory" (Said, 1993, p. 8).

During the early days of the administration of George W. Bush, much of the attention to foreign policy centered on matters involving China and Russia, consideration of the chances for peace in the Middle East, the development of a ballistic missile defense system, and responding to the US designated "rogue" states of Iran, Iraq, Libya, and North Korea. This agenda helped justify increased military and defense spending. Bush administration officials also debated the pros and cons of imposing new sanctions against Saddam Hussein and the Iraqi government, as well as the possible response in the event US planes enforcing the no-fly zones over Iraq were shot down (Leffler, 2011, p. 2). Even with the guidance left by the Clinton administration concerning ongoing and imminent terrorist threats and incursions, most administration officials, led by President Bush himself, neglected to assign the highest priority to terrorism. In August 2001, President Bush obliviously retired to his Texas ranch for vacation.

RESPONDING TO SEPTEMBER 11

While the September 11 attacks did not necessarily prompt a substantive change in American foreign policy, they did shift the emphasis to the war on terrorism and the conflict in the Middle East. Immediately following the attacks, the administration's posture changed from being passive to proactive in trying to bring about an expedient conclusion to the violence that was taking place between the Israelis and the Palestinians in the West Bank (Mansour, 2002). Despite the pressure from the Israeli government to support it in overcoming the threats posed by Palestinian suicide bombers, President Bush held fast regarding ending the violence, which was paramount in his Middle East policy due to the need to demonstrate sensitivity to the plight of the Palestinians. It was needed also because of the fragile nature of the coalition of Arab countries supportive of the U.S. war on terrorism (Mansour, 2002).

The Bush administration avoided isolating and focusing on Al-Qaeda singularly; rather, its approach involved focusing on terrorism generally as an integrated global threat. A complicating feature of the policy was that the United States would hold nonstate actors accountable for their actions. More significantly, it asserted that any state that harbored or succored any organization associated with terror would be dealt with accordingly. The US government employed what were eventually deemed questionable means and tactics for gathering actionable intelligence, further eroding its reputation and influence in the international community (Leffler, 2011, p. 2).

American citizens united in support of the efforts of President Bush and his administration's declaration of the war against terrorism. Even African Americans closed ranks with the rest of the nation to support Bush's plans, despite the fact that his administration had supported many policies antithetical to their progress. Nonetheless, as they had done in the past, black Americans rallied in support of the president. Among the black members, the bulk of whom represented majority black districts, Congresswoman Barbara Lee (D-TX) was the lone black member of the House of Representatives to vote against H.J. Resolution 64 (Stanford, 2002, pp. 96–97). This resolution authorized the President . . . to use all necessary and appropriate force against those nations, organizations, or persons he determines planned, authorized, committed, or aided the terrorist attacks that occurred on September 11, 2001, or harbored such organizations or persons, in order to prevent any future acts of international terrorism against the United States by such nations, organizations or persons. (H.J. Resolution 64, September 14, 2001)

The Bush administration requested that Afghanistan's Taliban government under the leadership of Mullah Muhammad Umar extradite Osama bin Laden, the leader of Al-Qaeda. The Taliban's refusal to extradite bin Laden ignited action by the administration (with the authorization of the United Nations Security Council's resolution 1368) to activate on October 7, 2001, Operation Enduring Freedom. Upon its defeat in December 2001, the Taliban retreated to Pakistan from Kandahar. Operation Anaconda was initiated in March 2002 to dispel Al-Qaeda and Taliban forces from the Sha-I-Kot Valley, and on December 5, 2002, Defense Secretary Donald Rumsfeld hastily acknowledged the cessation of "major combat" (Indurthy, 2011, p. 8).

A cornerstone of US foreign policy in the aftermath of September 11 was the feature of preemption. Often referenced as anticipatory self-defense, preemption entailed the operational imperative that the United States would take any necessary action to defend itself, *even if only in anticipation of an attack*. President Bush further asserted that he would take action to prevent impending threats and that if necessary, he would act alone (Leffler, 2011). This stance led eventually to war not only in Iraq, but in Afghanistan as well. It is important to note that H.J. Resolution 64 made clear that not only would states, organizations, or individuals who "aided" those deemed to be terrorists be punished, the resolution stipulated also that anyone involved in the attacks in any way, shape, or form could be subject to the force of the US military at the direction of the president of the United States.

EXPLAINING SEPTEMBER 11

Nevertheless, why was America attacked? What were the motivations, and do they even matter? There are various explanations for September 11; however, they are dictated and shaped primarily by the self-interest of their proponents. This self-interest operates in a manner that substantiates the religious, ideological, and/or philosophical orientation through which a people's experiences are filtered. The utility of these explanations singularly or in combination with something else lie in their ability to inform us about a state's foreign policy responsiveness, and its tendency toward foreign policy justice. Interestingly, the major explanations illuminate diverse perspectives and interpretations of precursor events that shed light on the underlying causes of September 11, and they highlight the corresponding divergent sources of explanations by attuning us to the alternatives and often-competing options available to participating parties. In this manner, they provide insight into perceptions about the United States and its political and cultural treatment of the tragedy, as well as a backdrop for gauging foreign policy decision making in light of the ideal of foreign policy justice. Thus, in sum, these explanations allow us to see more clearly the perspectives, circumstances, and conditions that give rise to a historical event. They can point toward the resolution of conflict and a long-lasting peace, which in the end benefits the United States' position as global leader.

Arguably the most powerful country in the world, foreign policy justice calls on the United States to consider explanations for the tragedy that emanate not only from within, but rather, from the range of explanations, including any earnestly presented by its adversaries. History demonstrates the difficulty of this charge, and in the aftermath of September 11, to do so was particularly challenging. However, it may be that in this instance introspection and self-criticism were deficient due to the need for US leadership to quickly formulate and justify policies related to the war on terrorism. There was also the potential for inflicting "damage" to the country abroad and at the domestic level with the suggestion that America indeed may in some way have been complicit in motivating September 11. Notwithstanding the consequences, there is little debate regarding the influence of September 11 on US foreign policy. Indeed, the event fueled the war on terrorism and led to outcomes not necessarily consonant with the ideal of foreign policy justice.

Although the plausibility of bin Laden's explanation of the central cause of September 11 continues to be debated, it is indisputable that the Israeli-Palestinian conflict has been one of ongoing contention since Israel's establishment in 1948. Yet, the motivations for the September 11 attack are considerably more complex than this issue when viewed through the prism of experience of either Al-Qaeda or the United States. To lend order to understanding the occurrence of September 11, Steve Yetiv (2011) suggests a multilevel approach that allows for the classification of these motivations. This schema facilitates the ordering of a series of random developments in a manner that illuminates the motivations and thus the explanations for

September 11. According to Yetiv (2011), the motivations occurred on three planes: (1) conceptual, (2) oil related, and (3) non-oil related. The conceptual level focuses on the perceptions of Al-Qaeda as filtered by their religious view of the world as self-declared Islamic fundamentalists. The second category, oil-related events, is a broadly inclusive category, which includes events in the Middle East, notably the 1990–91 Gulf War, and US intervention in the region. These factors motivated and enabled the attack (Yetiv, 2011, p. 56). The third dimension involves the range of non-oil-related factors, which are often disregarded in studies of terrorism. These factors include the zeal to establish Taliban-like states, the effects of the perceived global decline in the stature and influence of Islam, the ineffectiveness of Muslim states, the impact of failed states, global poverty, and personal factors associated with the Al-Qaeda rank-and-file (Yetiv, 2011, pp. 76–86).

King's vision and the ideal of foreign policy justice lend themselves to a balanced assessment of the war on terrorism by demanding consideration of the range of perspectives and developments that may have triggered it. Research conducted prior to September 11 demonstrates a clear interest in the causes and nature of terrorism; however, since that time, in actuality, little systematic work has been carried out that connects the event to recent related developments worldwide. The reason for this may be that "this event does not easily conform to its [political science and international relations] theoretical paradigms and because of sensitivities related to discussing issues about radical Islam" (Snyder, 2008, p. 1).

President Bush justified the American response by strenuously emphasizing the reasons he believed explained the attack. He did so by promoting normative values believed to resonate with the American people. Operating fully and in tandem were nationalism and patriotism, both of which intensified following the attacks, prompting broad support that enabled the justification and subsequent framing of the official response in a manner that Americans would find acceptable. Through his speeches, President Bush masterfully framed the "official" rationale for the attacks. Early on, in his "September 11 Address" delivered from the Oval Office, he declared, "America was targeted for attack because we're the brightest beacon for freedom and opportunity in the world" (Bush, 2001). The official position was reinforced by conservative media pundits and radio talk show hosts, including Rush Limbaugh and Sean Hannity, who cemented Bush's explanation by reiterating that September 11 was precipitated by the jealousy of radical Islamists long bent on the destruction of American culture and civilization as a world-defining force. In advancing this perspective in a January 2005 broadcast,

Limbaugh lambasted former Colorado University professor and chairman of ethnic studies Ward L. Churchill over a published essay titled "Some People Push Back: On the Justice of Roosting Chickens." In this essay, Churchill asserted that the September 11 attacks were retaliatory for the 1991 bombing raid, which killed Iraq children, and by and the economic sanctions imposed by the United Nations in the aftermath of the Persian Gulf War. Especially irksome for Limbaugh was Churchill's assertion, as he put it, "that Iraq was behind 9/11. Not bin Laden, not Al-Qaeda, not Mullah Omar, not the Taliban. It was Iraq, because of the Iraqi children killed in a 1991 U.S. bombing" (Limbaugh, January 28, 2005). The Limbaugh view reinforced the notion that the success of the United States had set fundamentalists against them and reinforced the belief that there was no chance of unintentional complicity or otherwise on the part of the government.

The regional politics/externalization explanation provides yet another option for analyzing the motivations for September 11. It asserts that Al-Qaeda attacked the United States with three major purposes in mind: to promote itself within the region, to provoke Washington to retaliate by killing Muslims, and to undermine "moderates" in the region deemed too close to America (Snyder, 2008). Related to this is still another explanation that focuses squarely on the effects of US foreign policy. Accordingly, Robert Pape (2006) maintains that US foreign policy was a significant stimulus for the broader issue of suicide terrorism. He notes that the action of suicide terrorists is motivated by their desire to drive "foreign occupiers" from their homeland.

Foreign policy justice, as noted above, dictates consideration of the motivations for the September 11 attacks from the vantage point of Al-Qaeda and its leadership. Widely viewed in the West as propaganda, on the sixtieth anniversary of the creation of Israel, the media arm of Al-Qaeda released a nine minute and forty second audio recording that featured Osama bin Laden. The communiqué was titled, "A Message to the Peoples of the West: From Sheik Osama bin Laden," with the subheading, "The Reasons for the Struggle on the 60th Anniversary of the Creation of the Occupation State of Israel." In this address, bin Laden stated that the Palestinian-Israeli conflict was a longstanding and primary reason for conflict between the West and the Muslim world—a struggle which he asserted was becoming increasingly difficult due to European partiality in Israel's favor. He stated, "The Palestinian cause has been the main factor that, since my early childhood, fueled my desire, and that of the 19 freemen [September 11 bombers], to stand by the oppressed, and punish the oppressive Jews and their allies." Bin Laden continued: "We shall continue the fight, Allah willing, against the Israelis and their allies, in order to pursue justice for the oppressed, and we shall not give up one inch of Palestine, as long as there is still a single true Muslim alive" (CBS Interactive Inc., 2009).

Thus, several explanations for September 11 have been prevalent. However, a balanced assessment of the predominant explanations of September 11 is essential from the standpoint of foreign policy justice in that it calls attention to the Islamic conditioned perspective of Al-Qaeda, which suggests that particular conditions within Islamic states and others stemming from Western influence may have been contributing factors. In the final analysis, an assessment of progress toward foreign policy justice dictates the understanding that there may be some degree of validity associated with each explanation. However, despite the claims made, independently the explanations fall short in that they provide only a granule of truth. In the following section, I discuss whether the United States is progressing toward a state of foreign policy justice and consideration of what Dr. King might say, were he alive, about the war on terrorism. To make such an assessment, the explanations of September 11 are considered since both their ideological basis and cultural vantage points provide useful insights.

TOWARD FOREIGN POLICY JUSTICE?

Since its initial declaration, the war on terrorism has been controversial due to questions it raised regarding encroachment on the rights and freedoms of American citizens and people abroad. We can therefore initiate the assessment of foreign policy justice in the post–September 11 era by focusing on selected outcomes related to the prosecution of the war on terrorism, which have yielded significant criticism in light of the policy decisions rendered. The war on terrorism has been criticized in at least three (3) important ways: (1) its encroachment on the freedom of American citizens and the erosion of these freedoms at home and abroad; (2) the ongoing imprisonment of suspected terrorists in Guantanamo Bay, Cuba; and (3) the US development and use of unmanned drones. While it may seem Pollyannaish to some, at issue is whether developments in each instance cited above tend toward objective assessments and balanced solutions that reasonably take into account the interests of the United States vis-à-vis those of Al-Qaeda. So if Martin Luther King Jr. were alive, what would be his view of these issues and the role played by the United States? Before proceeding, we briefly turn attention to the emergence of Barack Obama as a global leader. This is only fitting given that President Obama in many respects signifies an important dimension of the culmination of Dr. King's dream, and a powerful manifestation of his work.

OBAMA'S RISE TO GLOBAL POWER

As the first person of African descent elected to serve as the commander-in-chief of the United States, Barack Hussein Obama entered the Oval Office under the considerable weight of an overzealous public optimism—in particular, the pressure to distinguish his administration from that of his predecessor. The foreign policy challenges that beset President Obama upon taking office to serve his first term in 2008 were daunting. Especially pressing was the declining prestige of the United States abroad. Notwithstanding September 11, this was due in part to the perceived and real erosion of the effectiveness of the United States as a mediator in negotiations for peace between the Israelis and Palestinians. This may have been the strongest signal received by President Obama indicating a need to send a message different from that of President Bush. Compounding matters was the failure of the United States to locate in Iraq weapons of mass destruction (WMD), which had provided the pivot point for the invasion and overthrow of the regime of Saddam Hussein. The idea that WMD might fall into the hands of terrorists, of course, did not go unnoticed; it became a primary justification for war. For many of its allies and adversaries, the failure to locate WMD in Iraq pointed to a declining trajectory of US power and influence. However, an implicit irony of the war on terrorism has been diminishing democratization at home and abroad, and a heightened opportunity for the expansion of US and Western imperialist interests. This opportunity crystallized as the United States progressively backed off its earlier claims about the presence of WMD in Iraq due to the failure to locate any.

Candidate Barack Obama early on made it known that as president, he would reach out to Muslims around the world to mend the fissure in their relationship with America. This plan was made more urgent by the war on terrorism. The erosion of US global stature is illustrated poignantly by the difficulty encountered in assembling and maintaining the broad international coalition needed to continue the war against terrorism. In addition to the possibility of declaring an end to the war on terrorism, the task of reframing the US position presented President Obama with the option of deciding whether to continue the policy. Perhaps deliberately or otherwise, the president's actions were both ambiguous and obfuscating. On the one hand, upon taking office, to the chagrin of many Republicans and political opponents, President Obama embarked upon a worldwide tour geared toward enunciating the policy directions that his administration would pursue. Framed by his political opponents as the presidential "Apology Tour," Obama was roundly criticized for making the country appear weak, apologetic, and excessively conciliatory. Political opponents argued that by assuming the blame for actions that supposedly led to the September 11 attacks that the United States appeared to concede not only defeat, but also responsibility due to its own actions and policies. Despite the often heated and ideologically charged political rhetoric in response to the "Tour," many Americans applauded the president's message as a constructive one that would help reset America's position in the international arena. These developments largely resonated with Americans who viewed the president's action as potentially leading to a turning point in the country's foreign policy.

While it is impossible to know truly what Martin Luther King Jr. would say about the war on terrorism if he were alive today, given his iconic position in American and world history, it is not futile to raise the following query: What do developments in the war on terrorism portend about America's progress toward the achievement of foreign policy justice?

DISTILLING FOREIGN POLICY JUSTICE

In the arena of foreign policy related to the war on terrorism, to what extent if at all, did the Obama administration operate in a manner consonant with the ideals of Martin Luther King Jr. and thus, the major tenets of foreign policy justice? Did the change of presidential administrations prompt substantive change in US policy regarding the war on terrorism such that it demonstrates alignment with the conception of foreign policy justice? These questions are at the core of whether the Obama administration was interested in and able to redirect the course of foreign affairs away from that taken by the previous administration and instead advance a foreign policy consistent with King's ideals and the notion of foreign policy justice.

King's vision and work point to several tenets or provisions that facilitate distillation of the notion of foreign policy justice. Among these are the following: (1) might does not necessarily make right; (2) in situations of bargaining and mediation, as well as conflicts where the parties are of considerable unequal power and resources, the powerful and well resourced must strive to balance the scales of fairness and equity to avoid taking unfair advantage; (3) given that domestic politics are intertwined with foreign affairs and policy making, care must be taken to ensure that domestic conditions for the poor are not overlooked or exacerbated, and that basic individual rights are not subverted as a consequence of the country's foreign policy program; and (4) it is incumbent upon the powerful to respect and understand the needs and motivations of the weak and their perceived enemies. Taken together, these ideals form the basis of foreign policy justice. They provide a framework, which can be employed to ascertain whether significant differences exist in the operationalization of foreign policy from one presidential administration to the next.

Several issues have emerged as pivotal in characterizing the war on terrorism. As such, they are employed to help shed light on whether the United States made progress toward the achievement of foreign policy justice with the change of presidential administrations. The following salient emergent public issues are considered: (1) encroachment of the war on terrorism on the freedom and individual rights of American citizens and their erosion at home and abroad; (2) imprisonment of suspected terrorists in Guantanamo Bay, Cuba; and (3) the US development and use of unmanned drones.

ENCROACHMENT ON INDIVIDUAL RIGHTS AND FREEDOM

Intense debate ensued in the United States in the aftermath of September 11 about the protection of individual, civil, and human rights balanced against the rights and obligations of the federal government to protect the lives and property of its citizens. At the center of the debate was the Uniting and Strengthening America by Providing Appropriate Tools Required to Intercept and Obstruct Terrorism Act, or USA Patriot Act. Commonly known as the Patriot Act, this legislation was enacted one month following the horrific events of September 11 (USA PATRIOT Act, 2001). Legislative action revealed that there was enough of a consensus at that time to justify an approach that placed security above freedom. Ninety-eight votes in the Senate and 357 in the House were in support of the acts with only 1 and 66 against it in each chamber respectively (DOJ, 2001).

Although citizens initially supported the measure, this support later waned. Nonetheless, the bill was reauthorized under President Obama in May 2011. The legislation extended several key provisions of the Patriot Act before they were set to expire, including roving wiretaps, the pursuit of alleged "lone wolf" terrorists, and law enforcement's ability to obtain records deemed relevant to an investigation upon securing a federal court order. The bill passed both the House of Representatives and the Senate. The vote in the Senate to extend the Patriot Act provisions for an additional four years passed overwhelmingly by a 72–23 vote. Even though it was supported by a wide margin, the 250–153 House vote was tighter than that in the Senate, a reflection of widespread decline in the public's support of the legislation and the war on terrorism. Legislators on both sides of the political aisle were opposed to the extension for several reasons, including the impact on civil liberties. Still, while some members of Congress were concerned about the impact on civil liberties, others endorsed it in the belief that it should be permanent.

One of the three provisions of the Patriot Act, Section 206, provides for roving wiretap surveillance of targets who attempt to elude the Foreign Intelligence Surveillance Act (FISA). Without the capability of roving wiretap authority, law enforcement agencies would be forced to obtain a new court order whenever a change occurred in the location, phone, or computer that needs to be monitored. A second key provision, Section 215, permits the FBI to apply to the FISA court for permission to access any tangible items in foreign intelligence, international terrorism, and clandestine intelligence operations (Cohen, 2011).

Thus, the persistence of the war on terrorism as manifested in the reauthorization of the Patriot Act by President Obama likely reflects circumstances whereby interest advocacy (not necessarily national, but corporate and/or personal) overwhelms the democratic representation of average citizens and civilians abroad. Even more significant is that policies in both the domestic and international domains appear to intrude on the freedom of American citizens, and the lives and livelihoods of innocent citizens abroad. While there is evidence that Americans' knowledge and interest in foreign affairs has increased within the past decade, the fact remains that foreign policy making will likely continue to be the provincialism of elites, the implication being that regular citizens will pose little challenge to the status quo. Hence, in the case of the Patriot Act, the post-September 11 environment enabled elites, with little protest from the broader citizenry, in advancing policies widely believed to undermine the individual freedoms and rights of everyday citizens.

GUANTANAMO BAY NAVAL BASE

The 2001 Authorization to Use Military Force (AUMF) gave President Bush and the US military the authority to invade Afghanistan to pursue, detain, and punish those responsible for the attacks. This legislation enabled the establishment of the military prison, located at the Guantanamo Bay Naval Base in Cuba, in 2002 to detain and interrogate prisoners. In an apparent break with his predecessor, on his second day in office in 2009, President Obama signed an order declaring that the detention center be closed within the coming year. Obama's decision was based on critics' various accounts of detainee abuse, illegal detainment, and illegal interrogation. These allegations helped fuel questions surfacing worldwide about the credibility American values and morality. Despite developments pertaining to the release of prisoners, in 2014, the examination of former prisoners by doctors led Physicians for Human Rights, a US-based human rights organization, to report it found evidence of torture and war crimes (*CTV News*, 2014).

At its peak in 2003, about 660 prisoners were held at the detention center. In 2013, it was reported that 164 detainees remained in custody at the Guantanamo Bay facility. Most of the detainees had been released while Bush was in office. A total of 78 detainees have been released since 2009. President Obama reiterated in a major speech in May 2013 the view that "our nation is still threatened by terrorists." In the same speech, he called once again for Congress to permit trials and transfers for the majority of the remaining Guantanamo detainees. However, as it had done previously, Congress stood opposed to the transfer and resettlement of the detainees, arguing that they pose a security threat to the United States, and that resettlement would provide the opportunity for terrorists to regroup and continue the war.

In the last days of December 2013, the Pentagon announced that a "significant milestone" had been achieved toward closing the detention center at Guantánamo Bay, Cuba. While pointing out that the development was an important step toward President Obama's order to close the facility, it was also reported that 3 Chinese detainees had been transferred to Slovakia. They had remained from among a total of 22 ethnic Uighurs from China who were captured following the US invasion of Afghanistan in 2001 and sent to the prison at Guantánamo Bay. Although the military determined they were not at war with the United States, and that they should be released as a judge had ordered in 2008, they remained at the detention center because of issues associated with finding a safe and agreeable destination for their transfer (Savage, 2014). These 3 transfers brought the number of detainees who departed Guantánamo in December to a total of 9, and as of summer 2013, the total stood at 11. As of January 2014, 155 prisoners remained incarcerated at Guantánamo, and about half of these were approved for transfer, providing that security conditions could be met in the receiving country; the bulk of those approved for this transfer were Yemenis (Savage, 2013). Hence, the action taken by President Obama was delayed and has only recently begun to make inroads to fulfilling his campaign promise to close the Guantanamo Bay detention center.

However, there is the issue of whether the president is bound by constitutional requirements of due process and his role in deciding that a US citizen will be targeted for kill or capture by the CIA. This matter surfaced publicly following an April 2010 *Los Angeles Times* story that reported that Obama administration officials authorized the capture or killing of Anwar al-Aulaqi, a Muslim cleric born to a Yemeni couple in New Mexico (Cloud, 2010, p. 8). Indeed, there is much more to be done to improve the US global image, which was severely marred as a result of alleged torture and abuse of detainees during the administrations of Bush and Obama. While he would be encouraged by the transfer of most of the detainees, Dr. King would likely be especially critical of the detention center and the circumstances under which prisoners were and are being held in some cases. The absence of formal charges and the lack of a clear path of legal remedy for detainees in a country that professes to be a democracy is a travesty of justice and a stain on the American cloth of democracy. Nonetheless, it remains to be seen if politics will continue to be an obstacle.

USE OF DRONES

Since 2001, the use of drones by the United States has been on the rise. The application of drone technology was buttressed by the 2001 AUMF. This has resulted in the escalation of their use against Al-Qaeda and its affiliates, as well as some unfortunate collateral killing and destruction. Specifically, the AUMF has enabled the targeting of suspects in Pakistan, Yemen, Somalia, and other states. However, it appears that the Obama administration was reluctant to scale back its use of the policy as it justifies the application of drone strikes on suspected terrorist targets in the Middle East and North Africa. Moreover, Israel has played a pioneering role in developing drone technology. Since 1982, it has employed them for surveillance, although opponents have alleged that their drones fire missiles (Associated Press, 2013).

As developments continue to unfold in the Middle East, notably the US disengagement from the war in Afghanistan, the legal authority to hold detainees at Guantanamo Bay has diminished. Interestingly, an important issue has been the conditions under which Afghanistan would allow a force of about ten thousand troops to remain in that country. This is important in regards to the use of drones because technically speaking, when the war in Afghanistan is over, so too is the life of the AUMF, which has yielded broad flexibility for the application of drones. Given the legalities of the situation, there may be little incentive for the United States to completely withdraw its troops. This may leave some states and their leadership to question the sincerity of the United States in its stated goal of cessation of combat.

Perhaps devastating to the credibility of the United States and the West generally is evidence suggesting that since the beginning of drone strikes in Yemen in 2009, Al-Qaeda grew from about two to three hundred members to more than one thousand members in 2012. This membership growth surge may have been ignited by the drone strikes, which provided momentum for Al-Qaeda to assume power in places where government was nonexistent. It has been alleged, for example, that unlike in the past, in some jurisdictions Al-Qaeda "control[s] towns, administers courts, collects taxes, and generally acts like the government" (Morley, 2012, p. 1).

CONCLUSION

The achievement of foreign policy justice is a tall order for an international system comprised of many sovereign, self-interested states. These problems are exacerbated by the presence of transnational groups such as Al-Qaeda who operate essentially in geographic flux. Given this, King would agree that if any semblance of foreign policy justice is to be achieved, powerful countries such as the United States must assume a leadership role. This can be facilitated by acting in an independent and balanced manner when brokering deals and fashioning foreign policy in situations such as that longstanding between the Israelis and the Palestinians. Nonetheless, the linkage between the resolution of the ongoing dispute between these parties and sustaining the war on terrorism seems undeniable. Scholars have pointed out that despite the rhetoric, in his first two years in office, Obama did not formulate a clear policy vision that unequivocally rejected Bush administration policy and that he largely continued the course set by his predecessor (Shane, 2011/12, p. 29)-one that would have been roundly criticized by Dr. King.

The use of drone technology abroad appears to continue to gain political support in the United States and the rest of the West, despite the growing weariness and uneasiness among American citizens about its use and the implications for domestic life. For example, media reports have highlighted the possibility of deploying unmanned drones domestically. Their use has been touted for such purposes as surveillance of areas stricken with high rates of criminal activity and for more efficient package delivery. From the vantage point of Dr. King, drones would likely be construed as a potential invasion of privacy and possibly as problematic in the absence of legislative or judicial oversight. Overseas, the collateral damage inflicted on private citizens, especially women and children, by unmanned drones in pursuit of "terrorists" would be an unacceptable consequence for King in that it raises critical questions in regards to issues of fairness, equity, and balance in the prosecution of the war on terrorism.

The war on terrorism continues to affect people both abroad and in the United States. Given the criticism relative to the war on terrorism previously discussed, Dr. King would stress the urgency of the country to begin to take stock of the situation and conditions that may have contributed to the horrific actions on September 11. Although King would perhaps be encouraged by the increased public discourse concerning the freedom and individual rights of Americans (prompted to some degree by revelations made public by former National Security Administration contractor Edward Snowden), any concern about the effects of the Patriot Act on the erosion of American freedoms would remain, conceivably even prompting direct action in combination with formal political engagement.

The fact that the detention center in Guantanamo Bay, Cuba, continues to house individuals deemed enemy combatants persists as a blemish on the account of the Obama administration, despite the hard won progress it has made in reducing the number of detainees by transferring them to cooperating countries. Guantanamo Bay is demonstrative of the consistency of policy from one presidential administration to the next. It has been pointed out that there has been "operational continuity" when it comes to "the detention of alleged enemy combatants without any legal protections at Bagram Air Force Base in Afghanistan, the continued use of military commissions for trying enemy combatants for war crimes, and the indefinite incarceration of at least some military detainees without trial" (Shane, 2011/12, p. 35).

In the final analysis, Martin Luther King Jr. would likely be alarmed by the continuation of the war on terrorism and its effects on Americans and civilians abroad. He would probably encourage the Palestinians and Israelis to sit down in earnest to resolve their differences, and implore the United States to assume a balanced and fair role as mediator of their dispute. If this ongoing dispute is placed at the center of policy discussions and real progress toward peace is made, there can be a spillover effect that can quell the opposition. In a fictitious interview with Martin Luther King Jr. on his eightieth birthday, Professor Michael Eric Dyson (2008) asked him about his take on the war on terrorism. King responded in part:

> Since most Americans are ignorant of the tragic consequences of our foreign policy, the hatred we face as a nation comes as a surprise. But in fighting terror, we must also fight the impulse to be self-righteous and arrogant; we should practice a bit more humility, which might go a far longer distance in getting the sort of justice and balance and security we need—and that we need to guarantee for others as well. (Dyson, 2008, pp. 265–66)

Such is the challenge of contemporary US foreign policy. Whether or not the goal of foreign policy justice can become a reality remains to be seen as the world undergoes globalization—a process that can be beneficial to the proliferation of King's global vision and the ideals of foreign policy justice.

REFERENCES

Associated Press. 2013. *Israel's Air Force Developing Drones to Replace Aircraft.* April 21.

Boggs, C. 2005. *Imperial Delusion: American Militarism and the Endless War.* Oxford, Roman and Littlefield.

Bush, G. W. 2001. *9/11 Address to the Nation.* September 11. http://www.americanrhetoric .com/speeches/gwbush911addresstothenation.htm.

Carson, C., ed. 1998. *The Autobiography of Martin Luther King, Jr.* New York: IPM in Association with Warner Books.

CBS Interactive Inc. 2009. *Bin Laden: Palestinian Cause Prompted 9/11.* http://www.cbsnews .com/2100-224_162-4102367.html.

Clemons, M. L. 2010. "Conceptualizing the Foreign Affairs Participation of African Americans: Strategies and Effects of the Congressional Black Caucus." In *African Americans in Global Affairs: Contemporary Perspectives,* ed. Michael L. Clemons. Boston: Northeastern University Press, pp. 33–64.

Cloud, D. S. 2010. "Awlaki is Added to CIA Target List." *Los Angeles Times,* April 7. http:// articles.latimes/com/2010/apr/06/world/la-fg/yemen-cleric7-2010apr07.

Cohen, T. 2011. "Obama approves extension of expiring Patriot Act provisions." *CNN Politics.* May 27. http://www.cnn.com/2011/POLITICS/05/27/congress.patriot.act/, 9 February 2014.

Cone, J. H. 1987. "Martin Luther King, Jr. and the Third World." *The Journal of American History* 74(2): 455–67.

CTV News. 2014. "Vancouver Band Demands Compensation after Learning Music Used for Guantanamo Bay Torture." February 5. http://www.ctvnews.ca/canada/vancouver -band-demands-compensation-after-learning-music-used-for-guantanamo-bay-torture -1.1671312, 9 February 2014.

Dyson, M. E. 2008. *April 4, 1968: Martin Luther King, Jr.'s Death and How It Changed America.* New York: Basic Books.

Farwell, R. 2012. "Post 9/11 Foreign Policy: Continuation of 'New Imperialist' Ambitions?" August 14. http://www.e-ir.info/2012/08/14/post-911-us-foreign-policy-continuation -of-new-imperialist-ambitions/.

Goldstein, J., and J. C. Pevehouse.2013. *International Relations Brief, 2013-2014.* Update, 6th Edition. New York: Pearson.

Hancock, J. 2011. "Human Rights Narrative in the George W. Bush Administrations." *Review of International Studies.* 37: 805–82.

Hardt, M., and A. Negri. 2001. *Empire.* Boston, MA: Harvard University Press.

Hopkins, Dwight N. 2008. "The Last Testament of Martin Luther King Jr." *Theology Today* 65: 67–80.

House Joint Resolution 64. 2001. 107th Congress, 1st Session, September 14.

Huntington, S. 1993. "The Clash of Civilizations?" Foreign Affairs, summer.

Indurthy, R. 2011. "The Obama Administration's Strategy in Afghanistan." *International Journal on World Peace* 28(3)(September): 7–52.

Johnson, C. 2002. *Blowbac.* London: Time Warner Books.

———. 2004. *The Sorrows of Empire: Militarism, Secrecy and the End of the Republic.* London: Verso.

Leffler, M. P. 2011. "9/11 in Retrospect." *Foreign Affairs* 90 (5) (September): 33–44. *Political Science Complete*, EBSCO host.

King, M. L., Jr. 1967. "Beyond Vietnam." Address delivered to the Clergy and Laymen Concerned about Vietnam, at Riverside Church, New York City, April 4. https://ratical .org/ratville/JFK/MLKapr67.html

———. 1967. "Where Do We Go from Here?" Annual Report delivered at the 11th Convention of the Southern Christian Leadership Conference, August 16, Atlanta, GA.

King Center Archives. 2014. *Upbringing and Studies.* www.thekingcenter.org/upbring-studies, the King Center, Atlanta, GA.

Mansour, C. 2002. "The Impact of 11 September on the Israeli-Palestinian Conflict." *Journal of Palestinian Studies* 31: 5–18.

McCrisken, T. 2004. *American Exceptionalism and the Legacy of Vietnam.* London, UK: Palgrave.

Morley, J. 2012). "Hatred: What Dones Sow." Salon.com, June 12. http://www.salon .com/2012/06/12/hatred_what_drones_sow/print.

Obama, Barack H. 2013. "The Future of Our Fight against Terrorism." National Defense University, May 23.

Pape, R. 2006. *Dying to Win: The Strategic Logic of Suicide Terrorism*. New York: Random House.

Roskin, M. G., and N. O. Berry. 2005. *The New World of International Relations*. Sixth Edition. Upper Saddle River, NJ: Pearson Education.

Said, E. 1993. *Culture and Imperialism*. New York: Vintage Books, 1993.

———. 2000. *The End of the Peace Process: Oslo and After*. New York: Pantheon.

Savage, C. 2014. "U.S. Frees Last of the Chines Uighur Detainees from Guantanamo Bay." January 14. http://www.nytimes.com/2014/01/01/us/us-frees-last-of-uighur-detainees-from-guantanamo.html.

Shane, P. 2011/12. "The Obama Administration and the Prospects for a Democratic Presidency in a Post-9/11 World." *New York Law School Law Review* 56: 28–55.

Snyder, R. S. 2008. "On Explaining September 11." *Conference Papers—International Studies Association*, 1–13.

Stanford, K. 2002. "The War Within: African American Public Opinion and the 'War on Terrorism.'" In *The Paradox of Loyalty: An African American Response to the War on Terrorism*, ed. J. Malveaux and R. A. Green.

Walters, Ronald. 2002. "The U.S. War on Terrorism and Foreign Policy Justice." In *The Paradox of Loyalty: An African American Response to the War on Terrorism*, ed. J. Malveaux and R. A. Green. Chicago: Third World.

———. 2010. "Racial Justice in Foreign Affairs." In *African Americans in Global Affairs: Contemporary Perspectives*, ed., Michael L. Clemons,Boston: Northeastern University Press.

Yetiv, S. 2011. *The Petroleum Triangle: Oil, Globalization, and Terror*. Ithaca, NY: Cornell University Press.

MARTIN LUTHER KING JR. AND AFRICA

Then and Now

William G. Jones

Dr. Martin Luther King Jr.'s foreign policy thinking demonstrated a perspective consistent with his views on domestic issues. His views reflected several American foreign policy frameworks and traditions that scholars have embraced from both moralist and realist approaches (McCormick, 1998, p. 24). Additionally, scholars have described American foreign policy as moving from time to time from on a spectrum of isolationism to internationalism—activist foreign engagement. King's foreign policy philosophy was complex. His thinking was guided by the Christian moral principles he extolled, his civil rights movement experience, his human rights activism and international travel, his deeply historical perspective, and finally the turbulence of world events in his time. International events of his era influenced his perspective on foreign policy. The African national independence struggles, anticolonial efforts around the world, and travel grew both his understanding of international affairs and the civil right movement. Today, Martin Luther King Jr. and the civil rights and Black Power movements' legacy are continuing influences in African politics. This is particularly true of Africa's social movements and political activism.

Current Africa politics have numerous salient issues important to the continent's short-term progress and long-term prosperity. This examination of Dr. King's philosophy and concerns considers how he might have viewed current foreign policy toward Africa related to certain key issues and challenges. The principal issues to be weighed in this examination include democracy, alleviating poverty, finance and aid, conflict management, international relations, and Pan-Africanism. The methodology and approach will be to build the projection of King's perspective on current African foreign policy issues based on his writings, speeches, activities, and the scholarly record. Dr. King spoke to an array of foreign policy issues covering many regions and events. These include Western colonialism; the Vietnam War; world poverty; African, Asian, and South American development; human rights; world peace; communism; and democracy.

While a significant amount of time and events have passed since his death, as with other great world leaders and political philosophers, King's contributions have proven timeless. His intellectual contributions remain outstandingly visionary with currency toward practical implementation. In any examination of what he might say about current affairs, it is imperative to consider that little has happened that would have likely changed his principal positions or their applicability to the present era.

AFRICA, PROSPERITY, CHANGES, CHALLENGES, AND POVERTY

The major changes in Africa were taking place both during and after the civil rights and Black Power movements. Sweeping change occurred as Africa moved forward to successfully free itself from Western colonialism. In the 1950s and 1960s, most of Europe's former colonial territories in Africa obtained independence. African nationalism inspired many activists in the civil rights movement, including Dr. King (Jones, 2005), who remarked, "The nations of Asia and Africa are moving with jet like speed toward gaining political independence, but we still creep at horse and buggy pace toward gaining a cup of coffee at the lunch counter" (King, 1963a, p. 82). In January of 1957, Dr. King received a letter of invitation from Kwame Nkrumah, the Ghanaian prime minister, requesting his attendance from March 2through 10 for the new nation's independence ceremonies. The trip to Africa inspired a noteworthy sermon from King on Africa and Ghana that he would deliver in Montgomery, Alabama (Carson, 2000, p. 110).

Dr. King's speech "Birth of a New Nation" provides insight into his deep understanding of the significance of Africa's rise out of colonialism. In the speech, King shares his experience of visiting Ghana for several days during the newly independent nation-state's inaugural events. He provides a detailed historical account of the Ghanaian anti-imperialist movement and development of its leader, Kwame Nkrumah. The anticolonialists in the mass movement used nonviolent organizing with the involvement of a myriad of political and civic organizations in the former Gold Coast (King, 1957). He says of Nkrumah that "while in London, he came, he started thinking about Pan-Africanism, and the problem of how to free his people from colonialism. . . . [H]e always realized that colonialism was made for domination and for exploitation. It was made to keep a certain group down and exploit that group economically for the advantage of another" (ibid.). The speech illustrates that King grasped the political and economic conditions of the entire African continent in that period. In this speech, he mentioned a number of African countries/territories, including Egypt, Ethiopia, Morocco, Algeria, Belgian Congo, South Africa, Rhodesia (now Zimbabwe), Kenya, Tanganyika (now Tanzania), Uganda, Nigeria, Liberia, Libya, Tunisia, and Sierra Leona. His understanding of the colonial subjugation of Africa is explicit in his remarks, "[F]or centuries, Africa has been one of the most exploited continents in the history of the world. . . . It's been the continent that has suffered all of the pain and the affliction that could be mustered up by other nations . . . experienced all of the lowest standards that we can think about, and it's been brought into being by the exploitation inflicted upon it by other nations" (ibid.). The moral and biblical context for King was the Hebrew people's struggle against bondage and quest for freedom.

King attended the inauguration in Lagos, Nigeria, of the first president, Nnamdi Azikiwe, November 1960. In an interview after this visit to Nigeria, he remarked,

> I had the opportunity to talk to most of the major leaders of the new independent countries of Africa and also leaders of countries that are moving toward independence. . . . [T]hey are saying in no uncertain terms that racism and colonialism must go for they see the two are as based on the same principle, a sort of contempt for life, and a contempt for human personality. (Africa.com, 2013)

Throughout King's writings, sermons, and speeches, it is clear that he considered the African freedom movement and the African American freedom movement to have a symbiotic relationship along with other peoples considered to have a moral need or duty toward justice.

Since King's "Birth of a New Nation" speech, all fifty-four African states have freed themselves from traditional colonial rule. All of the states except Morocco are part of the United Nations and the African Union (Wikipedia, 2013). They continue to address the legacy of colonialism, which echoes into these countries' current economic challenges. While there are continuing barriers to Africa's entrenched poverty, there is economic progress. After the recent global financial crisis, progress has been mixed. African countries have recently experienced a modest level of recovery. Aggregate GDP growth was forecasted to rise to 5.0 percent by 2011 from 4.7 percent in 2010. This is a movement in the right direction, considering that African economies' exports shrank 32.4 percent in 2009 (UN Economic Commission, 2011, p. 2). African countries remain primarily commodity producers after centuries of Western and Middle Eastern domination. By 2010, demand for commodities was strengthened. Like other regions of the world, African states see industrialization as a means of furthering their self-reliance and achieving a better quality of life for their citizens.

African states have renewed their commitment to industrialization because of rising food prices, employment needs, energy prices, and the global financial crisis attributed to effects of the housing market and finance management in the fall of 2007 in Europe and America (UNIDO and UNCTAD, 2011, p. 3). The financial crisis was largely seen as the American financial sector's mortgage market mismanagement and fraudulent financial practices. In the 1980s African states' aspirations toward industrialization were muted by international finance institutions such as International Monetary Fund (IMF) and the World Bank, which enthusiastically promoted structural adjustment programs. The thrust of structural adjustment programs required a number of fiscal restraints and monetary reforms that resulted in less focus on industrial development and more focus on a "competitive advantage" approach. "Competitive advantage" concentrated states on using their special a niche in the global market to produce Gross National Product (GNP) and revenue. For African countries, structural adjustment and competitive advantage economists advised that commodity production was the path to the best possible outcomes. Also, these programs reduced expenditures on social development programs such as education, housing, food subsidies, and other social investments. The structural adjustment programs included trade liberalization, currency devaluation, interest rate deregulation, privatization of state-owned business, and removal of protections for indigenous enterprises. Structural adjustment program goals to "make African firms more competitive, trigger industrial development, and lay the foundation for sustained economic growth have not been realized" (ibid.). International financial institutions had appeared to generously provide support for infrastructure and other programs after semi-sovereignty was established in many of the former African colonies. Many economists, international engineering firms, consultants, and corrupt governments benefited from the projects. In a number of cases the projects addressed core needs, but were insufficient to raise the continent to a point of economic liftoff.

Dr. King saw modern technology and industrialization as blessings that held tremendous potential to address many of the contemporary dilemmas being experienced by poorer nations (King, 1963b). If used for good, modern technology and industrialization could cure the dilemmas of poverty, hunger, homelessness, and disease in America, Africa, and other regions. However, Africa's share of global manufacturing (Manufacturing Value Added—MVA) declined from 1.2 percent in 2000 to 1.1 percent in 2008 (UNIDO and UNCTAD, 2011, p. 105). In general, King was an advocate for political and governmental support for underdeveloped states' industrialization, progressively structured foreign aid, and antipoverty programs. During visits to Ghana and Nigeria, he was greatly disturbed by the poverty witnessed and viewed it as rooted in colonialism (King, 1993, p. 146).

A massive Marshall Plan by wealthy nations was advocated by Dr. King as a means of lifting underdeveloped nations out of poverty (Baldwin et al., 2002, p. 256). Africa, Asia, and South America were considered underdeveloped areas needing extensive funding to compensate for past exploitation and current deprivations of financial resources. Western nations were given the objective of annually contributing 2 percent GNP to alleviate poverty. The United Nations' target for development assistance was 0.7 percent of Gross National Income (GNI). When measured against the target of 0.7 percent of GNI, donor nations fell short by $153 billion in 2009 (United Nations Development Program, 2011, p. 148). According to the Organization of Economic Cooperation and Development (OECD) Scandinavian countries gave the highest percentage of their GNI (OECD, 2011). The OECD sprung from the Organization for European Economic Cooperation (OEEC), which helped administrate the Marshall Plan in Europe and a few select Asian countries. OECD produces reports on Official Development Assistance and promotes world trade and economic progress. Aid often has conditionalities that require African states to compromise on matters critical to their best economic interest. The depth of Dr. King's understanding of international affairs is illustrated in his writing on the foreign aid:

> The aid program that I am suggesting must not be used by the wealthy nations as a surreptitious means to control the poor nations. Such an approach would lead to a new form of paternalism and a neo-colonialism which no self-respecting nation could accept. Ultimately, foreign aid programs must be motivated by a compassionate and committed effort to wipe poverty, ignorance, and disease from the face of the earth. Money devoid of genuine empathy is like salt devoid of savor, good for nothing except to be trodden under the foot of men. (King, 1967b, p. 178)

With a clear understanding of the pitfalls of foreign aid and international finance programs, King cautioned against foreign aid with conditionalities and financial assistance usury. From 2010 through 2013 international organizations have continued to report a net decrease in global foreign aid but a general increase in financial assistance (loans) to Africa. King advocated a worldwide war against poverty.

AFRICAN LAND REFORM POVERTY AND EQUALITY

Decades after the independence movement, Africa still struggles with agricultural production and problems with land resource allocation. Land distribution is a continuing basic issue of equality and survival in Africa. Dr. Wangari Maathai, Kenyan leader of the Green Belt Movement and Pan-African Green Belt Network wrote about the need for land reform with integrity. She described how colonial powers had used dislocation, colonial authority, and force to dispossess native Africans of their land in favor of European settlers and favored African ethnic groups. Maathai indicates that not only did the imposition of colonial land structure cause disruption of agriculture, and further ethnic/tribal conflict, but it disenfranchised women. Formerly, land was considered community property allocation to families by traditional laws. Under colonialism where a system of land titling was imposed, generally deeds were provided in the name of the male head of household. Change has taken place in a number of states where effective challenges have been mounted (Maathai, 2009, p. 228). Like Martin Luther King Jr., Wangari Maathai was a Nobel Peace Prize laureate in 2004. Dr. Maathai won the prize for her contributions to the environmental consciousness, sustainable development, democracy, and peace. The Nobel committee said of her "that she thinks globally and acts locally" (NobelPrize.org.).

Since traditionally land was community property, traditional societal leaders depended on control of taxes and labor as power mechanisms to preserve social cohesion and guide progress (Beaver, 1996, p. 246). Colonialism impacted this relationship with traditional leadership and farmers as it imposed a new set of exploitative labor requirements and taxation requirements to aid sustaining a foreign domination. Traditional leadership was in cases compromised or alternatively sided with independence nationalists or took the role of collaborators with colonialists. Despite the historical fallacy, Africa always had widespread urban areas; however, modernization has intensive urbanization. This has impacted landownership, presenting a new set of land tenure and ownership challenges. Contemporary economic policies related to land reform in Africa are a mix of the traditional legacy, Western concepts, and a midground between the two approaches. Economic development initiatives and financial assistance supported by major international institutions and some bilateral trade agreements have generally attempted to further land privatization and a real estate legal regime to promote multinational corporate investments. This approach impacted land ownership and tenure, aggravating existing sources of conflict related to land resources. There remains a political agenda by the traditional agricultural sections and those with long-standing grievances to have land reform policies more aimed at equality and restoration as redress from the colonial era.

Martin Luther King Jr. saw land reform as an important concern at the heart of just resolution of many international altercations and internal societal tensions. In speaking to the Vietnam conflict, King put the historical demand for land reform as a core grievance driving hostiles and preventing peaceful resolution rather than ill-conceived notions, "Cold War" rhetoric, and ideologies. He said the Vietnam conflict was brought about by

> Western arrogance that has poisoned the international atmosphere for so long. With that tragic decision we rejected a revolutionary government seeking self-determination and a government that had been established not by China—for whom the Vietnamese have no great love—but by clearly indigenous forces that included some communists. For the peasants this new government meant real land reform, one of the most important needs in their lives. . . . A true revolution of values will soon look uneasily on the glaring contrast of poverty and wealth. With righteous indignation, it will look across the seas and see individual capitalists of the West investing huge sums of money in Asia, Africa, and South America, only to take the profits out with no concern for the social betterment of the countries, and say, "This is not just." It will look at our alliance with the landed gentry of South America and say, "This is not just." (King, 1967a)

His quote provides an insight into his understanding that land reform and distribution are salient issues in Africa and South America. Like Dr. Maathai, King saw it as a moral imperative that the political process leading to land reform be reasonable, just, and democratic. Maathai placed land reform, as did King, in a broad political context. Additionally, her direct involvement in the Green Belt Movement extended her thinking about land reform to consider environmental impacts which were less prominent during the civil right movement. Wangari Maathai noted,

> Given the inequitable distribution of land in many countries in Africa, and inequities perpetuated by governance and economic systems that are inherently unjust, it is difficult to wholly avoid incidents of people or peoples fighting for access to resources—especially when politicians use land to incite violence. Furthermore, those without land will find it difficult to accept that some in their country may own thousands of acres. Despite the passions and ongoing controversies inflamed by land ownership in Africa, however, there can never be any excuse to take another's life. (Maathai, 2009, p. 237)

Both King and Maathai would have advocated an eclectic approach to land reform that considers Milton Friedman's theory in *Capitalism and Freedom* on the importance of a middle and business class as possible contributors to separating political and economic power in the cause of democracy in Africa. However, African scholar Richard Sandbrook cautioned that a self-confident business class with an independent economic base that disciplines the holders of political power has yet to emerge (Sandbrook, 1994, p. 980). King and Maathai, both practical activists and intellectuals, would opt for a land reform approach that provided for justly compensated subsistence and collective farming, corporate ownership, and large-scale agriculture for domestic consumption and cash crops.

AFRICA, INTERNATIONAL FINANCE, AND DEBT

International finance and debt are contemporary issues for the African states posing a continuing impediment to economic progress, equality, and social stability. For Dr. King moral considerations were the principal guides for the purpose and structure of finance and aid to underdeveloped nations. A rigorous and "excessive altruism" was morally necessitated, recognizing the historical impact of Western colonialism on Africa, Asia, and South America. There is a traditional Christian ethic in King's thinking about self-interest in contrast to the inverse modern perversion of self-centered self-aggrandizement as self-interest promoted by some social groups as the best servant to the common good. His prophetic framework and guidance translated to an international level advocated that "true altruism is more than the capacity to pity; it is the capacity to sympathize" (King, 1963b, p. 21). Aid and financial support for underdeveloped countries should not have an objective of maintaining subservience of other nations or further exploitation according to King. While he set out specific parameters for minimum levels of support to poor nations, he ultimately set the standard as being one beyond that which law and statute can require. The moral standard he set is that financial and aid relations between nations should be governed by "love" and "unselfish" giving between rich and poor nations, based upon the moral and theological principals presented in "Year of Jubilee" and the "acceptable Year of the Lord" biblical references. Both principals are addressed to ending usury, social justice, and the plight of the exploited.

Dr. Obery M. Hendricks Jr. is a theologian scholar who has written extensively about Jesus Christ's political philosophy and practice. Hendricks investigated the historical, social, and political context for much language attributed to Jesus Christ. He found of particular significance a reference used in the Bible that is attributed to Jesus:

> Then he made the ultimate political pronouncement: he announced *liberation to those who were oppressed* by the crushing weight of empire. Not "bruised," as some translations render it, but "oppressed," from the Greek word *thrawo*, "oppress, crush." Jesus ended his inaugural sermon by proclaiming: the acceptable year of the Lord," an allusion to the year of Jubilee (Leviticus 25:8–10), the end of a fifty-year cycle, when all land that has been confiscated or otherwise unjustly acquired was to be returned to its original owners. When read in the context of his times, Jesus' sermon has the ring of a manifesto. It is pronouncement of his divine appointment to struggle for—to "bring"—economic, political, and social justice to his people. It is difficult to make a more radical political statement than this. (Hendricks, 2006, p. 8)

In interpreting this biblical reference Hendricks saw relationship between the term "the acceptable year of the Lord" and year of Jubilee. As described by Hendricks, the "Year of Jubilee" set forth a time of reconciliation between the wealthy and the poor. In addition to releasing slaves and returning land and property to the poor, usury was forbidden. King provided this reference in a less known and less popular sermon called "Guidelines for a Constructive Church." In many respects this is one of Dr. King's most important sermons as he addressed it to one of the broadest, most influential audiences. In the speech he engaged all the clergy, challenging them to live up to a theological requirement that he saw as indispensable to the modern day fulfilling church's mission.

> Jesus Christ, he said that, "There are some things that my church must do. There are some guidelines that my church must follow." And if we in the church don't want the funds of grace cut off from the divine treasury, we've got to follow the guidelines. (That's right) The guidelines are clearly set forth for us in some words uttered by our Lord and Master as he went in the temple one day, and he went back to Isaiah and quoted from him. And he said, "The Spirit of the Lord is upon me, because he hath anointed me (Yes, sir) to preach the gospel to the poor, (Yes, sir) he hath sent me to heal the broken-hearted, to preach deliverance to the captives, and recovering of sight to the blind, (Yes) to set at liberty them that are bruised, to preach the acceptable year of the Lord." These are the guidelines. (King, 1966)

King went on to outline a myriad of circumstances related to moral issues and injustices, social, political, and economic. His speech was addressed to his congregation and clergy on the church's role as a sanctuary and cure for the "broken-hearted" persons and to be an active agent of change to "preach deliverance" and "free the people." In the speech a clear message can be discerned that he extended his concerns about the "Acceptable Year of the Lord" to providing for a more literately effective foreign policy for financial assistance as well as private charitable giving. The message was that both public and private lending must be truly altruistic in nature. Aid would be provided in a form where donor advantage was not a structural feature, conditionality, or result. The reverend cautioned against wealthy nations using aid or financing or investment in ways that only took advantage of the poorer nations of Asia, South America, and Africa. The message to the church has even greater importance when contrasted with the contemporary theology promoted by some evangelists in Africa. Few address the underlying moral principles related to political and economic justice.

The Jubilee 2000 campaign recognized the oppressive foreign debt as a powerful force stifling African progress. "To be in a position of owing unpayable debt is a kind of slavery. . . . In a fair world, monies should flow from rich to poor to alleviate their sufferings. The debt burden [on poor nations] has been producing a considerable reverse flow, thus nullifying much of the effect of aid" (Dent and Peters, 1999, p. 15). The campaign sought to alleviate foreign debt burden or 100 percent debt cancellation for the underdeveloped countries in Africa, Asia, and South America. Its origins had both ecumenical and secular advocates. The campaign coincided with the Catholic Church John Paul III declaration in 1994 in preparation for the "Great Jubilee" to honor the work and person of "Jesus." Jubilee 2000 was supported by scholars such as Martin Dent of Yale University and celebrities such as Bono of the rock band U2, Quincy Jones, Willie Colón, Muhammad Ali, Bob Geldof, and others. Wangari Maathai, co-chair of the Kenyan Jubilee campaign, wrote that despite Jubilee efforts, many African states continue to be burdened by "huge and unfair debts" (Maathai, 2009, p. 89). International financial institutions and unilateral lending both during and after the campaign failed to find innovative approaches to jumpstart a more dynamic self-reliant economic base. Conditionality tied to both financing and trade agreements has become more extensive and customary. Many of the conditionalities limit government funding of necessary government programs and services; require dropping protections to local products and resources; and currency restrictions.

The United Nations Millennium Development Goals (MDG) have also been an international effort to promote development and alleviate world poverty. The participant United Nations members and financial institutions such as World Bank and International Monetary Fund set a goal in 2010 of providing $40 billion between 2010 and 2015 with the objective of reducing extreme poverty by 50 percent; stopping HIV/AIDS; and providing universal primary education. However, the United Nations has evaluated the impediments to the MDGs. Its assessment is consistent with traditional critiques of international finance and aid programs. This seems to indicate that the MDGs may have increased the quantity of assistance but without a parallel change in the nature and structure of finance and aid. The United Nations reported that development finance is of very poor quality as it is too frequently

- Highly unpredictable.
- Targeted at technical assistance and emergency aid rather than investments, long-term capacity, and institutional support.
- Tied to contractors from donor countries.
- Driven by separate donor objectives rather than coordinated to support a national plan.
- Overly directed to poorly governed countries for geopolitical reasons.
- Not evaluated or documented systematically for results. (United Nations, 2005, p. 197)

Still, Dr. King would have found the principal basis of the Jubilee campaign and MDGs worth pursuing through to a more permanent solution to progress and poverty. The need for a structural transformation in nature of development finance to African and other underdeveloped nations continues to be a contemporary issue among some nongovernmental organizations, advocates, and scholars.

UNITED NATIONS ON RACISM AND REPARATIONS FOR AFRICA

The United Nations has had several conferences on racism. These conferences assembled national representatives of former colonies, antiracism interest groups and organizations, activists, and former colonial/imperial and neocolonial state powers, and other interested parties. United Nations Organization for Education, Science and Culture (UNESCO) sponsored conferences in 1978, 1983, 2001, and 2009. The last conference, held in Durban, South Africa, promoted discussions of the historical and current impacts and dynamics of international racism. The last two conferences were not attended by the United States for various reasons, one by the Bush administration and the last one by the Obama administration in 2009. Reparations were a "substantive part of the Durban Declaration and Programme of Action and one of the outcomes of this Review Conference should have been the process of repairing the damage that had been done" (UN, 2009). It is likely that Dr. King would have supported the conference participants' recommendation that reparations were a necessary ingredient for moving toward a healthy global environment where people impacted by the racism of colonialism, neocolonialism, and internal colonialism could once again prosper.

In his speech at the National Cathedral in Washington, DC, Dr. King strongly supported reparations before the terminology was popular. He said "[T]hey never stop to realize the debt that they owe a people who were kept in slavery two hundred and forty-four years. . . . We must come to see that the roots of racism are very deep in our country, and there must be something positive and massive in order to get rid of all the effects of racism and the tragedies of racial injustice" (King, 1968). The writings and speeches of Dr. King consistently support compensation for the impact of historical injustices. His contemporary perspective would have likely been consistent with that of the late Dr. Ronald W. Walters. Walters offered, "The damage was done to Africa by European colonial powers that exercised sway over territories in Africa larger than individual countries. Thus restitution should take place on a regional and continental basis. . . . There is a reason for the poverty of Africa, and for the failure to force the global system to face up to the history that created African poverty is to occupy permanently the place of a footstool in the international system" (Walters, 2011, p. 207). Walters and King saw reparations as essential to the prosperity of Africa.

CONFLICT MANAGEMENT

Africa is subject to a number of sources of conflict. Many conflicts are bred by the legacy of colonialism and imperialism. Divisions are hyperintensified by the underlying social fabric of wealth, poverty, and tribalism and further exaggerated by the state boundaries drawn by Western nations across nature, culture, and communities of interest; the use of ethnic minorities as auxiliaries in colonial and postcolonial regimes; and resource competition. The issues often appear as differences by tribal conflicts, political parties, and state-to-state warring. Dr. King fervently believed in nonviolence as the only permanent solution to interstate conflicts. He strongly supported the United Nations as the organization to resolve conflict and promote world peace (Baldwin, 2012, p. 148). He would have likely also strongly supported the African Union as the peace-keeping organization in Africa. Further, like the African Union, he would have opposed any nuclear weapons in Africa while being apprehensive about the establishment of foreign encampment on the continent. The retirement of nuclear weapons in South Africa at the end of Apartheid would have been considered an exercise of global moral leadership and an international necessity. In treating African conflicts, the course would be bread over bombs and dialogue over destruction and peace keepers over ramparts. King's approach to conflict, whether those involved were individuals or state actors, was to use nonviolence as an irrevocable principal which produced permanent peace. Short of waging war, he indicated that the use of police powers by international or interstate organizations such as the United Nations and African Union might in some instances be appropriate as a last resort. King stated, "I am not at all an anarchist, I believe in the intelligent use of police powers" (ibid., p. 149). At the same time, he would have likely taken a position similar to many postcolonial African leaders considering foreign power encampments for the purpose of forcefully extending their influence and interest as retrogression.

SUMMARY AND CONCLUSION

Martin Luther King Jr. was an internationalist speaking his messages of hope, fidelity of social and political morality, and progressive engagement of injustice to a global constituency. His travels to Africa, Europe, and Asia deepened his consciousness of the conditions faced by the underdeveloped nations. He understood that the plight of the African American community and that of the emerging nations of Africa were intertwined. He saw a special value in the cultural affinity of African Americans to Africa. He dedicated a significant amount of time voicing the need to defeat Apartheid in South Africa and advocating improving the nature of foreign aid and development finance for Africa. Where the opportunity was afforded him, he joined in the celebrations of independence of African states. The foreign policy prescriptions promoted for Africa were consistent with the conceptualization of American foreign policy as having an underlying moral prerogative. King saw the promotion of freedom and democracy as important in American foreign policy toward Africa.

There is a long tradition of peace movements and antiwar movements that are part of the American foreign policies tradition. Historian Robert H. Ferrell cites concerns expressed by George Washington and Benjamin Franklin related to the need for restraint and avoidance of conflict (Ferrell). Martin Luther King Jr.'s stand on peace and progressive foreign assistance to developing African nations helped clarify what he saw as the root causes of conflicts—exploitation, poverty, and injustice. His views were extended into the contemporary era by movements such as Jubilee 2000 and by other international activists who advocate debt cancellation and the reform of development finance to African states.

Dr. Wangari Maathai and Dr. Martin Luther King Jr. would have been partners in a push for African land reform with integrity to justly distribute land along with the fruits of labor. Like Dr. Walters, King supported restitution for the impacts of slavery and colonialism. He would have seen reforms in finance, aid, and land as precursors to peace and conflict management in Africa. He would have been wholly supportive of the African Union's vision for a continental parliament and African solutions to African problems as he was an advocate for the right of underdeveloped regions to democracy, self-sufficiency, and self-determination.

REFERENCES

Africa.com. 2013. "Connecting Continents—Dr. Martin Luther King Jr. and Africa" Posted by Africa.com Editorial Staff on January 17, 2013 at 11:06am. http://www.africa.com/blog/king-in-africa/.

Baldwin, L. V., ed. 2012. *In a Single Garment of Destiny*. Boston, MA: Beacon.

Baldwin, L. V., et al. 2002. *The Legacy of Martin Luther King, Jr., The Boundaries of Law, Politics, and Religion*. Notre Dame: University of Notre Dame.

Beaver, E. 1996. *Africa, International Government and Politics Series*. Phoenix: Oryx.

Carson, C., ed. 2000. Nkrumah to Martin Luther King Jr., January 22, 1957, in *The Papers of Martin Luther King Jr., Volume IV, Symbol of the Movement, January 1957—December 1958*. Berkeley: University of California Press, 2000.

Dent, M., and W. Peters. 1999. *The Crisis of Poverty and Debt in the Third World*. Ashgate.

Ferrell, Robert H. 2013. "Peace Movements." *Encyclopedia of American Foreign Policy.*http://www.encyclopedia.com/topic/Peace_movements.aspx. Accessed July 13.

Hendricks, Obery, Jr. 2006. *The Politics of Jesus: Rediscovering the True Revolutionary Nature of Jesus' Teachings and How They Have Been Corrupted*. New York: Doubleday.

Jones, W. G. 2005. "Congress and Africa's Constituency: The Intersection of Racial Factors and Related Interests and Business Interests in the Development of the Africa Growth and Opportunity Act." Washington DC: PhD diss., Howard University, May 2005.

King, C. S. 1993. *My Life with Martin Luther King, Jr.* Revised Edition. New York: Henry Holt.

King, M. L., Jr. 1963a. "Letter from the Birmingham Jail." In *Why We Can't Wait,"*ed. Martin Luther King, Jr.

———. 1963b. *Strength to Love*. New York: Harper and Row.

———. 1966. "The Guidelines for a Constructive Church." Delivered at Ebenezer Baptist Church, Atlanta, Georgia, on June 5. The King Center. *http://mlk-kpp01.stanford.edu/kingweb/publications/sermons/660605_Guidelines_for_a_Constructive_Church.ht.*

———. 1967a. "Beyond Vietnam—A Time to Break Silence." Delivered April 4, Riverside Church, New York City. http://www.americanrhetoric.com/speeches/mlkatimetobreaksilence.htm.

———. 1967b. *Where Do We Go from Here, Chaos or Community*? New York: Harper and Row.

———. 1968. Speech Delivered at the National Cathedral, Washington, DC, on March 31. *Congressional Record*, April 9.

———. 2000. "Birth of a New Nation." Delivered in Montgomery, Ala. Dexter Avenue Baptist Church, April 7, 1957. In *The Papers of Martin Luther King Jr., Volume IV, Symbol of the Movement, January 1957—December 1958*, ed. Clayborne Carson. Berkeley: University of California Press. http://mlk-kpp01.stanford.edu/index.php/encyclopedia/documentsentry/the_birth_of_a_new_nation/#fn4.

Maathai, W. 2009. *The Challenge for Africa*. New York: Pantheon Books, Random House.

McCormick, J. M. 1998. "*American Foreign Policy and Process* 3rd edition. Itasca, IL: F. E. Peacock.

NobelPrize.org. 2004. *The Nobel Peace Prize 2004 WangariMaathai—Facts*. Nobel Foundation. http://www.nobelprize.org/nobel_prizes/peace/laureates/2004/maathai-facts.html.

Organization of Economic Cooperation and Development (OECD). 2011. *Statistics on Resource Flows to Developing Countries, February 2011.*

Sandbrook, R. 1994. *The Politics of Africa's Economic Recovery.* Cambridge University Press.

United Nations. 2005. *Investing in Development: A Practical Plan to Achieve the Millennium Development Goals.* New York: UN Millennium Project.

United Nations Development Program. 2011. *Towards Human Resilience: Conditionalities Sustaining MDG Progress in an Age of Economic Uncertainty.* New York: United Nations.

United Nations Economic Commission for Africa and African Union. 2011. "Economic Report on Africa 2011, Governing development in Africa—the role of the state in economic transformation."

United Nations Industrial Development Organization (UNIDO) and United Nations Conference on Trade and Development (UNCTAD). 2011. "Economic Development in Africa 2011 Report, Fostering Industrial Development in Africa in the New Global Environment."

United Nations–sponsored "World Conference against Racism, Racial Discrimination, Xenophobia and Related Intolerance (WCAR)." 2009. " Non-governmental Organizations address Durban Review Conference on Issues arising from the Objectives of the Conference." April 24.

Walters, R. W. 2011. *The Price of Racial Reconciliation.* Ann Arbor, University of Michigan Press. 207.

Wikipedia, the free encyclopedia, Wikipedia Foundation. 2013. "List of sovereign states and dependent territories in Africa, 18 June 18. http://en.wikipedia.org/wiki/List_of_sover eign_states_and_dependent_territories_in_Africa (accessed, June 27, 2013).

SOCIAL DEVELOPMENTS

Part III

A DREAM THAT OCCURRED OR A DREAM DEFERRED?

Race Relations from Dr. Martin Luther King Jr. to President Barack Hussein Obama

Byron D'Andra Orey, Lakeyta M. Bonnette-Bailey, and Athena M. King

The harvest has past the summer has ended, and we are not saved.
—JEREMIAH 8:20

On August 28, 1963, Dr. Martin Luther King Jr. stood on the steps of the Lincoln Memorial and gave one of the most inspiring and provocative speeches ever delivered on this nation's soil. Even today, this speech continues to be referenced by those who continue to fight injustices and serves as the most memorable moment of King's legacy. Following King's speech, America and the world witnessed as all branches of government worked collectively with civil rights activists to eliminate many of the structural barriers that had previously impeded the opportunity of blacks to be fully integrated into the nation's democratic fabric. Throughout the tumultuous 1950s and 1960s, King led the civil rights community in their quest for racial equality by challenging the status quo, focusing heavily on voting, economic equality, and integration. Consequently, more than fifty years after the passage of the Voting Rights Act (VRA), a black president sat in the White House.

Since King's death in 1968, America's racial progress can be described as "mixed" at best. Now, more than fifty years after the passage of the Voting Rights Act (VRA), the apex of that quest has been, so far, the election of the first black president, Barack Hussein Obama. The election of Obama as the nation's first black president was but a mere dream for King. According to Cory Booker, one of two lone blacks to be elected in the current US Senate, "Our country is showing its forward evolution. . . [T]he color of one's skin cannot inhibit one's ability, and that's worthy of celebration" ("What Obama's," 2008). The progress made in Deep South states, such as Mississippi, should also be applauded. Mississippi, a state that Dr. King referred to as "sweltering with the heat of oppression," and a state that possessed a black registration rate of only 6.7 percent in 1963, currently possesses the largest number of black elected officials in the country.

Dr. King's "I Have a Dream" speech is rooted in the American Dream, consisting of a set of ideals in which citizens can achieve equal opportunities to prosper economically and can expect to achieve upward social mobility. If King were alive today he would have witnessed massive improvements in economic growth by blacks, when compared to his era. There has been a vast increase in the black middle class when compared to this population in the 1960s, and the number of black homeowners has doubled from 22.8 percent in 1940 to 46.3 in 2000 (Leigh and Huff, 2007).

For some, however, the country has not advanced far enough in achieving racial equality. In his book, *And We are Not Saved*, Derrick Bell uses the above epigraph as a reference for the current status of civil rights in the United States. Despite progressive legislation and legal decisions, blacks continue to face inequities in almost every facet of life. Nearly sixty years following the Montgomery bus boycott, blacks find themselves in what appears to be a time capsule. In 2014, the world witnessed as an unarmed teenager, Michael Brown, lay dead for approximately four hours, after being killed by a police officer. For some, the visual of Brown lying in the street for hours served as a stark reminder of the 1950s when Mamie Till demanded that her son's (Emmett Till) badly beaten and swollen body be displayed for the world to see. To be sure, the black middle class has grown; however, the wealth gap between blacks and whites remains dismal, and the unemployment rate is double that of whites. Similarly, while homeownership for blacks has increased since the 1960s, the 2006 burst of the housing bubble disproportionately impacted blacks. Thus, for some, racial equality has not become a reality.

There is no question that there have been huge improvements since the civil rights era. Dr. King would be extremely proud to see such improvements. However, we also suspect that Dr. King would be disappointed in some areas where race relations continue to struggle. In this chapter, we investigate whether King's dreams of racial equality have been realized. We focus specifically on race relations, voting rights, and economic equality.

THE EBB AND FLOW OF RACISM

"Racism" is one of the most loosely used and abused terms in America. Almost any behavior toward a nonwhite group by whites that is deemed to be unacceptable is often casually labeled as being a racist act. The term has been used so much that America has arguably become desensitized to it. In this section, we trace the evolution of negative racial attitudes toward blacks dating from the pre-King era to the Obama era. We then follow up with a discussion of recent incidents that some have classified as racist.

According to *Webster's Encyclopedic Unabridged Dictionary*, racism is "a belief that human races have distinctive characteristics that determine their respective cultures, usually involving the idea that one's own race is superior and has the right to rule others." In this vein, the old-fashioned racism that existed during the days of slavery placed focus on white supremacy. In order to justify slavery, for example, blacks were deeded as biologically, mentally, and socially inferior to whites. Such racism was institutionalized even among government officials as seen in Query 14 of Thomas Jefferson's *Notes on the State of Virginia* and subsequent Supreme Court decisions (Jefferson, 2014). Indeed, the Supreme Court in *Scott v. Sanford* (1857) ruled that blacks were not citizens. Justice Taney stated that the framers believed that blacks "had no rights which the white man was bound to respect; and that the negro might justly and lawfully be reduced to slavery for his benefit. He was bought and sold and treated as an ordinary article of merchandise and traffic, whenever profit could be made by it." But these beliefs were not just exacerbated by politicians and through political institutions; the use of science was also implemented to detail these fallacies. Using the pseudoscience of eugenics, scientists provided erroneous support for black inferiority. Of course, these findings had huge implications, as blacks were deemed to be incompetent, for example, to serve in government positions. These findings were also used to help justify Jim Crow laws that successfully worked to disenfranchise black voters and to maintain a segregated society. However, following World War II, probably because of America's criticism of Adolf Hitler and his treatment of the Jews as an inferior people, scientists began to provide evidence that challenged the eugenicist approach to race. In fact, biological racism held by whites began to subside. In 1942 only 41 percent of whites believed that blacks "are as intelligent as white people—that is can . . . learn things just as well if they are given the same education and training." By 1956, 77 percent of whites answered this question in the affirmative. Particularly surprising was that whites in the south doubled from 21 percent in 1942 to 59 percent by 1956—perhaps related to the rise of the "Sunbelt states" and subsequent mass migrations from the North and Midwest.

The eugenicists were replaced by "racial environmentalists," who found that the persistent inequalities between blacks and whites were a function of the social environment and not because of biological reasons. Despite these changes, whites actively resisted efforts to desegregate following the 1954 *Brown v. Topeka Board of Education* decision, often resorting to violence to challenge desegregation efforts and to intimidate blacks in the South. One such example of intimidation and murder of a black child occurred in Money, Mississippi. In 1955, the same year that we observed the Montgomery bus boycott take flight in Montgomery, Alabama, fourteen-year-old Emmitt Till was murdered in Money, Mississippi, for allegedly speaking to a white woman. In reference to Till's murder and after the public viewing of his mangled body, King commented that the murder "might be considered one of the most brutal and inhuman crimes of the twentieth century" (King, 1955).

Only a few months prior to Till's death, NAACP field worker Reverend George Lee was shot at point-blank range after attempting to vote. A few weeks later, after casting a voting ballot, Lamar Smith was murdered in broad daylight in front of the courthouse. Collectively, these deaths served as the impetus behind the 1955 Montgomery bus boycotts. From the urging of E. D. Nixon and the formation of the Montgomery Improvement Association, King, who was only twenty-five, found himself at the center of the movement. In the book *My Life with Martin Luther King, Jr.*, Coretta Scott King states,

> Montgomery was the soil in which the seed of a new theory of social action took root. Black people had found in non-violent direct action a militant method that avoided violence but achieved dramatic confrontation, which electrified and educated the whole nation. . . . Without hatred or abjectly bending their knees, the demand for freedom emerged in strength and dignity. Black people had been waiting for this, and instinctively they seized the new method and opened a new era of social change. (As Quoted in King, 1984, p. xiv)

CONTINUED VIOLENCE

While concessions were received in the South after the aforementioned murders and the Montgomery bus boycott, civil rights were not applicable to all parts of the nation. Many blacks still lived in fear of retaliation for fighting for the rights that King and others were advocating. On July 18, 1964, fifteen-year-old James Powell was shot and killed by an off-duty police officer. Powell's death incited a number of race rebellions that occurred across America from 1964 through 1965. The rebellions that took place in the Watts neighborhood of Los Angeles, California, proved to be the most serious, resulting in thirty-four deaths, nearly thirty-five hundred arrests, and the physical destruction of the Watts community. Although this uprising received national attention, it was overshadowed by the violence that took place in the South, as the nation witnessed the turbulence during Freedom Summer and the nationally televised beatings of civil rights workers on "Bloody Sunday" in Selma, Alabama. Dr. King accurately describes the transition of white racial attitudes in the opening quote to this section by calling out moderate whites and their beliefs of law and order.

Following the passage of major civil rights legislation (in 1964, 1965, and 1968), whites began to change their focus from supporting the end of *de jure* segregation to rejecting the social unrest reignited following the death of Dr. King and Bobby Kennedy, as uprisings sprung up all across America. During this period, whites saw their efforts to create equality as finished and now began to focus on the perceived threats to their safety. As King states,

> I have almost reached the regrettable conclusion that the Negro's great stumbling block in his stride toward freedom is not the White Citizen's Counciler or the Ku Klux Klanner, but the white moderate, who is more devoted to "order" than to justice; who prefers a negative peace which is the absence of tension to a positive peace which is the presence of justice; who constantly says: "I agree with you in the goal you seek, but I cannot agree with your methods of direct action"; who paternalistically believes he can set the timetable for another man's freedom; who lives by a mythical concept of time and who constantly advises the Negro to wait for a "more convenient season." (King, 1963b)

During this focus on "law and order," we see movement toward a different focus for the nation and moderate whites. To be sure, whites no longer believed that blacks were biologically inferior; however, they now believed that blacks did not subscribe to the morals and principles rooted in American democracy. With the diminishing of old-fashioned racist attitudes, whites began to acquire new racial attitudes that have been categorized as a *new racism*.

OUT WITH THE OLD, IN WITH THE NEW [RACISM]

New racist attitudes were observed prominently in politics, specifically through election results. In 1969, Tom Bradley, a two-term black city councilman in Los Angeles, challenged the incumbent mayor of Los Angeles, Sam Yorty. Bradley's decision to run was a direct function of the social unrest that occurred during the 1960s. Yorty was able to defeat Bradley by running a campaign that painted Bradley as being weak on the issue of law and order. This strategy played on the fears of whites who saw these uprisings as a threat. Yorty's campaign was consistent with that of Richard Nixon, who also ran a campaign that focused on law and order. These campaigns were derived from Barry Goldwater's efforts to recruit Southern whites by employing such racial rhetoric as "states' rights." Goldwater's approach was popularized as the "Southern Strategy."

The use of the Southern Strategy became the norm in elections. White candidates began creating campaign messages using racial code words that resonated with white voters. Himelstein described these words as follows: "[a] word or phrase which communicates a well-understood but implicit meaning to part of a public audience while preserving for the speaker deniability of that meaning by reference to its denotative explicit meaning" (Himelstein, 1983, p. 156). One of the most telling descriptions of the Southern Strategy was given by Republican strategist Lee Atwater during a 1981 interview. According to Atwater:

> You start out in 1954 by saying, "Nigger, nigger, nigger." By 1968 you can't say "nigger"—that hurts you. Backfires. So you say stuff like forced busing, states' rights and all that stuff. You're getting so abstract now [that] you're talking about cutting taxes, and all these things you're talking about are totally economic things and a byproduct of them is [that] blacks get hurt worse than whites. And subconsciously maybe that is part of it. I'm not saying that. But I'm saying that if it is getting that abstract, and that coded, that we are doing away with the racial problem one way or the other. You follow me—because obviously sitting around saying, "We want to cut this," is much more abstract than even the busing thing, and a hell of a lot more abstract than "Nigger, nigger." (Lamis, 1990, p. 26)

The use of the Southern Strategy prompted political scientists to study the perception of blacks in the minds of whites in the wake of the civil rights movement. Following the election of Yorty, David Sears, a psychologist at UCLA, and his student Donald Kinder, analyzed white racial attitudes in their support for Yorty. According to their research, a new racism was emerging. In principle, whites believed that blacks were equal. When faced with decisions to implement policies such as school desegregation, however, whites vehemently rejected such efforts. Schuman, and colleagues (1997) describe this phenomenon as the "principle-implementation gap." Kinder and Sears noted that individuals who possessed these new racial attitudes believed "that blacks violate such traditional American values as individualism and self-reliance, the work ethic, obedience, and discipline" (Kinder and Sears 1981, p. 416). According to Sears (1988), the "new racism" is comprised of an antiblack affect and attitudes that subscribe to the notion that African Americans violate the traditional American norms of individualism and moral values. These attitudes are said to develop over time. Indeed, Sears, Hensler, and Speer (1979, pp. 370–71) note that "people acquire in early life standing predispositions which influence their adult perceptions and attitudes. In adulthood, then, they respond in a highly effective way to symbols which resemble the attitude objects to which similar emotional responses were conditioned or associated in earlier life."

While these assertions were made in the late 1970s and early 80s, some have asserted that we now live in a postracial society. It is believed we live in a postracial society because blacks have top positions at companies, within institutions, and in media. Blacks have also acquired more homes, better vehicles, higher socioeconomic statuses, and better educational opportunities. Still, these advances do not compare in this argument to the election of the first African American president, Barack Obama. However, as you will see in the following passages the postracial society that is discussed does not exist, and instead there is evidence of explicit old-fashioned racism.

OLD-FASHIONED RACISM CURRENTLY

Administrators of schools located in the Deep South and known for their resistance to integration during the civil rights era have been silent as many school districts have segregated proms. Over fifty years after the *Brown vs. Board of Education* case, many students in these states are still experiencing *de facto* segregation. It should be noted that these proms are planned, organized, and sponsored by the parents and not the schools.[1] Although we see these types of instances in what is considered the "Deep South"—states such as Georgia and Mississippi-there have been various examples of *de facto* segregation in the North.

For instance, the Valley Club, located in Huntingdon, Pennsylvania, was under investigation the summer of 2009 for its alleged racial discriminatory practices. The parents of some African American and Latino American children complained that their children were not allowed access to its suburban pool because of their race. The director, who opposed this sentiment, reported that he denied the children access to the pool because the facility could not host such a large number of children at one time.

There are two problems with the director's argument. First, the parents paid for the children's access to the pool, and reportedly the children were in attendance because what they paid for was the institution's summer camp. It seems that the facility's administrators would have considered the number of children it could accept for the camp before the camp began. Second, the facility sits on ten acres with a reported "nice-size pool" and an additional pool for younger children (NBCNEWS.com, 2009). Yet, these examples are testaments to how the youth in this country are being exposed to these blatant forms of racism. Contrarily, one also has to recognize that adults who are minorities also bear the brunt of racial hatred and discrimination.

Harvard professor Henry Louis Gates is one of the most recognized authors, civil rights activists, and tenured professors in this nation. Despite a great number of publications and achievements that make his résumé a remarkable one, he was still a victim of racial profiling. On July 20, 2009, headlines detailed the arrest of Professor Gates at his home. This was, arguably, one of the most shocking headlines of the year-not just because of the arrest, but because he was arrested and booked for disorderly conduct at his own residence. Police officers were called to the scene because of a phone call they received from a neighbor about "suspicious characters" at the Gates' residence. Upon arrival, Professor Gates informed the police officer that this was his home, and he was not attempting to rob the place but attempting to gain entry into his home. The situation escalated into a possible racial incident when Gates was arrested on his front porch for "exhibiting loud and tumultuous behavior" (Thompson, 2009). Gates argues that the reason why he was arrested at his own home was because of the alleged racial stereotyping by the (white) officer on the scene. Gates, who lives in Cambridge, Massachusetts, near Harvard Square, claims that because of his race and where his home is located, he was racially profiled.

In all of these prior examples one can recognize how *de facto* segregation and racial profiling still exist within the borders of this nation. And, although it is referred to as a "blatant" example of racism in this particular text, one can argue that in this case and the ones referenced earlier, describing such as "blatant racism" may be a misnomer. Perhaps the director at the pool made a mistake with his numbers and did not consider having such a large number of students at the pool. Perhaps the officer who reported to Gates' home really thought that he was a threat. And, although these cases seem to have substantial evidence to prove that they were indeed incidences of racism, perhaps they are insufficient to prove just how far the nation has to go in its quest toward racial solidarity. Perhaps an examination of certain public policies would convey a greater understanding of both undisguised and covert racial resentment—overt hostilities toward minorities, coupled with a lack of negative response by whites to such actions. Some of the reactions to the passing of the Affordable Care Act and Arizona's immigration law (SB 1070) demonstrate further hidden racial resentment.

After passing a landmark health care bill (Affordable Care Act), many Congressional representatives went outside to confront unruly protestors and discuss the significance of the bill. During the conference and afterward many protestors shouted racial slurs, including the word "nigger," at African American legislators (Stein, 2010). This incident followed many angry protests that occurred during the campaign season. Similarly, considerations of America as a "color-blind," post-racial nation can be debunked by observing the numerous implicit and explicit racial cues and messages prevalent during Obama's presidential campaign and his first year in office. In fact, presidential candidate Senator McCain and his running mate Governor Palin were charged with inciting and advocating racism and hatred at many of their political rallies where audience members shouted such things as "kill him" and "terrorist" in response to then-Senator Obama (Milbank, 2008; Teo, 2008).

Additionally, while speaking of politics within the nation (as this is a country that thinks of racism in terms of a "black-white" dichotomy addressing African Americans and whites), one of the most contemporary and controversial issues is the new immigration law (SB 1070) that was passed in Arizona. The law states that in Arizona suspected illegal immigrants can be asked to show documentation of their citizenship or face deportation (Motes, 2010). The law does state that officers can question anyone suspected of illegal alien status; however, the counties in which this law was passed have large Latino populations. Many argue that the law is discriminatory because it gives the legal authorization to stop, question, and harass anyone, and the only justification an officer needs to question anyone is that he or she "looks" like an illegal immigrant (Motes, 2010). These examples are among a small subset of incidences of racism observed in the country since the election of President Obama. Thus, the allegation that the nation is post-racial because of President Obama's election doesn't ring true. Yet, this assumption of post-racism has affected one of the key legislations Dr. King advocated, voting rights. In fact, Dr. King stated,

> So long as I do not firmly and irrevocably possess the right to vote I do not possess myself. I cannot make up my mind—it is made up for me. I cannot live as a democratic citizen, observing the laws I have helped to enact—I can only submit to the edict of others. (King, 1957)

VOTING RIGHTS AND THE QUIET REVOLUTION

On November 27, 1963, only five days following the assassination of President John F. Kennedy, President Lyndon B. Johnson addressed Congress for the first time. During that meeting, Johnson stated, "No memorial oration or eulogy could more eloquently honor President Kennedy's memory than the earliest possible passage of the civil rights bill for which he fought so long." The Civil Rights Act was passed on July 2, 1964. Embedded within this bill was a voting rights provision that would help to protect citizens' efforts to register to vote. Despite such efforts by Congress, Southern whites perceived the bill as having gone too far, and members of the civil rights community felt that the law had not gone far enough. In response to the law not going far enough, Dr. King and the Southern Christian Leadership Conference led a series of marches in Alabama. During this period, one protester, Jimmy Lee Jackson, was killed (February 17, 1965). Following his death, protesters attempted to march from Selma, Alabama, to Montgomery, Alabama. However, they were met by law enforcement in what proved to be one of the most violent attacks during the civil rights movement, currently referred to as "Bloody Sunday." Having been broadcasted on national television, President Johnson was forced to respond. Borrowing the civil rights mantra, "We shall overcome," the president appealed to Congress to pass a voting rights bill that would strengthen the Civil Rights Act by removing such structural barriers as both the literacy test and poll taxes. The bill also included Section 4 and Section 5, which included a formula based on states that had employed such devices, and those states where voting registration rates were less than 50 percent during the 1964 presidential election. If a state did not meet these requirements then they were held under a "trigger" mechanism that would require them to submit any electoral changes to the Department of Justice for preclearance. The VRA was easily passed on August 6, 1965, with large majorities in both the United States House and Senate. Despite the success of the VRA, there have been numerous challenges by those in opposition.

Table 7.1 Black Elected Officials by Office					
1965 Covered Jurisdictions as of 2002					
State	Total Number of Black Elected Officials	US & State Legislatures	City & County Offices	Law Enforcement	Education
Mississippi	950	46	646	121	137
Alabama	757	36	569	56	96
Louisiana	739	32	408	132	167
Georgia	640	53	413	48	126
South Carolina	547	32	345	12	158
North Carolina	523	28	369	31	95
Virginia	248	16	132	16	84
Source: Table 402: Black Elected Officials by Office, 1970 to 2002, and State, 2002. U.S. Census Bureau. http://www.census.gov/compendia/statab/2008/tables/08s0402.pdf.					

The Civil Rights Division of the United States Department of Justice (DOJ) states that the VRA of 1965 is "considered the most effective civil rights statute enacted by Congress." Indeed, the data in table 7.1 reveal that registration in Southern states increased exponentially. For example, in Mississippi, a state that has often served as the barometer for racial progress, registered voters increased from 6.7 percent before the passage of the VRA to roughly 60 percent immediately after the passage. However, the massive resistance staged by whites prevented blacks from electing candidates of their choice, as Southerners invoked a variety of the most strategic contrivances to dilute the black vote. For example, despite the close to 40 percent black population in Mississippi in 1970, blacks had only elected one black state legislator.[2] While structural barriers such as the literacy test and poll taxes had been repealed, whites adopted newly developed dilutive mechanisms which included multimember districts and racial gerrymandering. These strategies ensured that blacks would be unable to elect the candidates of their choice. In response to this massive resistance, blacks began filing lawsuits under the VRA, specifically using Sections 2, 4, and 5. Section 2 eliminates voting restrictions that are based on race, language, or ethnicity and efforts that target minority voters. Sections 4 and 5 support Section 2 by detailing ways to identify voter disenfranchisement based on minority status and providing solutions for when these rights were violated including those who were ineligible to register to vote because of language barriers. Additionally, these sections state that when language barriers exist, resources must be given to accommodate non-English speakers in their spoken language and assert a requirement of preclearance from the DOJ before voting laws are changed in a state. Because Sections 4 and 5 are meant to ameliorate voting irregularities in certain areas of the country over time, both are subject to periodic revision and renewal by Congress.

The lawsuits filed by blacks resulted in a quiet revolution, where black electoral gains increased considerably. For example, in the landmark case *Thornburg v. Gingles* (1985), the Supreme Court ruled that the North Carolina redistricting plan which created six new multimember voting districts made it difficult for blacks to vote for representatives of their choosing, thus violating Section 2 of the VRA. Prior to this redistricting cycle, black voters constituted a majority in only fifteen congressional districts nationwide. Following the 1990s round of redistricting, the number of majority black districts nearly doubled nationwide, up to twenty-seven.

According to figure 7.1, the overall increase in black congresspersons reached a high of 40 by 1994. At the state legislative level, the numbers prove to be even more impressive. The amended VRA resulted in the creation of 57 new state senate districts and 109 new state House districts in which there were African American majorities ("Where Minorities Are the Majority ..." 1993). The VRA not only increased the number of black elected officials at the national level, but it also aided in the increases that took place at the local and state levels. As is reflected in table 7.1, states in the South now lead the country in the number of black elected officials (US Census Bureau, 2011). Turning again to Mississippi, the barometer of racial progress, the observed increase in black politicians denotes the effectiveness of Sections 2, 4, and 5 of the VRA. For instance, in the late 1960s Mississippi had only one black state legislator, but by the early 2000s, it had more than nine hundred black elected officials. The positions of these elected officials varied with one serving in the US house, while more than forty were elected to the state legislature. Still, the majority of the elected officials held city and county positions, including positions with school boards and law enforcement. However, Mississippi wasn't the only state to see an increase in black elected officials. Both Alabama and Louisiana have more than seven hundred black elected officials in various

Figure 7.1 Black Members of the U.S.
House of Representatives
1954-2014

Source: *Fifty Years of the Voting Rights Act: The State of Race in Politics*, Joint Center for Political and Economic Studies, Washington, DC, 2015.

capacities. The fact that these states have large populations of black citizens has a huge effect on the election of these black politicians, although some of the literature points to the willingness of whites to vote for black politicians (Gillespie, 2010). While black officials have been elected in some states where blacks were not the majority, those situations are rare when observing overall black elected officials. In fact, Cannon (1999) asserts that between 1966 and 1996 fewer than 1 percent of the thousands of majority white federal districts elected black officials. This number is even smaller when you note that Ron Dellums (D-CA), one candidate, represents almost half of the elections of black representatives of that period by being elected a total of eleven times (Cannon, 1999).

However, in more recent times we have seen efforts to dismantle the VRA by attacking separate sections of this act. In a 2012 Supreme Court decision in the case of *Shelby County v. Holder* it was decided that Section 4 of this act was unconstitutional. The elimination of this act also made Section 5 defunct and unconstitutional because it violated the constitutional provision of state sovereignty. The argument was that states no longer were presenting the bad behavior that was evident when the VRA was signed into law; thus, these sections of the act were outdated and unconstitutional. With these new decisions, many worried that more problems would surface with voting laws and voting requirements which could decrease the black vote. In fact, there are numerous debates about the necessity and detriment of voter

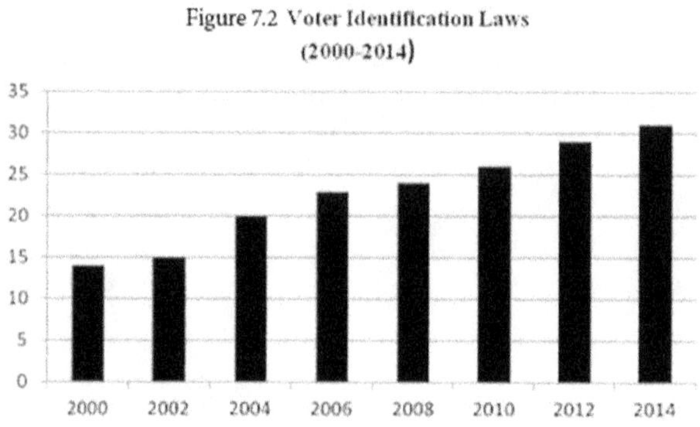

Figure 7.2 Voter Identification Laws
(2000-2014)

Source: National Conference
of State Legislatures, http://
www.ncsl.org/research/
elections-and-campaigns/
voter-id-history.aspx#Chart.

identification laws. Proponents state these laws are necessary to uphold the integrity of voting and prevent voter fraud. Opponents conclude that these types of laws only hinder a specific segment of the population, often young minority voters (Theis, 2013). While these positions do exist, we have seen an increase of voter identification laws among states with more than a 50 percent increase from 2000 until 2014 as observed in figure 7.2. Still, some states required individuals to have specific forms of identification to be allowed to vote, and if they did not have those forms of identification they would only be allowed to cast a provisional ballot, which would not be counted until identification was verified.

THE AFRICAN AMERICAN QUEST FOR ECONOMIC PARITY

The promises of the civil rights movement and subsequent legislation addressed the quest for blacks in America to achieve the "American Dream"— greater employment opportunities, improved wages, home ownership, and increased access to higher education. The strides taken by blacks as a result of the civil rights movement manifested themselves in socioeconomic gains; however, a half-century later, the goals of the movement and civil-rights legislation have not been sufficiently reached in this regard. Though the end of World War II saw the emergence of a relatively small black "middle class," the majority of blacks in the United States—especially in the South—prior to the civil rights movement still lived in or near poverty and were hampered in upwardly mobile socioeconomic opportunities.

The changes in economic status for blacks since King have been both positive and negative. On the positive end, blacks have made great strides in two areas: (1) occupations and increases in income, and (2) educational attainment. Combined, these two elements contributed greatly to the growth of the black "middle class," increase in black home ownership, and black participation in suburbanization. On the negative end, however, recent data indicates that half a century after the civil rights movement, (1) blacks maintain consistently higher unemployment rates (compared to other racial groups and the country as a whole) and rates of college completion lag considerably; (2) blacks are most likely to be affected by negative vicissitudes in the economic climate—most recently, by the burst of the housing bubble, the 2008 financial collapse, and the loss of public-sector jobs; and (3) the wealth gap for blacks has not narrowed since near the end of the civil rights movement.

THE POSITIVES: EMPLOYMENT AND SALARY/WAGES

Prior to the civil rights movement and passage of civil rights legislation, most black males in the South were employed as laborers or in agriculture, and black females, in "private service" (as domestics or nannies). Blacks who moved northward as part of the "Great Migration" were able to find jobs in manufacturing (albeit mostly in low-skilled or semiskilled positions). In 1959, the mean annual earnings for blacks were $2,848.67 for men and $1,412.16 for women, respectively (Maloney, 2014). The jobs in the North paid black workers less than their white counterparts (roughly 40 percent less), but the movement from the low-wage South represented progress for black workers. By 1969, black earnings nearly doubled, to $5,341.64 for males and $3,205.12 for females (ibid.). The antidiscrimination gains of the 1960s made it possible for blacks to expand into other industries and occupations, including those in the South. Title VII of the Civil Rights Act was particularly effective, as it "banned discrimination in hiring, firing, pay and working conditions, as well as created the Equal Opportunity Commission to investigate complains for workplace discrimination" (ibid.). As such, employment opportunities for blacks across the country expanded into white-collar, skilled blue-collar, and public-sector employment. Because migration from the South dropped considerably after 1965, blacks who remained were able to take advantage of these opportunities. Salaries for blacks continued to rise; by 2013, the median weekly earnings for blacks (full-time/salaried employees) were $606/week ($31,512/year) for woman and $664/week ($34,528/year) for men (Report 1051, 2014).

THE POSITIVES: EDUCATIONAL ATTAINMENT

The Supreme Court ruling in *Brown v. Board of Education* (1954) determined that segregation by race in public schools is unconstitutional. However, no plan to desegregate was implemented. The Court's ruling contained the provision that desegregation was to be implemented "at all deliberate speed," which meant that the courts would not establish a timetable for desegregation. Rather, the states and local government would do so at will. Of course, much of the racial animus in the South centered around black efforts to integrate local elementary/high schools and universities. This attitude was encouraged by the "Southern Manifesto"—a pledge led by Senator Strom Thurmond and signed by ninety-six US senators—to foment resistance to any attempts at federally mandated integration (Hannah-Jones, Zamora, and Thompson, 2014). Many of the sad yet iconic images of the civil rights movement include these examples of resistance—the meeting of the "Little Rock Nine" by white mobs, Ruby Bridges being escorted into elementary school by federal agents, and Governor George Wallace standing at the entrance of the University of Alabama-in defiance of federal orders to integrate these schools (ibid.). Fortunately, the civil rights movement and subsequent legislation such as the Elementary and Secondary Education Act, Higher Education Act, and judicial orders to integrate opened the doors at all-white schools of all levels to blacks. As such, black enrollment in higher education increased considerably and complemented enrollment in "historically black" colleges and universities. In 1965, the percentage of blacks enrolled in predominantly white institutions was negligible; by 1988, the numbers grew to 10.2 percent. Recent data indicates that blacks make up an estimated 14.9 percent of students in higher education. The percentage of blacks graduating with four-year degrees from undergraduate institutions has increased considerably as well, from 4 percent in 1964 (the year of the Civil Rights Act) to 10.3 percent as of 2009–2010 (US Census). Finally, the improvements in educational attainment extend to graduate school; in the 1960s, the overwhelming majority of graduate (master's) and professional degrees (PhD, ED, law, and medical) conferred on blacks were granted from historically black colleges and universities with only 3 percent of those degrees being graduate/professional degrees conferred; by 2009–2010, the percentages had reached 12.5 percent and 7.4 percent, respectively, and included degrees from predominantly white institutions (NCES, 2014).

THE NEGATIVES: UNEMPLOYMENT AND EDUCATIONAL ATTAINMENT

The movement of blacks from the South during the "Great Migration" (and through the 1960s) had the curious effect of increasing black unemployment. Though there was greater opportunity in the North and Midwest for higher wages and upward mobility, many blacks struggled to procure employment within the *de facto* segregated regions. Downturns in manufacturing were accompanied by layoffs or firings, which had a greater effect on blacks. Also, the overall decline of manufacturing across the country as the result of automation, outsourcing, and offshore relocation further increased black unemployment (and wage stagnation for those still employed). In 1972, less than a decade after the civil rights movement, black unemployment stood at approximately 10.2 percent; over the next four decades, the rate fluctuated between a "low" of approximately 9 percent to nearly 20 percent in 1980 (by comparison, white unemployment rates ranged from a "true" low of 3 percent in 2000 to nearly 8 percent in 2010) (NCES, 2014). Blacks in the inner cities have been particularly hard hit by chronic high unemployment and are in themselves a significant portion of this percentage. In addition to high unemployment rates, blacks have experienced wage stagnation and reductions in median income at disproportionate levels. Between June 2009 and June 2012, the median annual income declined across all races; the difference, however, is that black income declined 11.1 percent (to $32,498 from $36,567) compared to a 5.2 percent decline for whites.

Black unemployment rates have been exacerbated by forces which increased unemployment in all racial groups. The falling demand for unskilled labor, compiled with automation, relocation of jobs to the suburbs or offshore, and the transformation of central cities from manufacturing hubs to information processing and financial centers contributes to the increase in unemployment rates across the board (Maloney, 2014). However, blacks were particularly affected by industry relocations to the suburbs, as policies designed to protect *de facto* segregation in those areas (e.g., restrictive covenants and white backlash to black residents) made black relocation to employment sources in the suburbs impossible. Overall, one could argue that blacks have experienced a "negative effect" of the post-civil rights movement period: an increase in the jobless rate which has remained approximately 50 percent higher than that of whites. According to the Economic Policy Institute, black unemployment has averaged 15.8 percent over the past half-century, compared to 7.9 percent for whites (Pew Research, 2013). In addition, fluctuations in the unemployment rates for whites indicate that even in periods of relatively high unemployment, the rates are comparable to the *lowest* unemployment rates for blacks. Thus, black unemployment has remained high since the passage of the first civil rights legislation, with punctuations of even higher unemployment periods (ibid.). Finally, the economic recovery which began in 2009 is missing a key element present in past recovery periods: an expansion in the public sector. According to the US Department of Labor, 2009 marked the first time in forty years that the recovery was not accompanied by an expansion (of employment) in the public sector (Rice, 2012).

High school completion rate for blacks is one of the few areas where blacks are approaching parity with whites (along with voter participation and life expectancy). In 1964, approximately 27 percent of blacks (and 51 percent of whites) were high school graduates; by 2012, high school graduation rates for blacks were approximately 93 percent of whites'. While high school graduation rates for blacks are positive, college completion rates are less so. In 1964, 4 percent of blacks earned a college degree compared to 10 percent of whites; by 2012, 21 percent of blacks had earned a degree compared to 34 percent of whites, and blacks earned only 9 percent of all college degrees that year (Pew Research, 2013).

THE NEGATIVES: WEALTH GAP

Several factors influence the wealth gap between whites and blacks. Included in these are the lack of generational wealth (passed down from generation to generation), black employment in lower-wage occupations, comparatively higher levels of debt (especially for blacks residing in areas with higher costs of living), and restricted access to credit (which hampers acquisition to home mortgages). Despite the positive strides made by blacks, including the growth of the black middle class, the evidence indicates that the post-civil rights movement wealth gap between the races is nearly as wide as it has ever been. What is more, the economic downturn/stock market collapse of 2008 actually widened the gap. Between 2005 and 2009, the average black household wealth fell by more than half to $5,677 (compared to a 16 percent decline for whites, to $113,149) (Rice, 2012). According to the Pew Research Center Fact Tank, the median net worth for blacks in 2007 was approximately $19,200 (compared to $192,500 for whites), $16,600 in 2010 ($138,600 for whites), and a mere $11,000 in 2013 (compared to $141,900 for whites) (Kochar and Fry, 2014). Thus, the most recent indicators suggest that the median wealth of whites is approximately thirteen times higher than that of blacks, and is the largest gap since 1989 (when median white wealth was seventeen times that of blacks). Though most people lost some measure of wealth during the 2008 economic collapse, the amount of loss for blacks was staggering: according to the Urban Institute, whites lost a mere 1 percent of overall wealth, whereas blacks lost nearly a quarter (23 percent). Overall, the data suggests that black wealth is in a crisis and was not particularly helped by post-civil rights movement gains. For every dollar owned by blacks, whites held twenty dollars.

As previously stated, the burst of the 2006 housing bubble coupled with the 2008 stock market collapse/economic downturn had a deleterious effect on black wealth. Because most black wealth is concentrated in home owner-ship, the burst bubble and collapse were especially hurtful to blacks. Roughly 25 percent of black homeowners either lost their homes or became seriously delinquent; prior to these events, black borrowers with good credit scores were three times as likely to be steered toward subprime, predatory mortgage loans (a source of the 2008 collapse) compared to whites with similar scores (Rice, 2012).

Finally, the wealth accumulation gap between blacks and whites extends across generations. In 1983, the average family wealth for whites between the ages of thirty-two and forty was approximately $184,000 compared to $54,000 for blacks; by 2010, the gap increased to approximately $1.1 million for whites between the ages of fifty-nine and sixty-seven (the prime years for accumulating wealth), compared to $161,000 for blacks. Thus, white wealth in one's thirties is three and a half times greater than that of blacks of the same age range; by one's sixties, the gap for whites doubles to seven times the amount (The Urban Institute, 2014).

CONCLUSION

In the beginning, we raised the question as to whether black progress since the 1950s brings Dr. King's dream to fruition, or if the "dream" has been deferred. Overall, Dr. King would believe that considerable progress has been made by African Americans, particularly with regard to participation in the political process. He would point to the strong increase in African Ameri-can registration/voting percentages and the election of African American officials as proof that the VRA was a necessary tool for African American empowerment. However, though great strides have been made by African

Americans in the electoral realm, Dr. King would not assume the struggle was over and conclude that we are not in a "post-racial" society. He might point out that attacks on Sections 4 and 5 of the VRA threaten African American enfranchisement. He might also express concerns about the manipulation of district lines that have largely gerrymandered significant portions of the African American voting electorate into racially homogenous majority-minority districts. Though this was originally done under the pretense of fostering greater African American representation in Congress, redistricting has reduced the ability of African Americans to compete overall in other districts (or statewide), with a few exceptions (e.g., US representative-turned-senator Tim Scott of South Carolina).

With regard to race relations and economic equality, King would probably feel as if steps backward are being taken; the examples of racism and racial violence addressed earlier would suggest to King that the "unchecked cancer" of racism is no longer in remission. The quest for economic equality is also ongoing, as blacks continue to lag behind in income, personal wealth, and employment rates (despite educational and occupational gains) and are disproportionately affected by economic downturns.

Overall, King would acknowledge that his "dream" has been realized in part and deferred in part. The nation is, arguably, long overdue for a national forum on race relations: (1) to address the unfortunate endurance of racism (in all its forms) and racial resentment in American society; (2) to acknowledge that the positive strides made by many African Americans (including the president) may still be denigrated by whites who harbor racial resentment and choose to act on said resentment; (3) to address the socioeconomic and sociopolitical implications of white privilege (born out of a historical sense of white supremacy) and its continuing deleterious effects on African Americans; and, finally, (4) to address possible ways for people of all races to move past stereotypical notions of the "other" and attempt to understand those who differ phenotypically from themselves. All of these acts are necessary in order to reach the racial equity that King envisioned. Perhaps if this forum were to occur, positive strides could be made, realistically propelling the country a step forward towards becoming a "postracial" equal society. In the meantime, notions of racism and racial resentment that were present during King's era continue to be reminders of our nation's shameful past regarding race relations and its difficulty in achieving racial equity.

NOTES

1. Recently, changes have been made, and several of these schools now host integrated proms. Some of the first integrated proms in these states have been featured in the documentaries *Prom Night in Mississippi* (2009) and *For One Night* (2006).

2. The total population according to http://www.census.gov/population/www/documentation/twps0056/tab39.pdf was 2216912, and the black population in 1970 was 815,770.

REFERENCES

Cannon, D. 1999. *Race, Redistricting, and Representation: The Unintended Consequences of Black-Majority Districts*. Chicago: University of Chicago Press

Hannah-Jones, N., A. Zamora, and C. Thompson. 2014. "Timeline: From *Brown v. Board* to Segregation Now. Investigating America's Racial Divide." *ProPublica* (April 15). http://www.propublica.org/special/timeline-from-brown-v.-board-to-segregation-now#0.

Himelstein, J. 1983. "Rhetorical Continuities in the Politics of Race: The Closed Society Revisited." *Southern Speech Communication Journal* 48: 153–66.

Jefferson, Thomas. 2014. *Notes on the State of Virginia*. University of Virginia American Studies Program. http://xroads.virginia.edu/~hyper/JEFFERSON/ch14.html.

Kinder, D., and L. M. Sanders. 1996. *Divided by Color: Racial Politics and Democratic Ideals*. Chicago: University of Chicago Press.

Kinder, D., and D. O. Sears. 1981. "Prejudice and Politics: Symbolic Racism versus Threats to the Good Life." *Journal of Personality and Social Psychology* 40: 414–31.

King, C. S. 1984. *The Words of Martin Luther King*. New York: Newmarket.

King, M. L., Jr. 1955. "Pride versus Humility: The Parable of the Pharisee and the Publican." Sermon at Dexter Avenue Baptist Church, September 25. In *Papers* 6: 230–34. http://mlk-kpp01.stanford.edu/primarydocuments/Vo16/25Sept1955PrideVersus HumilityTheParableofthePhariseeandthePublican.pdf.

———. 1957. Address at the Prayer Pilgrimage for Freedom, Washington, DC. The King Center. http://www.thekingcenter.org/archive/document/address-mlk-washington -dc-prayer-pilgrimage-freedom#.

———. 1963a. "I Have a Dream" speech. Delivered at the March on Washington for Jobs and Freedoms.

———. 1963b. "Letter from the Birmingham Jail." Stanford University, Martin Luther King Research and Education Institute. http://mlk-kpp01.stanford.edu:5801/transcription/ document_images/undecided/630416–019.pdf.

———. 1964. *Why We Can't Wait*. New York: New American Library.

———. 1967. *A Time to Break Silence*. In *The Essential Martin Luther King, Jr.*, ed. Clayborne Carson. Boston: Beacon, 2013.

Kochar, R., and R. Fry. 2014. "Wealth Inequality has Widened along Racial, Ethnic Lines Since End of Great Recession." Pew Research Center Fact Tank. http://www.pewresearch .org/fact-tank/2014/12/12/racial-wealth-gaps-great-recession/. Accessed December 19.

Lamis, A. P., et al. (1990). *The Two Party South*. Oxford University Press.

Leigh, W. A., and D. Huff. 2007. "African Americans and Homeownership: Separate and Unequal, 1940 to 2006." Joint Center for Political and Economic Studies. http://www.northstarnews.com/userimages/references/African%20Americans%20and%20Home%20ownership.Brief_Joint%20Center%20for%20Political%20Studies.pdf.

Maloney, T. N. 2014. "African Americans in the Twentieth Century." Economic History Association. *http://eh.net/encyclopedia/african-americans-in-the-twentieth-century/*. Accessed December 20.

Milbank, D. 2008. "In Fla., Palin Goes for the Rough Stuff as Audience Boos Obama." *The Washington Post* October 6. http://voices.washingtonpost.com/44/2008/10/in-fla-palin -goes-for-the-roug.html.

Mitchell, G. 2008. "Racial Incidents and Threats against Obama Soar: Here Is a Chronicle." *The Huffington Post,* November 15. http://www.huffingtonpost.com/greg-mitchell/racial -incidents-and-thre_b_144061.html.

Motes, B. "Arizona's Immigration Law Is Racist (We Can Only Hope)." 2010. *The Huffington Post* (April 24). http://www.huffingtonpost.com/bart-motes/arizonas-immigration -law_b_550763.html.

National Center for Education Statistics (NCES). 2014. "Fast Facts; Degrees Conferred by Sex and Race." http://nces.ed.gov/fastfacts/display.asp?id=72. Accessed December 19.

NBCNEWS.com. 2009. "Pool Denies Turning Away Minority Kids." *NBC News.* July 10. http://www.nbcnews.com/id/31833602/#.UqOEp7-TN1M.

Pew Research Social and Demographic Trends. 2013. "King's Dream Remains an Elusive Goal; Many Americans See Racial Disparities." August 22. http://www.epi.org/publication/ african-americans-50-years-high-unemployment/.

Report 1051. 2014. Highlights of Women's Earnings in 2013: Median Usual Weekly Earnings of Women and Men Who Are Full-Time Wage and Salary Workers, by Race and Hispanic or Latino Ethnicity, 2013 Annual Averages. http://www.bls.gov/opub/reports/cps/highlights -of-womens-earnings-in-2013.pdf.

Rice, D. T. 2012. "30 Years of US Black Middle Class Economic Gains Have Been Wiped Out." *Chicago Tribune* (October 7). http://www.businessinsider.com/us-black-middle -class-is-suffering-2012-10

Schuman, H., C. Steeh, L. Bobo, and M. Krysan.1997. *Racial Attitudes in America: Trends and Interpretations.* Revised. Cambridge, MA: Harvard University Press.

Sears, D. O. 1988. "Symbolic Racism." In *Eliminating Racism: Profiles in Controversy,* ed. P. A. Katz and D. A. Taylor, 53–84. New York: Plenum.

Sears, D. O., C. P. Hensler, and L. K. Speer. 1979. "Whites' Opposition to 'Busing': Self-Interest or Symbolic Politics?" *The American Political Science Review,* 369–84.

Sears, D. O., and D. R. Kinder. 1971. "Racial Tensions and Voting in Los Angeles." In *Los Angeles: Viability and Prospects for Metropolitan Leadership,* ed. W. Z. Hirsch. New York: Praeger.

Stein, S. 2010. "Tea Party Protests: 'Ni**er, Fa**ot' Shouted at Members of Congress." *The Huffington Post.* May 20. http://www.huffingtonpost.com/2010/03/20/tea-party-protests -nier-f_n_507116.html.

Teo, D. 2008. "McCain-Palin and the Lucifer Effect: The Dangerous, Violent Rhetoric against Barack Obama." October 24. http://www.huffingtonpost.com/dawn-teo/mccain-palin-and-the-luci_b_136572.html.

———. 2009. "'Kill Obama' Painted on Phoenix-Area Campaign Signs." *The Huffington Post*. October 8http://www.huffingtonpost.com/dawn-teo/kill-obama-painted-on-pho_b_314751.html.

Theis, E. 2013. "Study Finds Voter ID Laws Hurt Young Minorities." *Politico* March 12. http://www.politico.com/story/2013/03/study-finds-voter-id-laws-hurt-young-minorities-88773.html.

Thompson, K. 2009. "Harvard Professor Arrested at Home." *The Washington Post*. July 21. http://articles.washingtonpost.com/2009-07-21/news/36874403_1_police-officer-front-door-african-american-lives (accessed December 2, 2011).

The Urban Institute. 2014. The Racial Wealth Gap Is Three Times Greater Than the Racial Income Gap: Ratios for Average Family Wealth and Income, 1983–2010. http://www.urban.org/changing-wealth-americans/lost-generations-interactive-race.cfm. Accessed December 21.

US Census. 2014. 1947, 1952 to 2008 Current Population Survey. http://www.census.gov/population/socdemo/education/tabA-2.pdf. Accessed December 20.

"What Obama's Election Really Means to Black America." 2008. *Time* magazine, November 6. http://content.time.com/time/nation/article/0,8599,1857222-2,00.html.

KING THE SELLOUT, OR SELLIN' OUT KING?

Hip Hop's Martin Luther King Jr.

James L. Taylor

The last conversation that Martin Luther King had before the bullet shattered his jaw concerned the performance of black music. "Sing it pretty," were his final words.
—JAMES L. TAYLOR

ON SELLING OUT IN AFRICAN AMERICAN POLITICAL THOUGHT

Differentiation in socioeconomic class, region, religiosity, levels of education, complexion, marriage preference, partisanship, racial attitudes, sexuality and gender, and political ideology readily sets "true believers" off against the duplicitous among African Americans in particular ways. The precariousness of African American life, in a society dominated economically, politically, penally, militarily, and totally by American whites and institutions, makes the issue of in-group disloyalty or "selling out" an enduring one. In the US Constitution, treasonous Americans are subject to punishments ranging from impeachment in high office, to imprisonment, fines, and the death penalty.

It is something of a perennial folk tradition among African Americans since at least the nineteenth century. Across ideologies, rivals have designated almost every prominent African American leader a traitorous "sellout" or "Uncle Tom." For Patrick Johnson, the practice of authenticating can be found in "the discourse of 'house niggers' vs. 'field niggers'" (Johnson, 2003, p. 4). Also during the earlier periods, many anonymous, ordinary individuals aided in the capture of fugitive slaves; in surveillance, in the suppression of slave uprisings, and in counterintelligence for the state in the later periods.[1] Yet these epithets are especially a birthright of black leadership in the United States, and according to Richard Keiser, "messianic leaders play a huge role in denying legitimacy to other leaders by condemning them as Uncle Toms"

(1997, p. 20). Dr. King, however, was understood to be both, respectively by his supporters and critics. Randall Kennedy insists that black leaders and organizations—including Martin Delany, Frederick Douglass, Booker T. Washington, W. E. B. Du Bois, Marcus Garvey, Elijah Muhammad, Martin Luther King Jr., Malcolm X, the NAACP, and modern black Republicans and conservatives—have been assigned the white badge of racial treason (Kennedy, 2008). The emergent black feminist and womanist projects of the late 1960s and after were charged with race betrayal by some men and women activists in black power; some even made the charge that they were one of many COINTELPRO schemes.[2] For Wilson J. Moses in *Black Messiahs* and *Uncle Toms,* Uncle Tom was not quite an "Uncle Tom," and definitely no sell-out (1993, pp. 55–56).[3] With some irony, given Garveyism's nod to Christian messianic racial destiny tropes, Garveyites would excoriate Uncle Tom and largely strip him of his loyalties and substitute them with unfettered perfidy and religious weakness. Understanding of both Uncle Tom and King is distorted; the former by Garveyites, and the latter by his contemporaries. The Nation of Islam's many critiques of black churchmen, pastors, and Christian otherworldliness, built on earlier critiques made by Booker T. Washington and Garveyites. Uncle Tom, like Stowe's book, garnered renewed importance during the civil rights movement; no single individual would be as widely associated with the caricature by critics as Martin Luther King Jr.

"April 4th 1968" is a striking visual created by an antiviolence graphic designer in support of the widespread reaction to the 2012 slaying of Florida teen Trayvon Benjamin Martin.[4] The illustration transposes the image of King into a "hoodie" sweatshirt to lend his antiviolence legacy to the cause of Trayvon Martin's supporters. King visually "became" Trayvon Martin, joining him in the hood precisely five decades after his famous "March on Washington" speech. Invoking King, and not, say, Malcolm X, is a reprieve from King's marginalization in the last two decades of hip hop's emergent influence in African American life, culture, and intellectual discourse.[5] With "the hyperpoliticization of rap music in the late 1980s," S. Craig Watkins noted how a "particular moment in the fusion of black nationalism and black popular culture was facilitated by important social, economic, and technological shifts that enabled black youth to assert their vision on black nationalism in imaginative ways" (Watkins,1998, p. 190). Hip hop's "golden age" (late 1980s-1993) in the East Coast has had a particular relationship to the legacy and social justice commitments of King and the larger movement. Hip hop's black community empowerment foundations asserted black consciousness ideological thinking in hip hop, but King was separated from it and put in abeyance. However, Martin Luther King was not totally ignored and unheralded in hip hop circles in the few decades after his death.[6] Young people did not so much isolate King, personally; after all, he (along with Ronald Reagan) was made an overarching point of black American life in the late twentieth century. Reiland Rabaka suggested, "[G]eneration after generation of African Americans have, whether consciously or unconsciously, followed in the footsteps of the New Negroes, who in forming their movement understood themselves to be breaking with the 'Old Negro' and/or blackface minstrel archetype" (2011, p. 61) (e.g., King). "Black conscious" hip hop, whether that of the Zulu Nation, Public Enemy, X-Clan, Boogie Down Productions, or early NWA, weighed and put King in abeyance, because it primarily understood him in *conventional* terms. According the late historian Vincent Harding, King told an SCLC meeting in 1965, "[S]omething is wrong with the economic system of our nation.... Something is wrong with capitalism." As a solution, he added that "maybe America must move toward a democratic socialism." King insisted to a select group of SCLC ministers, "*[W]e are not interested in being integrated in this value structure ... [A] radical redistribution of power must take place*" (Harding, 2008, p. xi). David Levering Lewis included Ralph Bunche, Adam Clayton Powell, Martin and Coretta King, A. Phillip Randolph, Louis Armstrong, and other leaders in the delegation to Accra, to celebrate Ghana's independence at the invitation of President Kwame Nkrumah (Lewis, 1970). King's visit to Africa before many of his radical contemporaries—including Malcolm X, Eldridge Cleaver, and Stokely Carmichael—was a signal experience in shaping his post-Montgomery leadership campaign in the United States. He was regarded as the most dangerous person in the United States by federal authorities by 1967, the SCLC organization was identified as a "*hate-type organization*" (along with SNCC, CORE, and the Nation of Islam), and he was the sole person named in the FBI's COINTELPRO directives to prevent the "rise of a black nationalist messiah," who was *not* an avowed black nationalist or Pan-Africanist such as Elijah Muhammad, Malcolm X, or Stokely Carmichael. Of them, Hoover noted, "King could be a very real contender for this position should he abandon his supposed 'obedience' to 'white, liberal doctrines' (nonviolence)." The Martin Luther King Jr. of Montgomery in 1955–1956, the March on Washington in 1963, Selma in 1965, Chicago in 1966, and Vietnam in 1967 is as intensely different as, say, the Sugar Hill Gang's jovial "Rapper's Delight," Kurtis Blow's "These Are the Breaks," Grandmaster Flash and the Furious Five's "The Message," or "White Lines," and the urban "gangsta rap" tracks and Thug Life nadir. Still, hip hop's Martin Luther King

Jr. is at times as statically rendered as in the conventional wisdom on him. This stale, deradicalization of Dr. King, in part, prompted Michael Eric Dyson to insist on a moratorium from "I Have a Dream," repetition (Dyson, 2000, p. 14). Indeed J. Edgar Hoover's COINTELPRO on King was prompted by the March on Washington's catapulting the minister to the fore of the still burgeoning movement; its aim, to "take him off his pedestal" (McKnight, 1998, p. 2).

HIP HOP IN INTELLECTUAL DISCOURSE

Princeton University professor Imani Perry suggested that "hip hop constantly references previous black music forms. This stands as testimony to the yearning for grounding in the post-civil rights era, to the nostalgia for the music of youth, but also to the definitive blackness of parents or grandparents generation." In the leading and popular thought that asserts hip hop to the center of contemporary academic discourses, the civil rights and black power movements and leadership are often put in service to hip hop, thus leading Perry to question, "[W]hy does the hip hop audience believe that it is ok to embrace the past, to converse with it, without adhering to its *ideological divides or rules?*" (Perry, 2004, p. 57). This points to an intergenerational tension in which the earlier stages have a utility that enables hip hop to borrow and sample without being obligated to community or accountable to it. Throughout this chapter, I argue, to the contrary, that the "ideological divides and rules" were indeed adhered to, at least with regard to Malcolm X and Martin Luther King Jr., and interpreted and recruited them to its purposes. Errol Henderson insisted that it was the "sampling aspect of hip hop" that facilitated "crossgenerational cultural trans-missions" among "the relatively apolitical generation of the 1970s and 1980s with a staunch Black nationalist African subculture of the 1960s" (1996, pp. 311–12). If sampling places hip hop in conversation with the past, so has "dissing." Like any first-rate rap icon, Martin Luther King Jr. and the broad civil rights movement have been subjected to well-known street poses of disrespecting (dissin') and challenging (battling) from upstarts, whether in lyrics or film or among the self-recognized "hip hop intelligentsia" seeking to make their mark. Imani Perry suggested likewise that *dis-* functions as a negative prefix (e.g., disrespect, dismiss, etc.), [and] gathered its meaning in the social context of inter-personal rejection, or what another generation might have referred to as "putting someone down" not in the white American dialect sense of insulting, but in the black American sense of *getting rid of someone as though setting someone on a table and walking away* (2004, p. 26). King was thus "dissed" ideologically in emergent "message" or "conscious" rap from the late 1980s through the 1990s.

Prior to Dyson's work, hip hop's King was largely status quo and without the benefit of emergent research and interpretive scholarship on King as a leader and thinker, or the broader movement. Primary source research and analysis today place King variously in quasi-black nationalist and social democrat radical traditions (Singh, 2004). But this "inconvenient" King was not—and is still not—widely available in popular portrayals as hip hop emerged over thirty years ago; it was in 1981 that some of King's SCLC papers were made available to scholars and researchers, revealing a "deep political radicalism" in King. King is uncritically cast as an essential moralist with accommodationist political inclinations suited to the needs and accouterments of bourgeois respectability and old guard white liberalism. Despite the emergent literature highlighting King's ever-deepening militancy and anti-capitalist commitments, hip hop has primarily settled on the King of August 28, 1963.

Some of this scholarship has so convincingly recast the conventional details and interpretations of many phases of the civil rights movement and its leadership that they warrant a broader reading. Investigating routine rapes of African American women in Alabama, for instance, was the motivation for Rosa Parks' militancy (and that of many other men and women) in the middle 1940s, as urgently, if not more so than dismantling Jim Crow codes. While King was yet a high school student in Atlanta, Rosa Parks kept faith with her *Garveyite* grandfather's militancy and activism, who, himself, helped raise funds and organize a defense for Alabama's Scottsboro Boys in the 1930s. To that end, "an analysis of sex and sexualized violence in well-known civil rights narratives changes the historical markers and meanings of the movement" (McGuire, 2010, p. xxii).[7] Perhaps knowledge of this "recovered" Rosa Parks, as consciously militant, Garveyite (or Garveyite-socialized), anti-rape crusader, would require a reframing of Parks in hip hop narratives, such as Ice Cube's *Barbershop* franchise, which, typically, projects Rosa Parks' militancy conventionally as a "sweet and reticent old woman, whose tired feet caused her to defy Jim Crow on Montgomery's city buses."

As hip hop's Rosa Parks is conventional, its Martin Luther King Jr. is a straight-laced moderate whose integrationist ideology appeased white anxiety in ways that Malcolm X and black power activists refused. Hip hop has not challenged the conventional interpretation of Dr. King as it did that of Malcolm X (rejecting, for example, the charges that he was "black supremacist" and anti-Semitic, to the point that they hardly stick in the mainstream of thought today); it largely accepted it and minimized King's harsh late social criticisms in the articulation of black conscious rap nationalism. The more subversive King in late criticisms in his final book, *Where Do We Go from Here: Chaos or Community?* (1968), took on precisely the major issues confronting the next two generations of black people in the United States and would be taken up by students of urban politics and sociology (Wilson, 1978). In 1967, King left the United States, and like in 1958 (Ghana), he chose a majority black country, Jamaica, in which to write his last book. Despite King's unprecedented direct action; staring down law enforcement, "White Citizens Council" and KKK members, FBI harassments, bombings and threats of bombings, looming assassins, a stabbing in Harlem, and moving into Chicago slum housing where he met with street gangs, are often minimized. It was not commonly known in the 1980s and 1990s that "by the end of his life, King viewed the idea of obtaining civil rights, for black individuals as an inadequate framework for combating the economic consequences and cultural legacies of white supremacy," (Singh, 2004, p. 3), on the US black population, specifically as a group.

The notion that King was a sellout was long promoted by contemporaries like Malcolm X and other Harlemite nationalists, for the young black power and black arts critics. In the words of Stokely Carmichael, "I respected Dr. King a great deal because he had found a tactic that put thousands of people in motion to confront racism . . . To be sure, the 125th Street nationalists did not support Dr. King. They attacked nonviolence, mocked his talk of redemptive suffering, and questioned the feasibility and desirability of 'integration' as a goal" (Carmichael and Thelwell, 2005). Subsequently, this shaped the early thinking of "rap nationalists" like Chuck D and Hank Shocklee of Public Enemy on Long Island, New York. Perkins noted that "the *early* trends in hip hop set the tone for the blossoming of rap during the Reagan years . . . the growing domination of the hip hop attitude, style, and music on youth culture; and, perhaps most important, its lurch into the crossover market made hip hop the defining expression of the eighties generation" (Perkins, 1996, p. 13). They, like many "first-generation" black college students in the 1980s and 1990s, experienced political socialization by academic black power—in the contested "Afrocentrism" movement. It was not significant to the nationalist intellectuals, rappers, and activists that King did not advocate (or have any formal) white membership in his SCLC organization or the dissolution of all-black organizations (he belonged to Morehouse College, Alpha Phi Alpha

Fraternity, Inc., and a majority black church), and called late for "temporary segregation," as a precondition to the Beloved Community religious social ideal.

For Dyson, liberal and conservative white establishment agendas have made King prisoner to his "Dream" speech. In a quest to find common ground between the legacy of King and hip hop, Dyson, unfortunately, did not address hip hop's role *among* the various criticisms he launched for those who "trampled," "distorted," "seized," and misappropriated his legacy and thought (Dyson, 2000, p. 14). Gary Peller suggested that "King has become more of an 'integrationist' in death, however, than in life" and that King and the civil rights movement were "domesticated" to fit within the reformist scripts of individualism, universalism, and civic equality, which necessarily downplayed the Americo-Eurocentric prerogatives of liberal integrationism (Peller, 2012, p. 43). In addressing these "civil rights myths," Nikhil Singh agreed that,

> today, no figure more fully embodies the notion that racial equal-
> ity is a U.S. national imperative than Martin Luther King, Jr. King's
> most cited rhetoric tied the fortunes of blacks to the status of the
> US nation-state and to its dominant and defining systems of belief:
> Christianity, liberal-individualism, and democratic-capitalism. . . .
> [Y]et this is also the King who has become part of a mythic national-
> ist discourse that claims his antiracist imperatives as its own. (Singh,
> 2004, p. 3)

Leading students of hip hop Mark Anthony Neal (2002, pp. 102-103) and Bakari Kitwana (2002, pp. 36-37) insist the US educational system has a vested interest in general "miseducation" concerning the radical implica- tions of King's broad social justice commitments and reduced them to a five-decades-old six-minute speech that offered no pathways out of the *nightmare* that would follow the movement for desegregation. Kitwana insists that hip hop has nevertheless provided young whites a voyer's view into the black predicament and King's signal role in challenging it. Estab- lishment liberals, race conservatives, and black power militants formed a collaborative in passing to posterity a caricature of King that is procapitalist, assimilationist, socially conservative, and more about sermonizing than organizing people for movement and social change. Young Turk intellec- tuals, street gang leaders, and ideological rivals felt they had better ideas, suited to their own circumstances. King's relationship to hip hop reflects a curious amalgam of recognition and renunciation. Some segments of the hip hop intelligentsia stridently rejected, ironically, the civil rights agenda (of integration) because hip hop has *succeeded* in garnering pop culture crossover appeal across US and international populations.[8] While a young person, still younger activists in SNCC, during the Greensboro, North Carolina, sit-ins, in the Lowndes County Freedom Organization in Alabama, and with "black power" did in relation to King's tactics and ideas, and as generational cohorts do, reject or revise inherited ideas and seek to carve their own niches, speak to their times, and engage their particular social, political and economic circumstances.

Hip hop intellectual discourse is increasingly the signal, post-black power intellectual development in African American life, thought, and culture.[9] Its influence in scholarship is increasingly international and "translocal," simultaneously (Morgan and Bennett, 2011). As a critical frame of "the Black predicament" (Jones, 2014), it has gained as wide recognition as Kimberle Crenshaw's critical "intersectionality" thesis or Paul Gilroy's "Black Atlantic" diaspora thesis. At its best, hip hop intellectual discourse has generated entirely new lines of inquiry, critical study, and discourse across several fields in arts, cultural studies, humanities, and social sciences.[10] Empirically grounded behavioralist research continues to emerge as hip hop studies receives wider recognition in journals, monographs, and books.[11] Where some students celebrate hip hop's break from civil rights claims, moralism, and leadership traditions, other interpretations suggest a set of complex intersections (Rabaka, 2011, p. xii). The intellectual sector of hip hop is, at points, more fiercely intense in those critiques of the previous generations than rap lyricists have been in lyrical jibes and criticisms. Todd Boyd's spirited, and at times gauche, rendering in *The New H.N.I.C.* (2003) epitomizes a triumphalist tendency in hip hop theorizing, particularly in its relationship to the civil rights movement. Subtitled *The Death of Civil Rights and the Reign of Hip Hop*, the book notes that "one of the biggest problems now facing the Black community is the divide between this civil rights generation and the hip hop generation. . . . *Hip hop has rejected and now replaced the pious, sanctimonious nature of civil rights as the defining moment of Blackness*" (2003, pp. xx-xxi). Boyd was onto something vital in acknowledging the religious dimension of hip hop's rejection of the civil rights movement. Hip hop's rejection seems less a dismissal of King and the movement than a passing on of its moralist political religion and its Christian integrationist foundation, which waned even *before* King's death in 1968. For many, hip hop has become the secular religion of black young people and many others in the twenty-firstcentury.[12] The full embrace of Malcolm X, who was likewise of King's generation (Malcolm was approximately four years older than King) and fanatically puritanical, points to a general confusion about hip hop's social justice genealogy and the particularity of its social aims and criticisms.

Boyd's work also acts creatively with being itself a hip hop performance in its wit and prose even as it elucidates hip hop's arrival as social and political discourse. This is evident in an identification "with hip hop," in his criticism of "these middle-class niggas who have become the gatekeepers of Black life," who fail to understand how "that civil rights sh[*]t is heavy and it in no way will work in today's society . . . [T]hat day is long gone" (2003, p. xix). Like many "O.G." hip hop generationers, Boyd identified the emergence of hip hop as having "more direct influence on my life than Martin Luther King Jr. did. His image and legacy were passed down to me by someone else, someone of another generation" (2003, p. xx). Recognizing its achievements as tantamount to a black analogue to Tom Brokaw's "Greatest Generation" thesis, Boyd nevertheless declared a break from it. Most bluntly, he wrote, "[T]he lawsuit filed by Rosa Parks and her attorneys is a gesture of unsurpassed arrogance and condescension. It is representative of the contempt that many older Black people feel toward their youthful descendants. In return, the hip hop generation says a collective 'f[*]ck you.' Asserting its independence and freedom of self-determination" (2003, p. 11). All of this is stunning, given the centrality of Boyd's own Detroit home as a contiguous site for black music production (interestingly, not hip hop, apart from Eminem),[13] political insurgency, ideological contestations, and leadership recruitment from Rosa Parks(who moved to Detroit one year after the Montgomery bus boycott) to Elijah Muhammad, C.L. and Aretha Franklin, Malcolm X, James and Grace Lee Boggs, Viola Gregg Liuzzo, Albert Cleage, Coleman Young, and many less prominent men and women (Shaw, 2009). According to the IWW, the "race and class struggles in the U.S.A. were concretely expressed at their highest levels in Detroit during the turbulent 1960s when Black nationalism was strong and the New Left was growing. The political confluence of these two movements produced the Dodge Revolutionary Union Movement (DRUM), which represented one of the most radical tendencies in America during that era."[14] It was also the site of two massive insurgency events (1943 and 1967) of the June 1963 "Walk to Freedom" where King tested his "I Have a Dream" theme following a march of more than 125,000 people, and of course Berry Gordy's Motown Records. Black power militancy played out in the city's neighborhoods and auto plants, and it produced the International League of Revolutionary Black Workers. And it was in Detroit where the Nation of Islam's first temple was established and where Malcolm X delivered the "Message to the Grassroots" in November 1963.

Bakari Kitwana concurred in principle that the socialization of 1980s and 1990s black youth in the United States, in general, has assembled a coherent national culture that is, at critical points, in conflict with the social, political, moral, and identity concerns of the civil rights and black power generations. He saw a "steadily intensifying war going on inside Black America itself. The divide between the hip hop generation and that of our parents (the civil rights/Black Power generation)" is the main obstacle to mobilizing for "workable solutions" to the ongoing social and cultural crisis that organizes hip hop's main themes (2002, p. 22). Nevertheless, this critique is not in conflict with the tenets of group solidarity, even as it distinguishes its own mission apart from previous generations. Kitwana noted, for instance,

> The core set of values shared by a large segment of the hip-hop generation—Black America's generation X—stands in contrast to our parents' worldview. For the most part, we have turned to ourselves, our peers, global images and products, and new realities we face for guidance. . . . Black pride is still an important part of this generation's identity. In fact, the hip-hop generation has embraced the idea of Blackness in ways that parallel the Black consciousness raising of the late 1960s and early 1970s. The popularization of the Afrocentric movement from the late 1980s through the 1990s, pro-Black lyrics on the contemporary rap scene, as well as traditional hairstyles (dreadlocks and braids, for example) adopted by many hip–hop generationers all speak to this. (2002, pp. 7–8)

Still emergent at the time, hip hop was an extension of contemporary African American culture, politics, and ideology, and it has not sufficiently demonstrated its autonomy from the modern black freedom struggle in general for Reiland Rabaka, who asserted that "when hip hop culture is connected to, and compared and contrasted with previous African American cultural aesthetic traditions and sociopolitical traditions and movements—rap music and hip hop culture are . . . nothing more than the ongoing evolution of black music and black popular culture" (2011, p. xii). The demand for independence is nevertheless anticipated. Mark Anthony Neal included himself as part of an informal Crusian group of "hip hop intelligentsia," which promoted a "post-soul aesthetic" and "ultimately render[ed] many 'traditional' tropes of blackness dated and even meaningless . . . [S]uch traditions are not just called into question but obliterated" (Neal, 2002, p. 3). In *Soul Babies* Neal summarily insisted,

> Our history—the history of the modern civil rights movement and its brash and angry offspring, the Black Power and feminist movements—was shared with us via its dominant icons. . . . Yet we [Soul Babies] remained uniquely poised—the first post-civil rights, post-nationalist, post-Black Power, post-Gary, Indiana, postintegration. . . . post soul generation—to interpret the political and cultural terrain of our own conflicted moment.(2002, pp. 100–103)

Labeling the hip-hop generation intellectual sector the "children of Cruse," Neal maintained, "[W]hat I am suggesting is that the generation(s) of black youth born after the early successes of the traditional civil rights movement *are in fact divorced from the nostalgia associated with those successes and thus positioned to critically engage the movement's legacy* from a state of objectivity that the traditional civil rights leadership is both unwilling and incapable of doing" (2002, p. 103) (emphasis added). This, without explanation, represents a clear shift on King and the movement in the few years following Neal's earlier book, *What the Music Said* (1999). That work was presented by Neal as a corrective, precisely "to counter assertions by the 'hip hop' generation that hip-hop was the first form of black music to 'speak truth to power' or in the language of contemporary black youth, the first form of black music to 'keep it real'" (1999, p. xi). King's impact is admiringly recognized where Neal notes how the slain leader previously,

> began to synthesize the most progressive elements of black radical thought with the prophetic and philosophical vision of the African American church. . . . The mass mediation of King's message, particularly given the increased influence of black nationalist thought, allowed him to reach a broader community of African American and progressive whites.[15]

Although hip hop emerged after the second major "civil rights cycle" (1954–1968), Cruse does not appear to have conceded, at any point for the decades that he observed it until his 2005 death, that it constituted a third civil rights cycle. In the aftermath of the 1960s cycle, Cruse imagined a black leadership that developed organizational and group solidarity mechanisms that were suited to the multiracial and multicultural American plurality milieu.

Cruse's observations concerning what might be considered specifically as the post-King phase of black politics were prescient. Confronted with the blunt reality of "more blacks being better off economically, and more blacks worse off, than their predecessors had been from 1900 to 1960," the 1980s opened with the law-and-order racial politics of Ronald Reagan. Neal noted, "[I]t is of course largely the policies of the Reagan Right, particularly as its eroding of civil rights era legislation aimed at addressing historic inequities experienced by blacks that helped further instigate the advent of hip hop music and culture as hip hop became the most visible site of an oppositional urban youth culture" (Neal, 2002, 103). Hip hop's original constituent group of younger urban blacks felt increasingly that King's political philosophy and moralist religious worldview were poorly suited for the conditions which Professor Marable highlighted as the contextual differences facing the "We Shall Overcome," and "Hip-Hop" generations"(Marable, 1995, pp. 204, 207).

These salient political socialization developments shaped their attitudes toward the antecedent struggle and generations. Civil rights leadership and politics, however, dominated most of the post-civil rights era, which might account for some of the acrimony from hip hop and its constant declarations of independence. A decade prior to the 2013 #BlackLivesMatter insurgency among young people in cities across the United States and abroad,[16] Kitwana admitted that "it is true that compared to our parents[sic] generation, we lack a sustained political movement (our activism, in fact, seems watered down by comparison). This may also explain why activism is less attractive to many of us" (2002, p. 153). Hip hop's specific critiques against the social, economic, and political system and its embrace of unfettered materialism (even if accompanied by militant pretense and prurient signifying language, style, film, dance, and antisocial attitudes) have not yet had the kind of systems-changing and challenging impact of some earlier generations of black people that preceded it. Hip hop is certainly implicated in the #BlackLivesMatter development of 2013, but its relationship is unclear. Still, Steinmetz and Henderson's (2012) content analysis of the lyrical themes of two hundred hip hop songs produced between 2000 and 2010 found consistent mention respectively of law enforcement and abusive policing, corrections, and courts. Michelle Alexander made the important point that mass incarceration and racial disparity, in every aspect of US law, received less urgency from civil rights organizations and black elected officials than preserving civil rights gains such as affirmative action or voting rights. Despite this policy blindspot among the black leadership establishment (and hip hop's keen attention to it), and the opening it provided, Lester Spence noted that "as political critiques against the growing role police play in the expansion of the American prison industrial complex. . . . black citizens in cities across the country rail as much against police brutality as they do black-on-black crime, [yet] there is no significant anti-police brutality movement led by prominent rap MCs" (Spence, 2011, p. 2). And this pattern is at the heart of Henderson's insistence that hip hop often "promoted a 'myth of action,' whereby political responsibility, knowledge, and activity [were] garnered by proclamation and not by demonstration" (Henderson, 1996, p. 323). A 1994 *Source* magazine editorial argued, for instance, that

> those of us who love this [gangsta] music are not only facing attacks from conservatives and white liberals, but also from a healthy chunk of *the generation of African Americans who marched with Dr. Martin Luther King.* . . . The saddest thing is that these attacks on rap have helped to set the stage for perhaps the most oppressive and wrong-headed crime legislation ever. "Three strikes out/" Mandatory sentences? More cops? More prisons? . . . Hardly a peep from [them]. (Quinn, 2004, p. 66)

Yet Todd Boyd conceded that,

> as the political edge of rap was taking hold in the popular imagination, opening up discussions surrounding a resurgent Black nationalism and ideas of Afrocentricity, gangsta rap was emerging as a defiant form which not only would threaten those on the outside, here represented by the overzealous FBI, but eventually would become *the antitheses of any sustained political discourse* in popular culture. In this sense, gangsta rap is, in many ways, about the *death of political discourse* in African American popular culture. (Boyd, 1997, p. 74)

According to Ronald B. Neal, King also stood as a major obstacle to hip hop's political discourse aspirations in the post-civil rights period. And it may be that hip hop has returned the favor participating inadvertently in what might be reasonably stated as an anti–civil rights agenda and weakening of the citizenship-rights claims of the movement establishment. Neal similarly insisted that King represents a historical pattern of black leadership that privileged "messianic idealism" over other possible modalities. It is fatally masculinist, since as a "messianic masculinism," it demobilizes democratic alternatives in black leadership styles, ideologies, and representation. With King at its center, this pattern has often combined "messianism, Christology, and masculinity [that] point to redemptive action in the world" (2013, p. 53). If King's death opened a space which black power sought to fill, it also "set a benchmark for masculinity in black America. It raised the stakes for what it means to be a black man in the United States. Overall, it created an impossible standard by which all black men are judged," (2013, p. 53). Neal offered an argument suggesting King remained a specter over hip hop, as he was first over the young of black power. He continued,

> [A]s a male centered cultural phenomenon with roots in the black underclass, hip hop has come to mirror and personify the trials, tribulations, and aspirations of young black men in the United States. These young men have been subject to intense demonization due to the distance between the messianic masculinity exemplified in Martin Luther King, Jr. and their lived experiences which defy this norm. (2013, p. 56)

Neal, pointing to Dyson's attempt to link King with hip hop, suggested that "although young black men have been pathologized and demonized by the messianic ideal and its norm for manhood, many young black men have been reluctant to surrender to its normative status, offsetting its stigmatizing effects."[17] It is unclear whether messianic masculinism has become a casualty of King's venerated status or just the opposite, King, a casualty of the rejection of the messianic masculine ideal as a leadership style that predated his public ministry.

Except, perhaps, for its deep obsession with being an articulable and independent generation, representative hip hop intellectual thought hasn't articulated a full-fledged theoretical synthesis of African American thought and ideology. Lester Spence rightly noted, "For scholars focused on the circulation of rap and hip-hop politics, *what looms large are comparisons with the civil rights movement* and discussions about its place in the public sphere (and within the black counter-public specifically)" (Spence, 2011, p. 7). Todd Boyd usefully advanced a reading of hip hop as a new black cultural ideology *in its hybridity*; it remains nevertheless one part black nationalist, one part integrationist, and infused with diasporic transnationality. Richard Iton insisted that "operating in deterritorialized arenas—for example, radio, television, and the internet—that confound the older understanding of the distinction between integrated and segregated spaces, artists in the post-civil rights era have been major contributors to the recalibration of the black discursive agenda" (Iton 2008, p. 22). Hip hop's early nationalist and late as-similationist trends are two interacting genealogical parts of a *black political tradition*.[18] As much as Harold Cruse thought 1980 closed the chapter on the "integrationist"-versus-"nationalist" traditions frame of the nineteenth and twentieth centuries, he later conceded that the black political and ideological traditions "still cast shadows over the black 1980s," simultaneous with emergent hip hop (Cruse, 1987, p. 387). If hip hop's origins are interlinked between its "black consciousness" turn in the late 1980s and 1990s and its current multicultural "cosmopolitan" stage, with its ideological "hybridity," it begs the question whether hip hop has fully escaped or transcended the fundamental question that previous generations sought to resolve: How does the black group in the United States mine the terrain ruled by the dominant white political, economic, law, and social order and maintain a semblance of cultural integrity and identity.

HEARD IT ALL BEFORE: KING AND BLACK POWER (DIS)CONTINUITY

In *Cycles of American History*, Arthur Schlesinger Jr. proffered how "generational experience" produces "generational cycles" that last roughly thirty years. For him, "each generation spends its first fifteen years after coming of political age in challenging the generation already entrenched in power. Then the new generation comes to power itself for another fifteen years, after which its policies pall and the generation coming up behind claims the succession." In this light, an appropriate generational cycle challenge would necessarily take up black power, critically, and the black arts movement substantially in some tandem *with* criticisms of civil rights. Thus hip hop's focus on the civil rights movement was somewhat misplaced as a succession movement in black politics and culture, unless it concedes that its criticism is not simply a generational one, and instead a crude and uncomplicated ideological one. If hip hop is more than a mere facsimile of the black power ideology of the 1960s and 1970s, it would seem paramount to launch a dialectical critique of black power in order to sustain its "break with the past," self-understanding, or it is traditional black aesthetics, culture, politics, and ideology in new forms (Cheney, 2005). Some important womanist and black feminist critiques draw sharp lines between "fallocentric" black Power and hip hop, with emphasis on transgenerational patterns and practices among men since the 1960s. Errol Henderson concurs, "[U]nfortunately, [hip hop's] nationalism also took the patriarchal focus of the 1960s and took a very misogynist approach to Black womanhood" (Henderson, 1996, p. 319).

Like generations before it, hip hop's generational cycle sought to understand the world and social context which it inherited. But hip hop rarely turned a critical lens to black power as a generational development. A blind spot in hip hop critical discourse is the tendency to focus on civil rights and black power as the "older generation," and not as analogous *youth* struggles in their own right. These considerations would require cross-generational as well as intergenerational frameworks. The tendency instead is to view the antecedent movement struggles in the rearview mirror rather than a split screen. If it is true that black power was a parallel movement to the civil rights campaigns, there was certainly a perceived generational dimension among them as well (Joseph, 2006). King was only a few years older than some of the student activists, organizers, artists, and political militants in SNCC. John Herbers favorably described them as "gifted and highly motivated youth"; the students in SNCC "taught in freedom schools, conducted voter registration drives, built community centers, set up health clinics, established black cooperatives, provided lawyers for taking discrimination and violence into the federal courts, established libraries, staffed day-care centers for pre-school children sponsored free theater" (Herbers, 1970, pp. 72–73). In Oakland and Chicago, for example, the Black Panther Party "Survival Programs" would become another example of black civil society at work among local young people. They were indeed some of the most extraordinary assemblages of black American youth, replete with gifts, skills, courage, inspiration, intellectual restlessness, and political consciousness. Their missteps, immaturities, and tragedies are well documented in scholarly literature. Their subsequent disenchantment with the direction the conservative and moderate civil rights cadres took and the violence, the question of interracial political coalitions, and the political setbacks (e.g., MFDP in 1964) were important among the factors leading to growing tensions. James Forman and others were particularly angered by the agreement between King and SCLC and Alabama authorities surrounding the second part of the Selma campaign in 1965 (Herbers, 1970, p. 78).

Whether taken up and extended by New York area black power babies like Chuck D, Sister Souljah, Nas, Mos Def, or Tupac, or among the hip hop intelligentsia, the rapnationalist moment in hip hop and black politics resonated more with Eldridge Cleaver's thinking and that of Harlem-centered black nationalists and Pan-Africanists (of late Garveyism) than with Carmichael's, particularly on the noted King dynamic and Malcolm X in black

in which Field Nigger Power and the grievances and goals of the Field Nigger—and the leadership of Field Niggers—will dominate the black movement for justice in America. (Scheer, 1967)

Cleaver wrote elsewhere, "[T]o black militants, Dr. King represented a stubborn and persistent stumbling block in the path of the methods that had to be implemented to bring about a revolution in the present situation. . . . much hatred, much venom and much criticism was focused upon Dr. King by the black militants (Scheer, 1967, p. 73). However representative Cleaver's sentiments were on King and Malcolm X, Stokely Carmichael wanted it noted that the conventional narrative that black power was a "declaration of independence" of black power youth, from the influence of King's leadership should be interrogated more rigorously and placed in the precise context of Selma in 1965. For Carmichael, it was not a matter of Malcolm *or* Martin; the lives and brutal murders of both weighed saliently on his generation's subsequent social and political movements. Carmichael's close relationship with King would deepen. King's shift of focus to more explicit economic critiques in Chicago (1966), on Vietnam (1965–1967), and the Poor Peoples' March (1968) were the results of King's interaction with the young people of SNCC in Mississippi—during black power.

Among works in hip hop literature that do partially treat civil rights and black power, there is a tendency to ignore hip hop's relationship to the black freedom struggle as an historical development, longitudinally (Rabaka, 2011). (John Gibbs) St. Clair Drake insisted, "if the struggle for Negro rights is viewed over the entire 350-year time span of their residence in North America, it can be conceptualized as involving several discrete social movements, including the abolition movement, the civil rights movement, and the black power movement" (1968, p. 23). Hip hop's discharge of King is consistent with some pre-civil rights era intellectual discourse. The likes of leading historian Rayford W. Logan, E. Franklin Frazier, Ralph Bunche,[20] St. Clair Drake, and the elderly W. E. B. Du Bois wrote and thought nothing significant about the young preacher-activist in the Southern movement who, by 1964, like Bunche, received international recognition, even becoming a world figure.[21] The sociologist Frazier, for instance, derided King's tactics as "self-abasement," through Christian concepts like redemptive love and redemptive suffering on the part of blacks.[22] For psychologist Kenneth B. Clark this doctrine was "pathological" and reinforced the centuries old "stereotype of the black man as long-suffering, meek, and more apt to resort to prayer than take decisive action against injustice."[23] Cedric Robinson insists that integration aspirations among black bourgeois leaders amounted to "soul murder," where for most ordinary people, "the America that King had dreamed of was impossible" (1997, p. 150).

A swatch of early King studies, provide important biographical and interpretive critiques of King, the mainstream of the civil rights movement, and the Christian liberal integrationist tradition he articulated and its relationship to black nationalism and especially, Malcolm X (Reddick, 1959; Bennett, 1968; Levering Lewis, 1970; Lincoln, 1984; Lomax, 1968; Walton Jr., 1970). Louis Lomax insisted that King benefited from a conflation of technological innovations in print and mass media and its need for a hero protagonist "upon whom they could focus as the racial drama unfolded." It also helped that national and regional newspapers began hiring then "Negro journalists," like Lomax. King was, in his twenties, among other things, a citizen tribune primed, as it were, where "one could not have created a black man who could have better filled the nation's television screens" (Lomax, 1968, p. 44). Yet Harold Cruse largely ignores King (who had been on the scene for more than a decade) in *The Crisis of the Negro Intellectual*, though later Cruse lists King with "a galaxy of outstanding black leadership personalities [who] came to the fore . . . outstanding spokesmen [and women] for a multiplicity of black trends that tried to translate a legal mandate for evolutionary social change into a Black Revolution" (1987, p. 31).[24] Cruse insists King was worthy of the "hero worship" that followed his death. Moreover, "King himself was unprecedented and unexpected among black leaders produced by the Fifties and Sixties" (p. 372). As part of a late critique of the judicial, political party, leadership and organizational politics of the second "civil rights cycle" (1954–1968),[25] Cruse ends the latter work with important insights on "post-King black politics" and what would be required in terms of leadership and institutions for any subsequent cycle; that is, *beyond* black power. Black power's relationship to hip hop is widely acknowledged in this literature, but some of its distortions and characterizations of King were uncritically taken up by the latter. Peniel Joseph suggests, "in the popular mind, black power is most often remembered as a tragedy—a wrong turn from Martin Luther King, Jr.'s hopeful rhetoric toward the polemics of black nationalists who blamed whites for the worsening urban crisis, on the one hand, and, on the other, gun-toting Black Panthers who vowed to lead a political revolution with an army of the black underclass" (2006, p. xvii).

William E. Perkins identifies three waves of hip hop commencing in the 1970s through the next three decades; to which one might add at least a fourth, marked by the death of Tupac Shakur; the persistent "Thug Life" phase (Ogbar, 2007). From its origins in New York City, to its emergence in the West Coast, South, and abroad, the various waves included different regional, lyrical, personalities, and technological innovations to set them apart from one another. We are concerned with Perkins's third wave hip hop; also "conscious rap," "rapnationalism," or "message rap." For Ogbar, the black nationalist militant style in rap and black culture almost seamlessly morphed into the thug type—"a new dimension of black militant or 'conscious' rap"—in the transition from the East Coast rapnationalist to the West Coast gangsta genre's increased influence. By the time hardcore or "gangsta rap" emerges in the late 1980s and 1990s, nevertheless, the legacy of Martin Luther King and the civil rights movement was largely sealed by black conscious rap and, ironically, conservative whites (who promoted King's social vision for color-blind implications), the liberal Civil Rights leadership establishment and organizations (SCLC, NAACP, NUL, and CBC) at its dead end, and liberal whites, who only conceived of King in terms of the August 1963 speech and moderation.

For Peniel Joseph, King's murder was "the very event that emboldened Black power activists to argue more vociferously than ever that America was an unrepentantly racist nation. . . . Black Power would fill the vacuum brought by King's death, its focus on politics and culture transforming race relations and black activism in the United States and beyond" (2006, p. 242). It continued to impact hip hop's pioneering personalities such as Chuck D, who explained, "I was in third grade when Dr. Martin Luther King was gunned down. My mother wore all black to work the next day. . . . I had been taught that Dr. King was a man of peace who fought for Black people's rights, and it was real deep to me that he would get killed like that. As a kid, checking all of that out made me ask a lot of questions" (1997, p. 26). As with black power, the most vocal and pronounced of black power activists (i.e., Amiri Baraka), tended to condemn US social and political relations from the ideological frameworks cast by Malcolm X and individuals other than King, with whom many fiercely and principally disagreed. Rapnationalism in the 1980s and 1990s period would retain proto-black power and (late) black power's nationalist criticisms of King, nonviolence methods, and political philosophy, but unfortunately didn't attribute this to its sources.

That Martin Luther King stood shoulder-to-shoulder next to Stokely Carmichael (being one of the four speakers that night) at the precise instance that the black power slogan was uttered, politically, during the June 1966 Meredith "March Against Fear," is often ignored (Carmichael, and Thelwell 2005, p. 511). King, Carmichael insisted, "never repudiated Black Power. Never."

Even before leaving Greenwood, where the black power tumult and subsequent police riots occurred (resulting in King being gassed and beaten with no cameras present), both King and Carmichael agreed, that "black power is not black nationalism or black racism. . . . King said Black power is too easily confused with black nationalism"(2005, pp. 510–11).[26] At the outset, and before its decidedly nationalist and internationalist turns, black power was ideologically *neutral*; hosting elements that represented the full spectrum of an ideological continuum of black thought, criticism, and organizing. Stripped of the myths, Carmichael insists,

> I learned a lot from Dr. King just from observing him. In the struggle I've been lucky to meet or been close to some extraordinary human beings, all of whom instructed me. I've met famous revolutionaries: Dr. Fidel Castro Ruz, Colonel Muammar Qaddafi [and] . . . Ho Chi Minh. I've studied under Kwame Nkrumah, President Ahmed SekouToure, and Madame Shirley Graham Du Bois. I knew Bayard, Malcolm, Mrs. Hamer. But at my most important, potentially confusing, and formative stage, *Dr. King was a true mentor, who instructed me by example.* (Carmichael and Thelwell, 2005, p. 663)

Speaking with a front-line view of developments surrounding the massive 1963 "Freedom Now March" in which King played a public role, *and* the 1965 Grassroots Leadership Conference, where Malcolm X delivered "Message to the Grassroots" in Detroit, Grace Lee Boggs, notes, "activists struggling for Black Power in Detroit, we identified much more with Malcolm X and tended to view King's call for nonviolence and for the beloved community as somewhat naïve and sentimental." Later Boggs would become critical of black power militancy that locked Malcolm X (and King) into static ideological positions, even as both of them changed considerably over the course of their respective thirteen years of public activism and ministries. As noted, for many since 1965, *Malcolm X has become ideology*; possessing all of the necessary explanatory, organizing, symbolic, and cultural functions. Boggs never renounces her full embrace of Malcolm X, but (like Eldridge Cleaver did before his 1998 death)[27] came to a late appreciation for King's insurgent politics and political style. Scott Kurashige insists, "this particular reading of King as a radical, which Grace would come to embrace, remains vastly underappreciated," (2012, p. 172).[28] In 2004, Boggs conceded, "it has become increasingly clear to me that King's prophetic vision is now the indispensable starting point for 21st Century revolutionaries" (p. 180). For many of its intellectuals and practitioners, hip hop's "black conscious" phase replicated, black power's "Malcolm X over Martin Luther King" line even as it thought itself altogether a radical break; not considering, that as "Civil Rights is dead" so, necessarily, would be Malcolm X's pertinent social and political critiques, which both took up with their own.

MALCOLM'S MESSAGE TO THE GRASSROOTS

Malcolm X took up the Little family's Garveyite jeremiads and railed against many religious contemporaries. Like early Garveyites, many who joined Elijah Muhammad's religious movement, the Nation of Islam, held most black Christian churches and ministers in contempt of representing the race's best interest. Still in the Nation of Islam, Malcolm X's fierce intervention, however, played *the* pivotal role in shaping *how* Martin Luther King would be interpreted ideologically, for adherents to black power, and hip hop's early nationalist phase, which they often coupled with their own critiques. Eldridge Cleaver confirmed the view of many young people in the 1960s, in noting, "the America out of which Elijah Muhammad call[ed] his people is indeed doomed, crumbling, burning, if not by the hand of God then by the hand of [humans]."[29] Before being ostracized as the greatest "traitor" and "a Judas" to Elijah Muhammad and the Nation of Islam, and extend himself to the civil rights mainstream, Malcolm X targeted Martin Luther King Jr., other liberal integrationist and Civil Rights leaders, (like the atheist A. Phillip Randolph) as "religious Uncle Toms."[30] Perhaps no single speech across Malcolm X's career solemnized King as a sellout more than "Message to the Grassroots" on Nov. 10, 1963, in Detroit. Two generations of African American young people, those corresponding to the black power and later hip hop generations (and attendant movements), were deeply impacted by the candid criticisms in Malcolm X's "Grassroots" speech. The speech focused on international and domestic events, including the anticolonial movements in Africa, Latin America, and Asia, and the massive March on Washington event, its leadership, Democratic coalition. Malcolm X panned, the plantation division of labor between house negroes and field negroes in slavery.[31] Malcolm plainly identified King as a "house Negro" and lined himself with the lumpen "field Negros" who were committed to revolution and the destruction of US white supremacy and European colonialism. To capture the influence of this single speech, Peniel Joseph notes,

> *Malcolm's speech at the Grassroots Conference brought together two generations of activists gathered in Detroit to organize a national movement for Black Power . . .* Over the next decade the speech became a quintessential example of Malcolm's rhetorical genius and political complexity and was widely distributed around the country. . . . The enduring legacy of Malcolm's speech would be reflected in the activism of a younger generation of Black Power militants who openly identified themselves as Field Negroes." (2006, pp. 89–92)

White establishment leaders in national government and media preferred moderates to militants. King's stature rose in relation to Malcolm X's among mainstream political and media decision makers. Dyson concurs in noting that "with the sudden and sharp rise of black militancy, King's challenging beliefs transmuted into terms that white America fully exploited. With the emergence of Stokely Carmichael and especially Malcolm X, King was seen as the humble, nonviolent messenger of integration" (Dyson, 2000). And as rapnationalists sought militancy over moderation, Malcolm X's stature rose in relation to King's in hip hop. For Dyson, one motive was to project King's early militancy as a patriotic counterpoint to the ominous (but less confrontational) presence of black nationalism among many remnant Garveyites, and individuals like Malcolm X, and young activists, intellectuals and organizers like Huey P. Newton, Bob Moses, Gloria Richardson, James Foreman, Stokely Carmichael, Nina Simone, Toni Morrison, Angela Davis and many others. Dr. King's more radical criticisms against capitalism, poverty, militarism, white moderates/liberals, and racism were (like noncommercial hip hop fulcrums) forced *underground*, in deference to the campaign for national recognition of the King holiday in the middle 1980s and conservative anti-affirmative action campaigns in the 1990s. This, in turn, contributed to King being quarantined from young people, as a resource while they sought to articulate their own policy concerns and political demands in the "new nadir" 1980s and 1990s period; they preferred Malcolm X and Louis Farrakhan (from 1983–1995).[32]

UNSAMPLING MARTIN LUTHER KING: HIP HOP, MALCOLM AND MARTIN

Martin Luther King was murdered a little over a decade and not a full generation before the earliest inklings of hip hop art and movement emerged in predominantly black and Puerto Rican communities in New York City. Black power was the intersecting force, linking the activists of the 1960s with those actually born in the 1960s and 1970s, who developed early hip hop. Kevin Gaines reminds us of the "sonic culture of Black Power," as he elaborates,

> During the 1960s and 1970s, popular music became a critical site for reflection on the meaning of blackness, and the historical relationship of African American to the United States, to the Africa diaspora, and the world. The global reach and influence of the Black Power movement was arguably achieved through the era's recorded music, as much as the iconography of images of US black liberation struggles brought by documentary photography, film, and television to overseas audiences, or the international touring of black and African activists and musicians.[33]

Well before Chuck D and hip hop nationalism, black power youth promoted—especially in Harlem—"the mass distribution of album and cassette recordings of the speeches of Malcolm X [which] gave a much wider circulation of the ideas of this pivotal figure, whose pervasive influence is evident in the anthology *For Malcolm: Poems on the Life and Death of Malcolm X.* . . ." (Gaines, 2012, p. 194). Early rapnationalist hip hop privileged Malcolm X and (simultaneously) Louis Farrakhan in its music and political thought and abandoned King, who was largely received as a race-compromising "Uncle Tom" unworthy of bringing out on any major tracks. Its imprint on politically conscious hip hop artists, particularly of the new nationalist sort, was deep.[34] Peniel Joseph provides a useful synopsis,

> The Influence of the Black Power movement's most revered icon, Malcolm extended beyond the era. . . . The rap group Public Enemy, in particular, helped to introduce the movement's legacy to a post-Black Power generation with anthems such as "Fight the Power," an objective further aided by the 1992 release of Spike Lee's film *Malcolm X. . . . Through Malcolm, contemporary black urban youth embraced other symbols of Black Power. Some of hip hop's angry young men and women were themselves echoes of the Black Power activists of four decades earlier. . . .* In some spectacular instances, both movements shared blood-line. (2006, pp. 296–97)

At different phases the likes of Public Enemy, KRS-ONE, and X-CLAN made more or less emphases on correct nationalist programs or dimensions; what they shared was often an uncritical valoriziation of the image and teachings of Malcolm X. Henderson noted, "Hip hop resurrected some deceased African American images, particularly Malcolm X, but it *didn't seem to elevate those leaders present today.* Politics was too often reduced to showing Malcolm X or Martin King in a video instead of incorporating their precepts into praxis on the part of the rappers who evoked the images of these African American leaders" (Henderson, 1996, p. 232)(emphasis added). This was a particular feature of rapnationalism until X-CLAN pushed Maulana Karenga's Kawaidinationalism and pushed Public Enemy toward a more strident nationalist critique at the core of its audio and video productions.

Chicago rapper Common (Lonnie Rashid Lynn Jr.) acknowledged this during a 2006 King-tribute collaboration with Black Eyed Peas' Will.I.Am, titled "A Dream." Like nearly all rap references to King, beginning at least with black radio DJ legend Joseph "Jack the Rapper" in the 1980s campaign with Stevie Wonder for the King holiday, "I have a Dream" is the starting point from which the duo's gritty song moves to elaborate the condition of declension in contemporary urban black life. A recent *Washington Post* online article on the subject of King's marginalization in hip hop details how some rappers and scholars have understood it.[35] One analyst described this in the article as a kind of resuscitation of King from near invisibility,

> [I]n the early days of hip hop . . . he wasn't sampled widely even though his speeches were readily available. . . . He *just wasn't making his way into hip-hop songs. . . . Once they bring out Malcolm X, King goes away again for 15 to 20 years. . . .* That Public Enemy sample [of] Malcolm—'Too black, too strong!' [in 'Bring the Noise']—it's one of the most iconic samples in hip-hop. They patented Malcolm X as the voice that should be associated with this particular hard-edged framework, connecting the music with the notion of militancy.

As Common noted, "Malcolm just represents more of the . . . fire of hip-hop" than King, who was "unsampled." Henderson concurred, in noting,

> It is impossible to consider the Black nationalist element in hip-hop without recognizing the seminal influence of Public Enemy. . . . Public Enemy broke out with one of the most heralded and respected institution[s] in the Black community—the NOI. The fusion of rap and Black nationalist political organization promoted a politically grounded rap focus that continue[d] to dominate the genre. . . .

Public Enemy focused youthful Black energy and consciousness in a way that no rap act ever had. Overtly promoted by and promoting Louis Farrakhan. Public Enemy helped bring thousands of young Blacks to the political philosophy of Black nationalism. (Henderson, 1996, p. 325)

Most of the lyrical recognition is based on the conventional framing and is used mainly as a cultural reference out of context, or in gest centering "dream themes."[36] Dead Prez's 2010 song "Malcolm, Garvey, Huey," is an important intervention particularly in the manner in which it showcases King's black power era criticisms in the "Black Is Beautiful," speech.[37] Along with the smattering of instances here, the compilation between Compton's The Game and Queens, New York, rapper Nas in "Letter to the King" is another tribute piece that goes beyond themes concerning King's "Dream."[38] At the end of the running hook "Malcolm, Garvey, Huey!," however, a very brief sampling of words from Malcolm X are followed by a *significantly* longer sampling of King's speech, with which the track ends; taking up nearly a fourth of the song's time. Here, Dead Prez offers a rare recognition in "conscious" hip hop of King's purported radicalization. Otherwise, hip hop generally views black power and civil rights along orthodox lines as more or less revolutionary.

Understanding the relationship between King and hip hop couldn't be achieved by simply reconstructing a hypothetical or "imagined Martin Luther King." Richard Iton insisted, "Bold declarations that the pressing questions of our time can be read backward into the past, or conversely that the past can be read without constraint, and without attention to context and flux, into the present and future invite doubt" (2008, p. 289). Still, cartoonist Aaron McGruder's 2006 animation of an encounter between Martin Luther King Jr. and hip hop culture and politics places them in conversation bluntly. By writing King as comatose since being shot in 1968, rather than assassinated, McGruder revived King for a confrontation with aspects of hip hop youth culture in which an elderly, balding "King,"[39] emerged to represent a generational critique and criticism about contemporary hip hop culture and lifestyle. It is at the same time, in actuality, McGruder's intragenerational bourgeois class critique of the prurient aspects of "ghetto-centric" hip hop culture. The salient assimilation orientation in contemporary mainstream hip hop is commonly viewed—especially among hip hop culture purists—as the nadir of the rap genre in particular. Indeed on cue, none less than Nicki Minaj ("N.I.G.G.A.S: Playtime Is Over") lyricized, "This ones for Malcolm this ones for Martin! Wish-a could have thanked them look what they started!" Which is one possible reply to the inquiry, Would Dr. Martin Luther King Approve of Hip-Hop's Current State?[40] McGruder's animation of King and hip hop suggests that King, at least, might be woefully perplexed with what Minaj claims Malcolm X and he "started" in terms of his call for "a revolution of values," in US society, ones opposed to rank individualism, materialism, violence, and its militarist underpinnings.[41] Upon arriving at a gathering of young, stereotyped black urban youth in party mode—it is *not* an interracial or multicultural hip hop gathering—with some fighting, King brings the room and music to a halt by jarringly calling the partiers "Niggas!/Niggers!" (insisting they "shut the hell up!"), to the younger generation's surprise and dismay. King then admonishes them about the violent beatings and martyrdom of others in the old movement. McGruder's King then prophecies, not a "promised land" like the last time speaking publicly before being shot in Memphis, but of a grave future for the young audience representing black American youth. In the end, King, like another great advocate of race integration in the twentieth century, namely W. E. B. Du Bois, announces he is leaving the United States for a life in Canada, where abolitionist and emigrationist movement leaders of previous generations moved in times past, ending King's encounter with hip hop.

Bakari Kitwana raised an important question in asking, "[A]re young Americans achieving Martin Luther King's dream via hip-hop?" Perhaps it would be instructive to explore, just briefly, the role hip hop as the principal cultural representation of black life, and in post-civil rights era race brokerage politics; the politics of representation in popular culture and society. Where Bakari Kitwana once boasted that hip hop is "crossover proof" in his celebration of the patterns indicating widespread appeal among US whites, by 2004 80 percent of hip hop's 45 million consumers were white" (2005, p. 82). He also readily acknowledged that "hip hop is *not the first time Black culture has been appropriated—nor will it be the last*. In fact Black culture is being appropriated in our lifetime" (2005, p. 156) (emphasis added). Tricia Rose specified the years 1995–2001 as critical to this development, noting that "by the late 1990s, most of the affirming, creative stories and characters that had stood at the defining core of hip hop had been gutted." And it is fiercely *race conscious*, as it refracts in *de facto* white and colorblind multicultural nodes, which Patricia Hill Collins argues are also "highly nationalistic" and grounded in current configurations of white supremacy (e.g., the "new racism") (2006, p. 7). It is conscious or unconscious participation in what Ronald Walters recognized as post-civil rights era "white nationalism" (2003). No single marker of this phenomenon makes this clearer than the torturous Internet photo image of Kanye West standing with the Confederate flag—while wearing a white angelic cherubim on his shirt—in 2013.[42] Very recently, the commercial form has not simply forged a "postracial" mystification and "generationally shared mental complexion" (Stoute, 2011, p. xvii) around ghetto-centric caricatures of black life and suffering in the United States; it has also taken on a perplexing animus toward highly valued symbols and figures in African American tradition and memory and appeared disinterested in the rescission of key provisions of the civil rights legislation addressing, for instance, antidiscrimination policy, voting rights, and education in the Obama presidential era. Consider the mutilating terms of the rappers FUTURE and Lil Wayne's "Karate Chop" remix, lyricized (by Lil Wayne) to link Emmett Till's notorious lynching with the torture that he promises to effect in a violent sex encounter with a woman; mutilating her sexually released in 2013 during the *very* campaign when Till's memory and images joined Trayvon Martin's in social media, as supporters demanded an arrest of Martin's killer. In addition, there was the 2013 spoof where an actress portrayed Harriet Tubman in a sex video with "Massah" in a quid pro quo arrangement that results in permission being granted to lead the Underground Railroad posted on an on-line site formerly owned and managed by hip hop mogul spokesman, and veteran Russell Simmons.[43] In July 2013, after the release of the popular *Holy Grail* album and after publicly supporting the family of slain Florida teen Trayvon Martin during organized demonstrations in one hundred US cities in response to the verdict in the case, the rap entrepreneur declared the *current* generation of nonblacks as being free of racism. Lost on most observers of the high-profile murders of both Trayvon Martin and Michael Brown (of Ferguson, Missouri) is the detail that their killers' ages at the time (twenty-eight) correspond with the popular hip hop generation of today. Jay Z's sold out concert teamed with Justin Timberlake, was held a few days later in Miami, Florida.[44] In early 2014, entertainer Nicki Minaj joined the fray when "Lookin' Ass N*gga" was released as a single on a social media site with the phrase "Lookin; Ass N*gga" embossed over the iconic 1965 *Ebony Magazine* pose by Malcolm X. Many critics interpreted this visualization as Minaj referring to Malcolm X, who is peering through a curtain while holding an assault rifle, as the "Lookin' Ass N*gga" in question.[45] This unfolded simultaneously with a second Florida murder trial and controversial partial verdicts over a white vigilante's killing of an African American teen (Jordan Davis) for listening to loud rap music with other teens and young men, who were also targeted by a gunman. Following scores of shootings of young, unarmed, criminally uninvolved

Wyclef Jean, and KRS-ONE—and its "universal" appeal as a world music form. It became a dominant force and international export of music, culture, and politics, as has hip hop over a good part of the same period and continues to valorize the likes of Paul Bogle, Sam Sharpe, Marcus Garvey, Haile Selassie, and Bob Marley in order to move from the impoverished margins of colonial Jamaican society to global influence across the majority (if not all) of the continents (Campbell, 2003). But its lesson seems to have been lost on money-getting hip hop, that it is vital to change the world on its own terms, in its own tradition or traditions—rejecting "Babylon" as the height of evil and "downpression" in the modern world. Hip hop intellectual discourse often celebrated hip hop's "break" with its ancestral foundations in the struggle for black liberation; a declaration of independence from it at the precise phase in black politics where a conservative and libertarian strain has effectively reversed the key legislative achievements of the civil rights/black power phase—on its watch. What remains, at least among hip hop studies and research, is the need for the formulation of a theoretical synthesis that provides a basis for the development of institutions and other independent fulcrums, that move beyond its concerns with its generational properties and leads to the kind of social and political transformation of African American life that has remained elusive since the struggles of the previous generations.

NOTES

1. David Walker cited an incident in his *Appeal*, where a woman slave aided a slave driver whom her compatriots overtook in a freedom attempt; all of the men were executed. The woman was an object of scorn for Walker. Likewise, it became widely known that the inspiration for Harriet Beecher Stowe's Uncle Tom was one Josiah Henson, a trusted slave who accidentally crossed into Ohio from Kentucky with a group of slave charges and then returned to Kentucky. As Henson tried to raise the money, his new master sold him to a new planter in New Orleans. While traveling to New Orleans with his owner to finish the transaction, the master's son got seriously ill. Henson was charged with bringing his master's son back home, and he could have escaped. Instead, Henson brought the son safely home and received no reward or appreciation. This was the last straw for Henson, and in 1830 he decided to flee to Canada with his wife and children. On October 28, 1830, Henson and his family settled in Dresden, Ontario. For the next four years, Henson worked as a farm laborer and preacher in the area and had his oldest son teach him how to read and write. He also became involved in the Underground Railroad, leading more than two hundred slaves to freedom. In 1842, he developed his own Afro-Canadian community, which taught practical skills to the fugitives he aided. In 1849, Henson published his autobiography, *The Life of Josiah Henson, Formerly a Slave, Now an Inhabitant of Canada, as Narrated by Himself*. In

1852, Harriett Beecher Stowe published *Uncle Tom's Cabin*, a fictional portrayal of slavery in America. Beecher later revealed that one of the novel's main characters, Uncle Tom, was based on Josiah Henson.

2. This was the case for Michelle Wallace and her much maligned work in 1979, *Black Macho and the Myth of the Superwoman*.

3. Moses insists that the messianic, long-suffering caricature of Harriet Beecher Stowe's protagonist, Uncle Tom, was rejected immediately by leading black contemporaries "because it made him submit to tyranny." This contempt would persist despite Tom's "passive defiance," rejecting the command by his master, Simon Legree, to beat an obstinate loved one named Cassy. Such life-threatening defiance haunted Tom's sadistic tormentor, Legree, thereafter. Often ignored was the stoutheartedness of Uncle Tom's death knell and blunt refusal to point his torturer to her whereabouts before calling him "a poor miserable fool," as death approached.

4. Nikkolas Smith is an architectural and graphic designer from Houston, Texas, who attended the historically black Hampton University. Please see http://www.nydailynews .com/news/national/image-martin-luther-king-jr-hoodie-viral-article-1.1399127#ixzz2 Z9°i7DB0. Please also see http://gunshowgallery.com/artistanda=4536. Miami artist and Vietnamese refugee Huong similarly created a mural titled *We Are All Trayvon Martin*, which includes the likeness of Trayvon's murderer firing a gun at a faceless, bloodstained hoodie and a likeness of Martin Luther King Jr. splattered in young Trayvon's blood.

5. I understand and use it in its broadest sense and in relation to Marcyliena Morgan and Dionne Bennett's definition: "Hip hop refers to the music, arts, media, and cultural movement and community development by black and Latino youth in the mid-1970s on the East Coast of the United States." See, Marcyliena Morgan and Dionne Bennett, 2011, pp. 176–96. I use the term "hip hop" to represent the current commercial form noted in several studies. I view the commercial form interchangeably with "popular hip hop" and "corporate" hip hop. Like most other scholarship, I see it as a phenomenon that came out of hip hop's organic base, before it was popularized and controlled by the few corporations that Tricia Rose identified in *Hip Hop Wars*.

6. The campaign for the federal holiday tribute to King (1976–1983) mattered as much to the likes of Sister Souljah, Chuck D, and Public Enemy as it did to Stevie Wonder, Coretta King, and others. Errol Henderson provided some context for understanding this dynamic in Public Enemy's use of King in "By the Time I Get to Arizona," (1991). He noted first how "nationalism in hip hop does not emerge exclusively from the lyrics of early rap music. In the early days of hip-hop in the 1970s, this nationalism developed from the collective ethos of the Black community that spawned this new genre." Within the contours of this nationalist turn, Henderson noted, "here PE takes the prototypic symbol of nonviolence, *Martin Luther King*, and depicts retribution for the sufferings visited upon African Americans before, during, and after the movements that he helped to lead." See Errol Henderson, "Black Nationalism and Rap Music." For an explanation of NWA's "message rap" dimensions, please see Jeffrey Ogbar's *Hip-Hop Revolution*, 2007, p. 110.

7. In Montgomery, Parks worked for (one-time) Garveyite E. D. Nixon (later of the NAACP); she was raised as a Garveyite antiracist militant before she took centerstage when she was kicked off a bus in Alabama for the second time by the *same* abusive bus

driver who had kicked her off in 1943. See McGuire, *At the Dark End*, 2010, pp. 12, 79. See also pp. xix, xvii. Another example might be found in Huey P. Newton's "Revolution Intercommunalism," which presciently anticipated late capitalist globalization and its effects on ordinary people, internationally. Foreseeing a move from US-dominated nation-states to US-dominated international regimes that transcend the nation state (e.g., World Bank, IMF, WTO, Haliburton) in intentional conglomerate "communities," intercommunalism offers a method to counter them, in ways that hip hop practitioners, activists, and intellectuals have yet to take seriously. Please see Huey P. Newton and Vladimir I Lenin, *Revolutionary Intercommunalism and the Right of Nations to Self-Determination* (2004). This is even as hip hop continues to have global reach and appeal. Maori and aboriginal studies in New Zealand and Australia recognize that black power had international impact and followings across the continents in these and other places, including Israel, South Africa, parts of West Africa, London, and (among Dalits) India. It would be instructive to map out the reach of both phenomena, not to compare the popularity of one over the other, but to learn whether there is a relationship to where both black power and hip hop have resonated globally, to assess whether and where hip hop's reception might have been primed by black power.

8. See Eldridge Cleaver, *Soul on Ice* 1967 [1991], p. 71. See also David Levering Lewis, *When Harlem Was in Vogue* [1981] 1997.

9. Prominent research universities and academic institutions today take hip hop critical discourse seriously as evidenced by a few highly visible faculty appointments, research publications, scholarly publications, forums, and new institutes; and individual courses offered across the curriculum of universities and colleges, nationally. Jimmy Lovine and Dr. Dre's $70 million gift to the University of Southern California and a "Nas fellowship" at Harvard University also received wide notice. Jimmy Lovine and rapper Dr. Dre (aka Andre Young) gave the school $70 million to create a new undergraduate program, the USC Jimmy Lovine and Andre Young Academy for Arts, Technology and the Business of Innovation.

10. Tricia Rose, Reiland Rabaka, Monica R. Miller, Marcyliena Morgan, Mark Anthony Neal, Richard Iton, Lester Spence, Imani Perry, Errol Henderson, Jeffrey Ogbar, Todd Boyd, Charise Cheney, Robin Kelly, Patricia Hill Collins, and Lakeyta Bonnette (whose recent book, *Pulse of the People: Political Rap Music and Black Politics*, I did not have the advantage of reading for this chapter), among many other students of hip hop studies, have strengthened hip hop as a critical lens through which to interpret African American, black diaspora, and youth cultures in the United States and internationally. The emergent body of research is mostly analytical, descriptive, and interpretive of social and political contexts, using content analysis, ethnographic approaches, and academic journalism.

11. See Lester Spence, *Stare in the Darkness: The Limits of Hip-Hop and Black Politics (2011)*. See also Kevin F. Steinmetz and Howard Henderson, "Hip -Hop and Procedural Justice: Hip Hop Artists' Perceptions of Criminal Justice," in *Race and Justice*; also see "Defiant Messages in Rap/Hip-Hop and Rock Music 1993 and 2003," *Journal of Medical Psychology: Theories, Methods, and Applications*; see also Charise Cheney, "In Search of the 'Revolutionary Generation': Engendering the Golden Age of Rap Nationalism," *The Journal of African American History*; *The History of Hip Hop* (Summer, 2005): 278–98.

12. The religious dimension of hip hop is an emergent line of inquiry that some of its students take seriously. See Monica Miller, *Religion and Hip Hop* (New York: Routledge, 2012); Monica R. Miller and Anthony B. Pinn, *The Hip Hop Reader* (New York: Routledge, 2014); Monica R. Miller and Anthony B. Pinn, *Religion and Hip Hop: Mapping the New Terrain in the U.S.* (London: Bloomsbury Academic).

13. Some of the most insightful analysis of hip hop culture, music, and politics can be found in the writings of native Detroiters like Todd Boyd, Michael Eric Dyson, and Lester Spence.

14. Yet Detroit has played no significant role in the production of breakthrough rap acts—Eminem's "8 Mile" is not viewed locally as "Detroit" proper; indeed it served as a psychological boundary, separating poor whites from the black community in nearby "7 Mile" and elsewhere. I am indebted to Professor Errol Henderson (of Penn State University), a Detroit native and University of Michigan alumnus, for his insights on most of these details. Please see the article by Luke Tripp, http://www.iww.org/history/documents/misc/Tripp, last accessed, 12/27/15.

15. See also Mark Anthony Neal, *What the Music Said: Black Popular Music and Black Public Culture* (New York: Routledge, 1998), p. 50.

16. It is not clear whether the current #BlackLivesMatter intervention can be attributed to developments in hip hop life and culture apart from contemporary developments in African American life, culture, and politics in general. It certainly cannot be fully understood apart from its Oakland, California, roots, where the catalytic Oscar Grant police violence protest predated it by half a decade, as it emerged there in response to the Trayvon Martin homicide verdict in 2013.

17. Ibid., p. 56. It has certainly continued beyond King at least through to the Jackson-Farrakhan period, and in the presidential campaigns and elections of Barack Obama. See p. 67.

18. See Clayborne Carson, "Foreword," in Scot Brown, *Fighting for US: Maulana Karenga, the US Organization and Black Cultural Nationalism* (New York: New York University Press, 2003), p. x. Also, in Du Bois, for instance, Hanes Walton Jr. argued that his many "shifts in posture reflected not uncertainty as to goals, but rather the constant need to reassess a theoretical position in the light of empirical losses and gains. Integration and racial solidarity were the two seemingly conflicted ideas that remained constant themes in Du Bois' writing, ideas that have persisted at the center of the black debate." Hanes Walton, Jr., *The Political Philosophy of Martin Luther King, Jr.* 1970), p. 21. Of course, dimensions of these can be detected in the thought of numerous "traditional" artists, intellectuals, and activists such as Du Bois, Paul Robeson, Ella Baker, Lorraine Hansberry, Maya Angelou, Martin Luther King, Gloria Richardson, Malcolm X, Huey P. Newton, and Toni Morrison, and in the noted attempts at national conventions. Where there is a coherent worldview for hip hop, generally, one component of it is found in hip hop's critiques of the ideologies, institutions, leaders, and symbols of the "old order," the modern black freedom struggle.

19. Stokely Carmichael, to the contrary, suggested that King was fully engaged in the black power episode in Greenwood, Mississippi, and on the front line of "field nigger" leadership. Rather than an apologist for the status quo, King, at least on site, contextualized

black power to Carmichael's satisfaction: "[H]e really understood us better, more sympathetically and was much closer to us in spirit than people think."

20. King became seriously ill on the second day of the trip after participating in several independence celebrations. David Levering Lewis, *King* 1970, p. 91. Lewis recognized the March on Washington as the key event that raised King's stature among civil rights leaders. He was awarded *Time* magazine's 1964 "Man of the Year" tribute, and donned its cover. See pp. 238, 260–63, for instance. Lewis also reported that King received a very encouraging telegram from Ralph Bunche for "the splendid work he was accomplishing in the 'vineyards of democracy." p. 72. Bunche also attended the historic 1963 March on Washington and sat on the dais with other dignitaries in attendance and participated in the 1965 Selma march. See pp. 225, 286. Bunche joined the chorus of King's critics on Vietnam, insisting "as early as October, 1965. . . . that Martin 'should positively and publicly give up one role or the other,' that of civil rights leader or that of international conciliator." P. 357. See also C. Eric Lincoln, *Martin Luther King, Jr.: A Profile*, pp. 44–46.

21. The left radicalism of most of these men and their class-based interpretive frameworks likely militated against a full appreciation of the religious dimension around which King mobilized. This includes Frazier, the great sociologist of African American family and church history, who died before most of key events of the civil rights and black power movements. King received the Nobel Prize in 1964 and increasingly saw himself as a "world citizen" or citizen of the world. Moreover, King is one of ten world martyrs of the twentieth century who are depicted in life-size statues at Westminster Abbey in London, memorializing the Innocent Victims of Oppression, Violence, and War circle, dedicated in 1996. At its west entrance, King is among the most well known of the martyrs. His statue stands near the center of the martyrs, between Bolshevik victim Grand Duchess Elizabeth of Russia and Archbishop Oscar Romero of San Salvador. Nazi victim Dietrich Bonhoeffer, whose thought and theology influenced King and Bonhoeffer's antinazi convictions were influenced by his encounter with US segregation and Harlem, New York. Several theological and biographical scholarly works favorably compare Bonhoeffer and King to one another.

22. Lerone Bennett, 1970. "When the Man and the Hour Are Met," in C. Eric Lincoln, *Martin Luther King, Jr.: A Profile*, p. 26. There is a well-documented history of Christian socialism that indirectly influenced King and the entire movement through such individuals as A. Philip Randolph, Ella Baker, Bayard Rustin, Du Bois, and Paul Robeson, who were not all Christian, but nevertheless embedded African American religious narratives, symbols, and traditions in their work.

23. Kenneth B. Clark (1961, pp. 36-37) cited in Hanes Walton Jr., *The Political Philosophy of Martin Luther King,* 1971, p. 99. Dr. Clark is known for the "doll study" included in the 1954 *Brown v. Board of Education* case.

24. Among the women Cruse includes in the redacted section of this quote are Rosa Parks and Angela Davis. Other men include Malcolm X, Medgar Evers, James Farmer, Stokely Carmichael, H. Rap Brown, Eldridge Cleaver, Huey Newton, Bobby Seale, and Jesse Jackson.

25. The "first civil rights cycle" was roughly 1868 through 1896.

26. This amounts to an extraordinary recognition on the part of Carmichael that places King at the center of black power's formation in Carmichael. Where he later distinguishes the Student Nonviolent Coordinating Committee (SNCC) from the Black Panther Party (BPP)—in terms of its organizational character and philosophical approach to community-based organizing—Carmichael notes precisely how SNCC, but not the BPP, had "the benefit of the highly experienced, politically activist adult membership that [SNCC] had. No Bayard, No Ella Baker, no James Lawson, no Dr. King." He accepted the principles of black power, called for it more or less forthrightly at times, while trying to discourage its open-ended susceptibility to racial threat, resentment, and violence.

27. Aside from the immediate recognition of King's impact by Cleaver, see the reference to the October 1968 Stanford University speech in this article. Also, see Peniel Joseph's description in *Waiting 'Til the Midnight Hour*, pp. 297–99.

28. Please see Scott Kurashige, "From Black Power to a Revolution of Values: Grace Lee Boggs and the Legacy of Martin Luther King, Jr.," in Nico Slate, ed., *Black Power Beyond Borders: The Global Dimensions of the Black Power Movement* (New York: Macmillan, 2012).

29. Cleaver, 1991, p. 94. The term "man" was replaced here.

30. Accompanying this characterization was regular reference to King and others as "handkerchief heads."

31. Here Malcolm X did not consider, for instance, that "house slaves" like Haiti's Toussaint L'Ouverture, "Black Gabriel," and Nat Turner (both of Virginia) led many of the more well-known insurrection plots of the nineteenth century Or that many field slaves betrayed the confidence of conspirators. David Walker, author of the incendiary *Appeal*, was born free, though he likely witnessed enslaved blacks firsthand in late eighteenth century of his childhood and youth and later in his travels South. He failed to mention the very influential Haitian Revolution as he covered the period "back during slavery" in his speech. Malcolm X also chose to ignore the 1859 antislavery uprising led by John Brown and his sons, white militant abolitionists. Apart from this, however, Malcolm X also bluntly demystified the march as a veritable coup against revolutionary black militancy, which was taken over by white and black liberal leaders, government officials (e.g., JFK), and civil society. Indeed, the march, viewed as the culmination of a century of struggle by King and others, for Malcolm X, coopted the "grassroots" of a broad black revolutionary impulse. Established black leaders including King and other members of the civil rights "big six" leadership group were juxtaposed to the "masses" of black people who were in the process of rejecting the "Negro revolution" and embracing the anticolonial "black revolution." Malcolm X offered one of the broadest conceptualizations of black nationalism ever constructed by a major leader or intellectual, one which incorporated all-nonwhite peoples' antiracist and anticapitalist struggles, globally.

32. For an expanded treatment of this argument, please see my *Black Nationalism in the United States: From Malcolm X to Barack Obama*.

33. Kevin Gaines, "Music Is a World: Stevie Wonder and the Sound of Black Power," in Nico Slate, ed., *Black Power beyond Borders: The Global Dimensions of the Black Power Movement* (New York: Macmillan, 2012), p. 191. While his essay provides a sketch of Stevie Wonder's importance in being influenced by the broad movement, it actually outlines the global transmission of US black militancy through noteworthy figures including Bob

Marley (of Jamaica), Duke Ellington, Aretha Franklin, Max Roach, John Coltrane, Billie Holiday, James Brown, Curtis Mayfield, Marvin Gaye, and Nina Simone—among others.

34. The argument in this section is not based on empirically grounded content analyses or leadership preference polling and would be considerably strengthened by an actual breakdown of the sampling patterns of African American leaders in rap music's various stages and genres. We are unaware of any such work, but it would not be sufficient to merely quantify, for instance, whether Public Enemy, Dead Prez, KRS-1, or X-CLAN sampled King say, *more or less* than Malcolm X in their tracks during the "Golden Age" of hip hop; it is the case regardless that the genre is more associated with Malcolm X.

35. See Thomas Conner, "Martin Luther King Jr.'s Dream Has a Place in Hip Hop: But It Wasn't Always That Way," *Washington Post*, August, 20, 2011. Please see for the full article http://www.washingtonpost.com/lifestyle/style/martin-luther-king-jrs-dream-has -a-place-in-hip-hop—but-it-wasnt-always-that-way/2011/07/15/gIQAQNmpSJ_story.html.

36. See the *XXL* compilation of 20 Songs that Reference Martin Luther King, Jr., http:// www.xxlmag.com/news/2014/01/20-rap-songs-reference-martin-luther-king-jr/.

37. The actual footage of the short piece is widely distributed on Youtube and other social media sites. Cornel West, ed., *The Radical King* (*Martin Luther King, Jr.*) (Boston: Beacon, 2015) adds to the existing literature on King's radicalization.

38. Please see the lyrical references to leaders such as King, Jesse Jackson, Hillary Clinton, and philanthropist Bill Gates. http://www.azlyrics.com/lyrics/game/lettertothek ing.html.

39. McGruder's approach brings to mind Julian West, the narrator/protagonist of Edward Bellamy's utopian classic *Looking Backward: 2000–1887*. It used a device widely employed in European and Victorian American literary works. In brief, the plot shows West to be tormented in 1887 by insomnia and the excesses of the Gilded Age and the Industrial Revolution. He goes to a silent chamber and falls asleep until the year 2000, when the world has evolved into a condition of equality, public art works, and unnamed socialism, without violence; his sleeping state, of the sort of the fictional character "Rip Van Winkle" (1819) insinuates a nonviolent Fabian socialism. Of course Washington Irving's Rip Van Winkle slept through the brutal American Revolution and awoke twenty years later. King's coma condition can thus take on a meaning about the times when he was in a thirty-five-year-long coma, even as his condition was prompted by history-shattering violence aimed at him. King sleeps for decades following the assassination attempt and through every major development in African American life since. But I do not mean to stretch the point.

40. For a summary of some of the criticisms of hip hop, please see http://hiphop wired.com/2012/01/16/would-dr-martin-luther-king-approve-of-hip-hops-current-state -editorial/#sthash.a7n0Fkek.dpuf.

41. But it can be taken from King's very careful "management" of the black power event and furor that he may have reacted to these developments in hip hop with a middling position; he routinely condemned the abject living conditions of the poor among black Americans and simultaneously insisted on traditional black Protestant moral codes and respectability.

42. As part of an explanation for selling a T-shirt line of Confederate flags, West, the son of a Fulbright Scholar and English professor Donda West (deceased), insisted, "I just

think people look cool in it. They look nice. And it's colorless also. . . . It's super hood and super white boy approved at the same time." See this link, for instance: http://www .huffingtonpost.com/2013/10/29/kanye-west-confederate-flag-shirt-explained-_n _4173200.html. The 2015 massacre of nine worshippers in Charleston, South Carolina, led to a widely covered debate and ongoing confrontations among groups and also with law enforcement. #BlackLivesMatter repudiated the Confederate flag, leading one young woman to mount the flagpole and take down the flag. Governor Nikki Haley and the South Carolina state legislature lead in the removal of it from state property.

43. Moreover, there were controversies centering on the Quentin Tarantino film *Django* and LL Cool J's "Accidental Racist" duet with country singer Brad Paisley, a song where hip hop's gold chains are portrayed as offensive to American whites, as the chains of enslaved Africans and Negroes would be to most present-day black Americans). Consider Jay Z responding to criticizing Harry Belafonte by referring to the eighty-six-year-old, as "boy" in "Nickel and Dime" July 16, 2013. On a new track, "Nickles and Dimes," he says: "I'm just trying to find common ground/ 'Fore Mr. Belafonte come and chop a n*gga down/ Mr. Day O, major fail/ Respect these youngins boy, it's my time now/two door homie/ You don't know all the sh*t I do for the homies." To be fair, this response was prompted in part when Mr. Belafonte stated that Bruce Springsteen "is black" in social justice commitments in comparison to Jay Z and Beyonce.

44. The seventy-four-year-old Lost Poets member Dahveed Nelson (formerly David) insisted, from Ghana, Africa, in 2013, "[T]his whole Hip-Hop generation, is the devil. It's Satan. It's hedonism. It's the pursuit of pleasure. There's no soul. They've captured our medium." For him, "[Jay-Z] is one of the most wealthy people in America, certainly one of the wealthiest blacks and most influential, for being a n***er, for putting on blackface and cooning. That's what he's getting paid for. . . . You can put the blame squarely on Hip Hop. . . . The enemy has its responsibilities, but you've got the collaborators. That's what the whole Hip Hop culture is." Please   http://allhiphop.com/2013/07/15/dahveed-nelson -of-the-last-poets-says-hip-hop-is-now-the-devil-calls-jay-z-a-coon/.

45. The 2:56-minute song makes no reference directly to Malcolm X, but it uses "n*gga" just short of forty times (this reflects an emergent rap genre that might be properly labeled "nigga rap"). This nonetheless prompted Brooklyn-based hip hop journalist and activist Kevin Powell to direct his "BK Nation" alliance in a petition and boycott of Minaj. See for instance Bobby Shmurda's "Hot Nigga."

46 Several months of protest, confrontation, and rioting, and rage was unleashed on the local police department and its surrounding area police forces, a massive paramilitary police riot, after the death of eighteen-year-old Michael Brown.

47. It was created to mock mass media representations of black youth caught in the crosshairs of official misconduct and vigilante violence aimed at black young people in the twenty-first century. The hashtag started trending on Twitter after media outlets circulated scandalous images of Michael Brown, in a manner done also in the Trayvon Martin case. Many of the tweets containing the hashtag showed contrasting images of the same person in the photos in "respectable" and stereotyped imagery and poses. At one point, the link became so frequently spread in the intensity of the violence in Ferguson that it was

shut down for a period. See http://www.chron.com/news/article/IfTheyGunnedMeDown
-hashtag-goes-viral-in-the-5684202.php 8/24/14).

48. Common mournfully lyricizes over hip hop's move to its "gangsta rap" phase and
eventual unrecognizability. Indeed throughout the piece, hip hop is unrecognized as the
subject, until its very end, when he reveals, that "her" was hip hop, and not a woman with
whom he had parted.

REFERENCES

Bennett, L., Jr. 1964. *What Manner of Man: A Memorial Biography of Martin Luther King Jr.* Chicago: Johnson.

———. 1970. "When the Man and the Hour Are Met." In *Martin Luther King, Jr.: A Profile,* ed. C. Eric Lincoln. New York: Hill and Wang.

Bonnette, L. 2015. *Pulse of the People: Political Rap Music and Black Politics.* Philadelphia: University of Pennsylvania Press.

Boyd, Todd. 1997. *Am I Black Enough for You? Popular Culture from the 'Hood and Beyond.* Bloomington: Indiana University Press.

———. 2003. *The New H.N.I.C.: The Death of Civil Rights and the Reign of Hip Hop.* New York: New York University Press.

Campbell, H. 1987. *Rasta and Resistance: From Marcus Garvey to Walter Rodney.* Trenton, NJ: Africa World.

Carmichael, S. (Kwame Ture), and E. M. Thelwell. 2005. *Ready for Revolution: The Life and Struggles of Stokely Carmichael (Kwame Ture).* New York: Scribner Books.

Carson, C. 2003. "Foreword." In Scot Brown, *Fighting for US: Maulana Karenga, the US Organization and Black Cultural Nationalism.* New York: New York University Press.

Charnas, D. 2011. *The Big Pay Back: The History of the Business of Hip-Hop.* New York: New American Library [Penguin Books].

Charise C. 2005. *Brothers Gonna Work It Out: Sexual Politics in the Golden Age of Rap Nationalism.* New York: New York University Press.

———. 2005. "In Search of the 'Revolutionary Generation': Engendering the Golden Age of Rap Nationalism." *The Journal of African American History; The History of Hip Hop* (Summer, 2005): 278–98.

Cleaver, E. 1967. "The Death of Martin Luther King: Requiem for Nonviolence." In *Eldridge Cleaver,* ed. Robert Scheer. New York: Ramparts Books [Random House].

———. 1967 (1991). *Soul on Ice.* New York: Random House.

Conner, T. 2011. "Martin Luther King Jr.'s Dream Has a Place in Hip Hop: But It Wasn't Always That Way." *Washington Post,* August 20.

Council of Black Internal Affairs. 2002. *The American Directory of Certified Uncle Toms.* Trenton, New Jersey: Lushena Books.

Cruse, H. 1987. *Plural but Equal: A Critical Study of Blacks and Minorities and America's Plural Society.* New York: William Morrow.

Dyson, M. E. 2000. *I May Not Get There with You: The True Martin Luther King, Jr.* New York: Simon and Schuster.

Gaines, K. 2012. "Music Is a World: Stevie Wonder and the Sound of Black Power." In *Black Power beyond Borders: The Global Dimensions of the Black Power Movement*, ed. Nico Slate. New York: Macmillan.

Harding, V. 1981. *There Is a River: The Black Struggle for Freedom in America*. New York: Harvest Book [Harcourt, Brace, and Company].

———. 2008. *Martin Luther King: The Inconvenient Hero*. Maryknoll, NY: Orbis.

Henderson, E. 1996. "Black Nationalism and Rap Music." *Journal of Black Studies* 26(3) (January): 308-39.

Henson, J. P. 1849. *The Life of Josiah Henson, Formerly a Slave, Now an Inhabitant of Canada, as Narrated by Himself*. Boston: Arthur D. Phelps.

Herbers, J. 1970. *The Lost Priority: What Happened to the Civil Rights Movement in America?* Clarion, IA: Funk and Wagnalls.

Iton, R. 2008. *In Search of the Black Fantastic: Politics and Popular Culture in the Post-Civil Rights Era*. Oxford: Oxford University Press.

Johnson, P. 2003. *Appropriating Blackness: Performance and the Politics of Authenticity*. Durham, NC: Duke University Press.

Jones, M. 2014. *Knowledge, Power, and Black Politics*. Albany: State University of New York Press.

Joseph, P. 2006. *Waiting 'til the Midnight Hour: A Narrative History of Black Power in America*. New York: Owl Books.

Kelly, R. 1996. *Race Rebels: Culture, Politics, and the Black Working Class*. New York: Verso.

King, M. L., Jr. 1968. *Where Do We Go from Here: Chaos or Community?* Boston: Beacon.

Keiser, R. 1997. *Subordination or Empowerment?: African-American Leadership and the Struggle for Urban Political Power*. Oxford: Oxford University Press.

Kennedy, R. 2008. *Sellout: The Politics of Racial Betrayal*. New York: Vintage.

Kitwana, B. 2002. *The Hip Hop Generation: Young Blacks and the Crisis in African-American Culture*. New York: Basic Civitas Books.

Kurashige, S. 2012. "From Black Power to a Revolution of Values: Grace Lee Boggs and the Legacy of Martin Luther King, Jr." In *Black Power Beyond Borders: The Global Dimensions of the Black Power Movement*, ed. Nico Slate. New York: Macmillan.

Lewis, D. L. 1970. *King: A Biography*. Urbana: University of Illinois Press.

———. *When Harlem Was in Vogue*. [1981] 1997. New York: Penguin Press.

Lincoln, C. E., ed. 1970. *Martin Luther King Jr.: A Profile*. New York: Hill and Wang.

Lomax, L. 1968. *To Kill a Black Man*. Los Angeles: Holloway House.

Marable, M. 1995. *Beyond Black and White: Transforming African American Politics*. New York: Verso 1995.

McGuire, D. L. 2010. *At the Dark End of the Street: Black Women, Rape, and Resistance: A New History of the Civil Rights Movement from Rosa Parks to the Rise of Black Power*. New York: Vintage Books.

McKnight, Gerald D. 1998. *The Last Crusade: Martin Luther King, Jr., the FBI, and the Poor People's Campaign*. Boulder: Westview.

Miller, M. R. 2012. *Religion and Hip Hop*. New York: Routledge.

Miller, M. R., and A. B. Pinn. 2014. *The Hip Hop Reader*. New York: Routledge.

_____. 2015. *Religion and Hip Hop: Mapping the New Terrain in the U.S.* London: Bloomsbury Academic.

Morgan, M., and D. Bennett. 2011. "Hip-Hop and the Global Imprint of a Black Cultural Form." *Daedalus, the Journal of the American Academy of Arts and Sciences* 140(2) (Spring).

Moses, W. J. 1993. *Black Messiahs and Uncle Toms: Social and Literary Manipulations of a Religious Myth*, 1982; Revised edition: Pennsylvania State Univ. Press.

Neal, M. A. 1999. *What the Music Said: Black Popular Music and Black Public Culture*. New York: Routledge.

———. 2002. *Soul Babies: Black Popular Culture and the Post-Soul Aesthetic*. New York: Routledge.

Neal, R. B. 2013. "Savior of the Race: The Messianic Burdens of Black Masculinity," *Exchange* 42, pp. 51-67.

Newton, H. P., V. I. Lenin, and A. Gdala, eds. 2004. *Revolutionary Intercommunalism and the Right of Nations to Self-Determination*. UK: Cyhoeddwyr Superscript.

Ogbar, J. 2007. *Hip-Hop Revolution: The Culture and Politics of Rap*. Lawrence: University Press of Kansas.

Peller, G. 2012. *Critical Race Consciousness: Reconsidering American Ideologies of Race*. Boulder: Paradigm.

Perkins, W. E. 1996. *Droppin Science: Critical Essays on Rap Music and Hip Hop Culture*. Philadelphia: Temple University Press.

Perry, I. 2004. *Prophets of the Hood: Politics and Poetics in Hip Hop*. Durham, NC: Duke University Press.

———. *Black Nationalism in the United States: From Malcolm X to Barack Obama*. 2011. Boulder, CO: Lynne Rienner.

Quinn, E. 2004. *Nuthin' but a "G" Thang: The Culture and Commerce of Gangsta Rap*. New York: Columbia University Press.

Rebaka, R. 2011. Hip Hop's Inheritance: *From the Harlem Renaissance to the Hip Hop Feminist Movement*. Lanham, MD: Lexington Books.

Reddick, L. D. 1959. *Crusader without Violence: A Biography of Martin Luther King, Jr.* New York: Harper's and Brothers.

Robinson, C. 1997. *Black Social Movements in America*. New York: Routledge.

Rose, T. 1994. *Black Noise: Rap Music and Black Culture in Contemporary America*. Middletown, CT: Wesleyan University Press.

———. 2008. *Hip Hop Wars*. New York: Basic Books.

Shaw, T. 2009. *Now Is the Time!: Detroit Black Politics and Grassroots Activism*. Durham, NC: Duke University Press.

Schlesinger, A. M., Jr. 1986. *The Cycles of American History*. New York: Houghton Mifflin.

Scheer, R., ed. 1967. *Eldridge Cleaver*. New York: Ramparts Books [Random House].

Singh, N. P. 2004. *Black Is a Country: Race and the Unfinished Struggle for Democracy*. Cambridge MA: Harvard University Press.

Slate, N., ed. 2012. *Black Power beyond Borders: The Global Dimensions of the Black Power Movement*. New York: Macmillan.

Spence, L. 2011. *Stare in the Darkness: The Limits of Hip-Hop and Black Politics*. Minneapolis: University of Minnesota Press.

Steinmetz, K. F., and H. Henderson. 2012. "Hip–Hop and Procedural Justice: Hip Hop Artists' Perceptions of Criminal Justice." *Race and Justice* 2(3)(July): 155–78.

Stoute, S. 2011. *The Tanning of America: How Hip-Hop Created a Culture That Rewrote the Rules of the New Economy*. New York: Gotham-Penguin Books.

Taylor, J. L. 2011 [2014]. *Black Nationalism in the United States: From Malcolm X to Barack*. Boulder: Lynne Rienner.

Umoja, A. O. 2013. *We Will Shoot Back: Armed Resistance in the Mississippi Freedom Movement*. New York: New York University Press.

Wallace, M. [1978] 1999. *Black Macho and the Myth of the Superwoman*. New York: Verso.

Walton, H., Jr. 1970. *The Political Philosophy of Martin Luther King, Jr*. Westport, CT: Greenwood.

Watkins, S. C. 1998. *Representing: Hip Hop Culture and the Production of Black Cinema*. Chicago: University of Chicago Press.

Wilson, W. J. 1978. *The Declining Significance of Race: Blacks and Changing American Institutions*. Chicago: University of Chicago Press.</bib>

ON REDEFINING CIVIL RIGHTS

Amardo Rodriguez

On every Martin Luther King Jr. holiday in January, King's "I Have a Dream" speech will be played again and again and again. There will be endless black-and-white images across the media of the 1963 March on Washington that supposedly changed everything and made everything better. We will hear about that coming day when black and white children will walk arm in arm. We will also hear many calls for racial healing and view endless images of diverse peoples praying, hugging, singing, swaying, kissing, and hand-holding. Our impression of Dr. King as being the person who united the races will be reinforced. He will be cast as a kind of patron saint of the races. Throughout the day, discussions of Martin Luther King will be confined to issues of race, racial equality, and discrimination, although King said in 1964, "I'm much more than a civil rights leader" (Bond, 1993). We will debate how much of King's dream of inclusion and integration has been achieved, although King said that "There must be a better distribution of wealth. . . . We can't have a system where some of the people live in superfluous, inordinate wealth while others live in abject, deadening poverty" (ibid.).

Martin Luther King Jr. has been properly sanitized and scrubbed of all politics. He has been packaged for mass appeal and put in service of a national narrative that stresses our racial progress and moral superiority. On every Martin Luther King Jr. holiday there will be hardly any mention in the media of King's positions on poverty, equality, and, most of all, violence and war, though King publicly voiced those positions again and again (Dyson, 2000; Smiley, 2014). About the sanitizing and depoliticizing of King's legacy, William Lamar, director of the Foundations of Christian Leadership Program at Duke University's Divinity School, noted, "We have essentially made him a nice Negro who brings us toys in January [and] who tells us that we are a colorblind society" (Ross, 2013).

What is striking about our continuing sanitizing and depoliticizing of King is that the United States is still waging war on many fronts, and poverty, hunger, and homelessness are on the rise as the gap between rich and poor now reaches record levels. What is also striking about this sanitizing and depoliticizing of King is that many African Americans remain trapped in a new Jim Crow—unsurpassed numbers of African Americans incarcerated, politically disenfranchised, and economically ostracized as a result of having a felony conviction for a nonviolent offense (Alexander, 2010; Petitt, 2012; Weiman, Western, and Patillo, 2006). Marian Wright Edelman (2011), founder and president of the Children's Defense Fund, contended that the unsurpassed incarceration of African Americans constituted "a historically punitive form of social control and social death" that threatened to overwhelm and "destroy millions of our children's futures."

On nearly every January 17 there will also be no airing, or discussing, or quoting of Martin Luther's King's "A Time to Break Silence" speech that was delivered on April 4, 1967, at a meeting of Clergy and Laity Concerned at Riverside Church in New York City, declaring his opposition to the Vietnam War. There would also be no mention of the backlash and harsh criticisms that King received for publicly opposing the war and giving the speech. There would therefore be no reminders that the New York Times editorialized that King's opposition to the war was "wasteful and self-defeating" and likely to be "disastrous for both causes" ("Dr. King's Error," 1967, p. 36). The New York Times said that King was fusing "two public problems [civil rights and peace] that are distinct and separate," and, besides doing "a disservice to both," would presumably only make for confusion rather than solutions. Nor would there be any reminders that the Washington Post editorialized that King had "done a grave injury to those who are his natural allies in a great struggle to remove ancient abuses from our public life; and he has done an even graver injury to himself. Many persons who once viewed King with respect will never again accord him the same confidence. He has diminished his usefulness to his cause, his country, and his people" ("A Tragedy," 1967, p. A20). Time magazine said King's speech was "demagogic slander that sounded like a script for Radio Hanoi," and Life magazine declared that King had done a disservice to the civil rights cause.

Milton Sacks of Brandeis University and past director of Vietnamese affairs in the State Department's intelligence bureau said that King's Riverside speech did a "disservice to the American people, the Vietnamese people, and to the cause of people in a troubled world." Ernest W. Lefever (1970), founder of the Ethics and Public Policy Center, an organization "dedicated to applying the Judeo-Christian moral tradition to critical issues of public policy," said that "King's Riverside speech gave aid and comfort to the enemies of peaceful change in Southeast Asia as well as to their allies in Moscow and Peking. It directed anger against the US Government—perhaps the major temporal force for peace in the world. It pronounced an indirect benediction upon the revolutionary and nihilistic agencies seeking to destroy the foundations of Western justice and freedom" (p. 12). Moreover, for Lefever, "King's Riverside Church speech seriously violated the moral limits of public debate and advocacy. His unrelenting attack on American society and government, its distortions and falsehoods, all presented in the garb of self-righteousness, was a disservice to the American people and a service to the forces of revolutionary violence" (p. 12). Lefever concluded that "King's attempt to join the causes of "freedom" and "peace" appears to have had the effect of sowing confusion in both camps, thereby making more difficult the achievement of equality under the law at home and a sound policy toward the Third World" (p. 14). In sum, on every January 17 there would be no commemoration of King's "Time to Break the Silence" speech like that given to King's "I Have a Dream" speech.

The Martin Luther King Jr. found in the "I Have a Dream" speech poses no threat to the status quo. We can comfortably celebrate this King. He makes us feel good about ourselves. He reinforces our view of ourselves as good, decent, tolerant, and morally progressive. However, his "A Time to Break the Silence" speech challenges everything we value, believe, and assume. It torments our conception of ourselves and openly calls into question our civility and decency. King knew that there would be consequences for challenging us this way. He knew that he was supposed to be a race man, and there would be consequences for speaking on a matter—the Vietnam War—that seemingly had nothing to do with race and civil rights. But King knew well that in this case "silence would be a betrayal." He would be forsaking the call of moral courage. He now had to "speak from the burnings of [his] own heart." So that evening at Riverside Church in 1967 Martin Luther King Jr. began by addressing the issue head on: "Why are you speaking about war, Dr. King? Why are you joining the voices of dissent? Peace and civil rights don't mix, they say. Aren't you hurting the cause of your people, they ask?" King said he was "greatly saddened" by such questions because they reveal that even many in the civil rights movement did not really understand "my commitment or my calling." However, "I believe that the path from Dexter Avenue Baptist Church—the church in Montgomery, Alabama, where I began my pastorate—leads clearly to this sanctuary [Riverside Church] tonight" (King, 1967).

King turned next to explaining why the promotion of peace and opposition to the Vietnam War were integral to the success of the civil rights

movement. According to King, there were many "major reasons for bringing Vietnam into the field of my moral vision." To begin with, the war was
taking resources away from improving the lives of the poor in the United
States. As such, the "war was an enemy of the poor." Moreover, "the war
was doing far more than devastating the hopes of the poor at home. It was
sending their sons and their brothers and their husbands to fight and to die
in extraordinarily high proportions relative to the rest of the population."
There was also "the cruel irony of watching Negro and white boys . . . kill
and die together for a nation that has been unable to seat them together in
the same schools."

Still, for King, the matter of opposing the Vietnam War went much further.
It was about moral consistency. He had to speak out because the US government was "the greatest purveyor of violence in the world today." Thus for "the
sake of those boys, for the sake of this government, for the sake of hundreds
of thousands trembling under our violence, I cannot be silent." Then there
was a moral obligation that came with being a Nobel Peace laureate—the
obligation to oppose war and violence. King said that the Nobel Prize for
Peace came with a commission "to work harder" for "the brotherhood of
man." This meant moving "beyond national allegiances" and struggling for
the liberation of all human beings from misery and oppression. Finally, there
was for King the matter of simply trying to be a decent Christian and finding
the courage to embody the life and teachings of Jesus Christ. According to
King, "I must be true to my conviction that I share with all men the calling
to be a son of the living God." This living God, said King, is deeply concerned
about the suffering of those who are "outcast." As Christians, "We are called to
speak for the weak, for the voiceless, for victims of our nation and for those
it calls enemy, for no document from human hands can make these humans
any less our brothers."

Ultimately, King's point was that our conception of civil rights is highly
narrow. It limits the stakes involved in the struggle and the sacrifices the
struggle requires. Civil rights is about the right of every human being, regardless of race or creed, to be spared from misery as a result of the actions
and decisions of others. Moreover, our conception of civil rights limits our
understanding of the struggle's ambitions. It assumes that the struggle is
merely about the inclusion and accommodation of those who are racially different and have been historically brutalized and marginalized. But, for King,
civil rights was ultimately about speaking for "the weak, for the voiceless, for
victims of our nation and for those it calls enemy." For "these humans" are

"no less our brothers" and sisters. For King, viewing civil rights in terms of race impeded moral courage, as in the courage necessary to speak on behalf of "the victims of our nation and those it calls enemy." He returned to this point again and again that evening at Riverside Church. For King, moral courage meant calling for empathy for those waging war upon the United States in Vietnam.

To understand the enormity of King's challenge merely requires us to ask who would make such a call in a post–September 11 world in the United States? If King were to make such a call today, the reaction would be no different than that in 1967. He would once again be rebuked for giving moral and political comfort to the enemy. In many ways what King was saying that evening at Riverside Church—exactly one year from his death—was what Frederick Douglas said long ago: "No man can put a chain about the ankle of his fellow man without at last finding the other end fastened about his own neck." For King, the civil rights struggle was really a struggle to save the soul of all of humanity by removing all the conditions that make violence possible and justifiable. To subject any person to violence is to subject all of humanity to violence. Thus, on that evening at Riverside Church Martin Luther King was compelled to "speak as a citizen of the world," "a child of God," and "a brother to the suffering poor" to cease immediately the "madness" that is war.

Violence is ultimately responsible for the misery that has tortured the lives of black folks. Poverty is violence. Discrimination is violence. Indifference is violence. This is why, for King, nonviolence had to be foundational to the civil rights movement. As King said in 1957, "The end of violence or the aftermath of violence is bitterness. The aftermath of nonviolence is reconciliation and the creation of a beloved community." For King, war was a moral and spiritual abomination that eroded the humanity of those waging war and as well as those who are the victims of war.

Yet King's position on the Vietnam War was also publicly opposed by many in the civil rights movement and the African American community. Carl T. Rowan (1967), in an article titled "Martin Luther King's Tragic Decision," said that King had alienated "many of the Negro's friends and armed the Negro's foes . . . by creating the impression that the Negro is disloyal" (p. 37). Indeed, soon after the Riverside speech, the NAACP said in a statement that King had made a "serious tactical mistake" and the effort to merge the two movements would neither serve the cause of "civil rights nor of peace." The NAACP unanimously passed a resolution declaring,

Civil rights battles will have to be fought and won on their own merits, irrespective of the state of war or peace in the world. We are not a peace organization nor a foreign policy association. We are a civil rights organization. The N.A.A.C.P. remains committed to its primary goal of eliminating all forms of racial discrimination and achieving civil rights and equal opportunities for all Americans. We are, of course, for a just peace. But there already exist dedicated organizations whose No. 1 task is to work for peace just as our No. 1 job is to work for civil rights. (N.A.A.C.P. Decries Stand, 1967, p. 1)

Henry Lee Moon, director of public relations for the NAACP, said that the organization believed that "it was time to make a declaration, to make our position clear." Whitney M. Young Jr., director of the National Urban League, also agreed that the civil rights movement and the peace movement had different goals and fusing them would be a mistake. He said that "urgent domestic programs of civil rights and the issue of the war in Vietnam should remain separate" (Robinson, 1967, p. 10). Ralph J. Bunche, the first African American Nobel Peace Laureate, also criticized King for trying to be involved in two movements that "have too little in common" (Sibley, 1967, p. 1). He said King should "positively and publicly give up one role or the other" as "he is making a serious tactical error which will do harm to the civil rights struggle" by alienating "many friends and supporters of the civil rights movement" (p. 32). For the civil rights movement and many African Americans, "[t]he violence of the cities had nothing to do with the violence of the war" (Bromwich, 2008).

But how did so many in the civil rights movement come to believe that the struggle for justice and the struggle for peace had nothing to do with each other? Put differently, how did so many in the civil rights movement come to believe exactly what opponents of the civil rights movements believed and propagated? Yet this belief persists within the modern civil rights movement as seen by the unwillingness of any civil rights organization to make any declaration calling for the end of the different kinds of wars the United States is now waging around the world. Indeed, nearly fifty years after the Civil Rights Act of 1964, what has come from the separation of the struggle for justice from the struggle for peace? How valuable has this separation proven for African Americans and other peoples who have been historically brutalized and marginalized?

To contend that the struggle for justice is separate from the justice for peace obligates us to make the case that the enormous resources allocated to military spending and financing different wars had no significant bearing on the lives of peoples who have been historically deprived or could have significantly contributed to improving the lives of these peoples. But meeting this obligation is impossible. There is always a morality that guides the allocation of resources. The resources that waging war demands must be taken from other places that are also in competition for resources. One key point King was making at Riverside Church that evening was that war is an enemy of the poor. It consumes the resources that the poor need most. In many ways King has been vindicated by history. All of the resources (both human and monetary) spent in Vietnam and many other wars since could have been better utilized in improving the lives of many peoples who have been historically deprived of many valuable resources. Thus, what have the poor achieved from our continuing separation of the struggle for justice from the struggle for peace? How does the unsurpassed incarceration of black and poor peoples—the New Jim Crow, to use Michelle Alexander's words—testify to the value of sustaining this separation?

ON THE NATURE OF PEACE

Martin Luther King Jr.'s vision of civil rights, as eloquently articulated that evening at Riverside Church in 1967, remains on the margins of many politics for social justice. As found in "just war" discourses, there is still a deep belief that certain wars are necessary and morally defensible. Even a large number of Nobel Peace laureates contend that many wars are just and moral. To advocate for peace is still seen as reflecting a profound naiveté, one that has, according to one famous Nobel Peace laureate, no "recognition of history, the imperfections of man and the limits of reason" (Obama, 2009). For instance, in criticizing King's position on the Vietnam war, Milton Sacks (1967) said, "We live in a free world where free men cannot survive without mastering the techniques of violence, even granting the arguments that pacifists make. . . . And this is one of the hard and bitter facts of the world we live in." However, to promote peace is to oppose violence, especially the everyday and ordinary violent practices that ultimately give rise to all manner of racism, ethnocentrism, and terrorism that make war inevitable. War is an ultimate outcome. Peace is about removing all the practices and conditions that cultivate and legitimize violence. Without violence, war is impossible. To cast peace as the negation of war is misleading, as doing so fosters the impression that peace is the absence of war. This is false as slavery and Jim Crow were found in places where war was absent.

To promote peace is to cultivate practices and conditions that undermine the possibility and legitimacy of violence. It is about cultivating a new vision of the world that makes violence impossible. King believed that violence is a threat to all of humanity. Violence torments the marginalized and disenfranchised. Violence makes us less human. Violence is the antithesis of love, which King believed is the only path to prosperity. Violence begins in our failure to recognize that our own humanity is bound up with the humanity of others. This is why, for King, the civil rights movement had to be fundamentally about ending violence. He believed that to be included in a society that values and promotes any kind of violence represents no kind of moral and political evolution.

If there is any supposed "harsh truth" of history it is that violence makes war inevitable and justifiable. As King said that evening at Riverside Church, "Those who make peaceful revolution impossible will make violent revolution inevitable." We lessen the possibility of war by impeding or removing the conditions that promote and legitimize violence. There is simply no such thing as a morally just war. To accept the premise of a just war is to mask all of the violence that ultimately makes war possible. This indeed is the height of naiveté. No less naïve is believing that in a world that is increasingly laden with nuclear weapons, any war, regardless of however just and moral, is winnable and even survivable. For "just war" advocates, "our challenge" is to reconcile "two seemingly irreconcilable truths—that war is sometimes necessary, and war at some level is an expression of human folly." But this is another false schism as war will always reflect a lack of moral imagination. This can be seen in the fact that any future war involving nuclear weapons, regardless of however just and moral, will most likely vanquish us all. What then is the value of planning and resourcing for such a war? For persons like King who oppose violence, the challenge is to remove all the practices and conditions that promote and legitimize violence. There are no illusions about our capacity and even proclivity for evil. Opposing violence and promoting peace is fundamentally about being committed to removing all the ideological, social, and material conditions that excite, encourage, and legitimize violence, such as ending our own incarceration of so many peoples for nonviolent offenses, reversing the growing gap between rich and poor, ending poverty and despair, reconfiguring our relation to the planet so as to lessen our impact, encouraging self-determination for all peoples, releasing peoples from the structures and forces of imperialism and colonialism, fostering cooperation between different peoples, and ending retribution as a foundation for justice.

We can understand well the case for just war and the anguish that comes with supporting such wars. But no war, regardless of our capacity and proclivity for evil, evolves out of an ideological and material vacuum. This is "a plain fact" and "a hard truth." To promote peace and oppose violence is to recognize only too well our abundant and stubborn capacity to create misery and wage war. However, to promote peace and oppose violence is also about recognizing that peace rather than violence ultimately constitutes a more constructive path to our survival and prosperity.

FINAL THOUGHTS

Ideology makes memory selective. To remember the King at Riverside Church is to remember how King by 1967 was poorly treated by a significant portion of the African American community (Smiley, 2014). This is the King that many prominent black pastors publicly said in April 1967 was unwelcome in Chicago and also an "outsider" who should "stay in Alabama" ("Negro Pastors," 1967). To remember this King is also to remember the harsh words spoken to him by liberal elites and members of the civil rights movement for opposing the Vietnam War and condemning the US obsession with war. Naturally, many would now prefer to forget this King at Riverside Church or simply pretend this King never was. This is why the "I Have a Dream" speech must be played again and again. We use this King to mask the King at Riverside Church. Reconciling the King at Riverside Church with the King of "I Have a Dream" is hard. The King at Riverside Church can be tormenting. Whereas the King of 1963 works well as a history lesson, the King of 1967 remains as relevant as ever as the US continues to wage many wars and devote enormous resources toward readying for and waging war. Thus, what of the complicity of the black community and the civil rights movement in helping marginalize and even silence the King of 1967? What and whose interests are best and least served in the marginalizing and silencing of this King?

On that evening at Riverside Church, Martin Luther King Jr. was challenging us to come to a fundamentally new conception of what being human means: the condition of our own humanity is bound up in the condition of others' humanity. Any abuse of others falls back on all of us. This is King's case against war and violence. Those who wage war and promote violence also become disfigured and dehumanized by war and violence. On that evening at Riverside Church in 1967 King was challenging our worldview and how our society is organized. He was calling into question the legitimacy of our commonly held notions of decency and civility. Our belief in the necessity of violence cannot be separated from our unsurpassed incarceration of black, brown, and poor peoples for nonviolent offenses; the ever-widening gap between rich and poor; and the ecological peril that now looms as a result of our own doing.

But the modern civil rights movement remains obsessed with race and ending discrimination. It continues to show no profound understanding of how the United States is ideologically situated and organized in ways that legitimize and promote violence and war. That the country can elect a black president who will do nothing to disrupt the existing conditions shows well how race and a politics of inclusion pose no threat to the status quo. We can now have a black president and still believe that violence and war are morally defensible. We can now have a black president and still bear witness to the rise of a new Jim Crow, an ever-widening gap between rich and poor, and an unrelenting onslaught on the planet. In many ways, this is what Martin Luther King Jr. was warning us against on that evening at Riverside Church: mistaking the struggle for inclusion for the struggle for justice. The latter involves changing our view of the world as well as how we view ourselves in relation to each other.

REFERENCES

"A Tragedy." 1967. *Washington Post*, April 6, p. A20.

Alexander, M. 2010. *The New Jim Crow: Mass Incarceration in the Age of Colorblindness.* New York: New Press.

Bond, J. 1993. Remember the Man and the Hero, Not Just Half the Dream. *Seattle Times.* *http://seattletimes.com/special/mlk/perspectives/reflections/bond.html.*April 4.

Bromwich, D. 2008. Martin Luther King's speech against the Vietnam war. *http://antiwar* *.com/orig/bromwich.php?articleid=12844.* May 16

"Dr. King's error." 1967. *New York Times*, April 7, p. 36.

Dyson, M. E. 2000. *I May Not Get There with You: The True Martin Luther King, Jr.* New York: Touchstone.

King Jr., Martin Luther. "Beyond Vietnam." Address delivered to the Clergy and Laymen concerned about Vietnam, at Riverside Church, New York City, April 4, 1967. https:// ratical.org/ratville/JFK/MLKapr67.html.

Lefever, E. W. 1970. "Reckless Rhetoric and Foreign Policy." *Worldview* (November): 9–12.

"N.A.A.C.P. Decries Stand of Dr. King on Vietnam." 1967. *New York Times*, April 11, pp. 1, 17.

"Negro Pastors in Chicago Bid Dr. King End Marches." 1967. *New York Times*, April 20, p. 38.

Obama, B. "Acceptance Speech." Remarks by the President at the Acceptance of the Nobel Peace Prize, Oslo City Hall, Oslo, Norway, December 10, 2009. https://www.whitehouse.gov/the-press-office/remarks-president-acceptance-nobel-peace-prize.

Petitt, B. 2012. *Invisible Men: Mass Incarceration and the Myth of Black Progress*. New York: Russell Sage.

Robinson, D. 1967. "Jewish Veterans Attack Dr. King's Stand on War." *New York Times*, April 6, p. 10.

Ross, J. 2013. "Obama's Inaugural Speech Salutes King, but Highlights Differences." *Huffington Post*. http://www.huffingtonpost.com/2013/01/21/obama-king_n_2521679.html

Rowan, C. T. 1967. "Martin Luther King's Tragic Decision." *Reader's Digest*, September, pp. 37–42.

Sacks, M. 1967. *An Answer to Dr. Martin Luther King*. Speech given in New York, April. Part of the Schomburg Center Oral History Tape Collection.

Sibley, J. 1967. "Bunchie Disputes Dr. King on Peace." *New York Times*, April 13, pp. 1, 32.

Smiley, T. 2014. *Death of a King: The Real Story of Dr. Martin Luther King Jr.'s Final Year*. New York: Little, Brown.

Weiman, D., B. Western, and M. Patillo. 2006. *Imprisoning America: The Social Effects of Mass Incarceration*. New York: Russell Sage.

Wright Edelman, M. 2011. "The New Jim Crow." *New York Beacon*, March 17, pp. 8, 25.

EPILOGUE

King's Enduring Relevance

Michael L. Clemons

The chapters in this volume are a bold pronouncement of the timelessness of the King legacy, which for the foreseeable future will be a guiding light for the world in general and the United States in particular. Unfortunately, many of the problems faced during the life of Dr. King persist in some form or fashion. America is starkly marked today by a profound demographic transformation. It is feared by many to represent a challenge to the status quo in the United States, and even more ominous, for some it reeks of the decline of white dominance. Interestingly, the rapidity and depth of demographic change have increased the general attention Americans give to matters of social equity and justice in the midst of population increases among Latinos and the concomitant general decline in the white population. Critically important to a diversifying society are the active pursuit of social equity and social justice and/or eventually their demonstrated achievement. This is essential for instilling and maintaining societal peace and stability, which help form the fundamental basis for a nation's prosperity.

The prevalence of the evolving condition of diversification and other trends poses important opportunities for the application of the tremendous untapped potential in the wisdom and legacy of Dr. King's work, which lies well beyond our society's shallow acknowledgment of his dream of domestic racial equality and integration. The King Center website points out:

> He [Dr. King] is revered from small villages to great halls of power, and his name is invoked by countless social causes and movements. Schoolhouses and community centers from Boston to Bosnia bear his name, and in the United States, he is the only non-president with a national holiday dedicated in his honor. And yet, in many ways the true power of his legacy remains untapped. Children across the

country celebrate his life with a day off from school each year, but too many don't understand the reasons why. (The King Center)

This quotation captures the overarching motivation of this book. The contributors attempted to delve into some of the most significant social issues and cultural developments of the day from the vantage point of the political thought, ideals, and activism of Dr. Martin Luther King Jr. Unfortunately, Dr. King did not live long enough to see the myriad of societal and global challenges that would confront the nation and the world as his life was cut short by the bullet of an assassin. Admittedly, this work presented an arduous task as we could only speculate, despite well-grounded arguments and advancement of a defense based on the historical record. Had he lived, it seems likely that his influence would have even more profoundly influenced America's social trajectory and world culture, as well as the pace of change with respect to the achievement of social, political, and economic justice, not only for African Americans, but for everyone. However, the celebration of heroes more often than not does not occur until they have departed the material world.

The social, political, and economic challenges that prevail in the twenty-first century are testaments to the importance of scholars' continued efforts to ferret out details from Dr. King's extensive legacy—an analytical process arguably fraught with considerable subjectivism. We considered within the contemporary context, What might Dr. Martin Luther King Jr. say? in response to selected current political and social matters. This hypothetical question led us to reflectively analyze and apply the motivations and principles of King's work to form a framework of sorts for the analysis, consideration, and possible resolution of the issues. While clearly the subjects and issues covered in this book are not exhaustive of those that could have been examined, this work nonetheless provides an extraordinary glimpse into the applicability and potential public policy utility of King's ideas and work.

As we demonstrate in this book, Martin Luther King Jr. was much more than a dreamer, although he was frequently depicted as such by mass media and white national leaders. Indeed, King was a "revolutionary" as has been carefully articulated by Professor Cornel West, whose book goes far in demonstrating the contemporary utility of Dr. King's political and social thought. Books such as that edited by Professor West and this anthology are necessary because of the fact that some of the most controversial views espoused by Dr. King have been submerged, skewed, or utterly adulterated in scholarly and public discourse and policy applications. There is a great need to continue such work not only for the clarification of the King legacy, but also for ensuring the proper and accurate application of his ideas to today's problems.

King's work, particularly that formulated in the heyday of the civil rights movement, is destined to be relevant well into the future and will be a significant influence in shaping American values and culture, and a national and eventually global consensus of the idea of justice that people the world over can embrace. King's legacy will remain relevant for a number of reasons. For example, America's growing diversity (in the broadest of terms—racial, ethnic, gender, special needs, children, and immigrants) and the associated social challenges will continue to present opportunities to understand, apply, and celebrate Dr. King. Indeed, those who comprise the tremendous strength of diversity in the United States and are interested in social justice and equity, will look toward King's vision to highlight and resolve problems and issues as seen through their experiential lenses. King's work is inspirational for many, and its broad complexity allows the latitude to interpret and apply it in a manner consonant with an individual's or group's own unique circumstances and experiences.

Trends indicative of increasing economic inequality and concentration of wealth in the United States easily lend themselves to King's preoccupation with and analysis of issues such as poverty, maldistribution of wealth, and educational access as American society presumably strives toward the achievement of true democratic practice. Indeed, there are developments occurring on the US economic front that seem to indicate that classism, and thus class conflict, within and outside the Western world will become increasingly pronounced in the future. Moreover, since Dr. King's death in 1968, technological innovation has drastically reduced the time and space needed for information dissemination and the movement of people around the globe. In effect, technology has altered the quality, frequency, and nature of human interaction on both the national and international levels. Technology, while in many respects serves to enhance the quality of life of humankind, it can also increase the likelihood of misunderstanding and conflict among people. Future applications of King's philosophy and activism can shed light on these matters, as well as other critical issues such as the response to terrorism, the shrinking US middle class, the erosion of voting rights, same-sex marriage, the effects of the welfare state, gun ownership, immigration, and diversity, to name a few. Dr. King's life remains a reservoir from which the nation and the world can continue to draw knowledge and strength into the foreseeable future.

REFERENCES

The King Center. 2016. *Dr. King Today.* Atlanta, GA. http://www.thekingcenter.org/dr-king-today.

West, Cornel, ed. 2015. *The Radical King.* Boston: Beacon.

CONTRIBUTORS

Rosa M. Banda is assistant professor of educational leadership at Texas A & M University-Corpus Christi. Formerly, Dr. Banda was a research associate to the Samuel DeWitt Proctor Chair in Education in the Graduate School of Education at Rutgers, the State University of New Jersey. Dr. Banda earned her PhD in higher education administration and human resource development from Texas A & M University-College Station. She holds an MEd in adult and higher education with a cognate in bicultural/bilingual studies and a BA in communications with a concentration in public relations from the University of Texas at San Antonio, respectively. In addition to numerous national and international presentations, Dr. Banda's most recent publications include two co-edited books titled *Priorities of the Professoriate: Engaging Multiple Forms of Scholarship across Rural and Urban Institutions* and *Black Faculty in the Academy: Narratives for Negotiating Identity and Achieving Career Success*. Dr. Banda's primary research interests include high-achieving Latinas in engineering, gifted poor students of color, and faculty diversity.

Lakeyta M. Bonnette-Bailey is a political science professor at Georgia State University. She received her doctorate and master's in political science from the Ohio State University. Her research interests include popular culture, political behavior, black women and politics, political attitudes, African American politics, political psychology, and public opinion. She is the author of *Pulse of the People: Rap Music and Black Political Attitudes* (University of Pennsylvania Press, 2015). Dr. Bonnette-Bailey currently teaches classes on American government, black women and politics, black political behavior, black politics, and hip hop and politics.

Donathan L. Brown is an associate professor; former editor of *The Journal of Race and Policy*; lead author of *When Race and Policy Collide: Contemporary Immigration Debates* (2014) and *Voting Rights under Fire: The Continuing Struggle for People of Color* (2015); and recipient of the 2015 Ithaca College

Faculty Excellence Award. Dr. Brown conducts research focused on the inter-section of race, rhetoric, and public policy, particularly pertaining to African Americans and Latinos. His research has appeared in the *Harvard Journal of Hispanic Policy* (2013); the *International Journal of Discrimination and the Law* (2013 and 2012); the *Journal of Latino and Latin American Studies* (2013); *The Journal of Race and Policy* (2012); *Counterterrorism: From the Cold War to the War on Terror* (2012); *Studies In Ethnicity and Nationalism* (2012); the *Routledge Companion to Race and Ethnicity* (2012); *Communica-tion Law Review* (2011); *Anti-Immigration in the United States: A Historical Encyclopedia* (2011); *Widener Journal of Law, Economics and Race* (2010); *Racism, Slavery and Literature* (2010); and *Domestic Policy Discourse in the New World Order* (2010).

Michael L. Clemons is professor of political science and African American studies and internship director at Old Dominion University in Norfolk, Virginia. He is the founding editor of *The Journal of Race and Policy* and the founding executive director of the Consortium for Research on Race, Diver-sity, and Policy. His research has been published in a variety of periodicals, including *National Political Science Review, Political Geography, Journal of Latino and Latin American Studies,* and *Review of Black Political Economy.* Dr. Clemons is editor of *African Americans and Global Affairs: Contempo-rary Perspectives* (Northeastern University Press, 2010), and his most recent book (with Donathan L. Brown) is *Voting Rights under Fire: The Continuing Struggle for People of Color* (Praeger, 2015). He is currently completing a book entitled *The Logic of African American Global Participation: A Theoretical and Contextual Approach.*

William H. L. Dorsey is a third-generation black educator. He is a graduate of Jack Yates Colored High School in Houston, Texas. While at Swarthmore College he majored in sociology-anthropology and minored in psychology. He completed graduate work in sociology at the University of California at Berkeley, concentrating on role theory, race and ethnic relations, and social change. Professor Dorsey served for two years on staff at the Institute of the Black World and became involved in varied editorial work beginning in 1970. He has served as a sociology and African American studies professor at Atlanta Metropolitan State College since 1972. He has also served as a professional copy editor for a number of publications, including *The Journal of Race and Policy, Berkeley Journal of Sociology,* and *International Journal of Africana Studies.*

Hannah Firdyiwek received her bachelor's in sociology at the University of Virginia in 2012. Following her undergraduate studies, she completed a master's of social work, with a concentration in mental health, at the George Warren Brown School of Social Work at Washington University in St. Louis. She is currently living in St. Louis where she facilitates a youth development program at a middle school in the Ferguson-Florissant school district.

Alonzo M. Flowers III is assistant professor in the Department of Policy, Organization and Leadership, and Foundations at Drexel University. Dr. Flowers specializes in such educational issues as academic development of African American males, STEM education, diversity, and college student transition. Dr. Flowers' research focuses on the academic experiences of academically gifted African American and Latino students in the STEM disciplines, particularly engineering, mathematics, and science. Recently, he was selected to join the Massachusetts Institute for College and Career Readiness at Boston University as a senior research fellow. He has presented more than thirty-five peer-reviewed papers at national conferences, including several at the Association for the Study of Higher Education and Texas Association for the Gifted and Talented. In addition, he served as a keynote speaker at the first annual Texas African American Males in College Achievement and Success Symposium in Austin, Texas, where he discussed Giftedness at a Crossroads.

Helen Taylor Greene is professor of administration of justice at Texas Southern University in Houston. She is the co-author (with Shaun L. Gabbidon) of *Race and Crime*, fourth edition (Sage, 2015). Her research interests include race and crime, law enforcement, and juvenile justice. Her most recent research includes the school-to-prison pipeline in Texas and racial socialization and African American offending.

William G. Jones holds a doctorate in political science from Howard University. He specializes in American politics with an emphasis on African American politics and affairs and urban politics. He has worked as a researcher for national interest groups and has held several significant positions in local government and the nonprofit sector, including posts as director of planning for the cities of Portsmouth, Virginia, and Harvey, Illinois.

Athena M. King is lecturer of political science at Eastern Michigan University. She received her PhD in political science and a master's in public administration from the University of South Carolina. Her major field is

American politics, with research emphasis in US racial and ethnic politics, African American politics, urban policy, electoral behavior, and American political development. Her dissertation explores past and present policies that have fostered racial stratification, as well as the role of policy entrepreneurs in bringing said policies to fruition. Her current research includes projects on black electoral complexity and environmental justice. She teaches courses in American government, public policy, urban policy and state/local government for African American male college students in STEM.

Taj'ullah Sky Lark is a civil and human rights advocate, with an expertise in diversity, equity, equality, and inclusion. She earned her bachelor's at Rutgers University, New Brunswick; MA ED at the University of Illinois Urbana Champaign; MS ED at Fordham University; and PhD ED at Hampton University.

Jamela M. Martin is assistant professor of nursing at Old Dominion University in Norfolk, Virginia. She completed a BA in healthcare administration from North Carolina State University in 2000 and earned a BS in nursing in 2004, a MS in nursing with pediatric NP post-master's certificate in 2008, and a PhD in nursing in 2013 at the University of Virginia. Dr. Martin's scholarship focuses on global maternal-child health in the West Indies and neonatal intensive care nursing.

Marcus L. Martin is professor and past chair of the Department of Emergency Medicine at the University of Virginia. At the University of Virginia, he served as assistant dean in the School of Medicine and assistant vice president, associate vice president, interim vice president, and chief officer for diversity and equity. He is the principal investigator of the Virginia-North Carolina Alliance, a National Science Foundation-funded Louis Stokes Alliance for Minority Participation (LSAMP) program. He earned bachelor's of science degrees in pulp and paper technology (1970) and chemical engineering (1971) from North Carolina State University and was employed as a production chemical engineer at WESTVACO in Covington, Virginia. A member of the charter class of Eastern Virginia Medical School, he earned his medical degree in 1976.

Byron D'Andra Orey earned a BS from Mississippi Valley State University, MAs from the University of Mississippi and the State University of New York at Stony Brook, and a PhD from the University of New Orleans. He has taught at the University of Mississippi, and the University of Nebraska, Lincoln, and currently teaches at Jackson State University, where he is a full professor and chairman of the Political Science Department. He has published more than thirty scholarly articles and book chapters, presented his research at more than one hundred conferences, and is currently working on two book-length manuscripts. He was selected as the national teacher of the year in 2008 and the mentor of the year in 2011 by the National Conference of Black Political Scientists. He was also selected as teacher of the year for Jackson State University and nominated for teacher of the year for the state of Mississippi in 2011. D'Andra currently serves on the executive committees of the American Political Science Association, Southern Political Science Association (APSA), Pi Sigma Alpha, and the editorial board for *State Politics & Policy Quarterly* and the Pi Sigma Alpha undergraduate journal.

Amardo Rodriguez (PhD, Howard University) is a Laura J. and L. Douglas Meredith Professor in the Communication and Rhetorical Studies Department at Syracuse University. His research and teaching interests look at the potentiality of new conceptions of communication to redefine and enlarge contemporary understandings of democracy, diversity, and community. His book-length monograph, *Communication: Colonization and the Making of Discipline*, was published by Public Square Press in 2014.

Audrey E. Snyder is assistant professor of nursing at the University of Northern Colorado, Greeley. She earned her nursing diploma at the Memorial Hospital School of Nursing in Danville, Virginia, in 1984. She subsequently completed her RN-BSN, MSN with a clinical nurse specialist focus, postmaster's acute care nurse practitioner, and PhD in nursing at the University of Virginia, Charlottesville. She has worked in critical care, emergency, and flight nursing. She developed an elective course in culture in health for undergraduate students across curriculums. Her areas of specialization include emergency and critical care advanced practice nursing, disaster preparedness and response, public health, international health, community engagement, and nursing education. Her research focuses on rural and underserved populations, access to care, prehospital triage, complementary therapies, nursing education, interprofessional education, and nursing history.

James L. Taylor is professor of politics at the University of San Francisco and lecturer of African American and African Diaspora studies at UC Berkeley. He is the former president of the National Conference of Black Political

Scientists (NCOBPS), and chair of the Committee on the Status of Blacks for the American Political Science Association. He is also the author of a number of books, including *Black Nationalism in the United States from Malcolm X to Barack Obama* (2010). He works in the Bay Area, where he lives with his family.

Leslie Walker received her bachelor's in Spanish from Wake Forest University in 2011. She began employment with the University of Virginia Office for Diversity and Equity in 2013, prior to which, she taught Spanish language and culture at the high school level in Charlottesville, Virginia. She served as co-editor for *West Indies Health Care and Disaster Preparedness* (2015).

Jason M. Williams is assistant professor of criminal justice at Fairleigh Dickinson University in Teaneck, New Jersey. His research interests are social justice, urban critical ethnography, criminological theory, race and crime, culture and conflict, and the sociology of knowledge. He is currently conducting critical ethnographic research in Ferguson, Missouri, and Baltimore, Maryland, following the untimely deaths of Michael Brown and Freddie Gray.

INDEX